枕
戈
待
旦

Above, in the author's own calligraphy, is the
Chinese title of this book—literally, "Pillowed
[on] Spears Awaiting [the] Dawn." The fitness of the phrase is apparent throughout the
book and particularly in the closing passage.

BOOKS BY LIN YUTANG

Published by THE JOHN DAY COMPANY

MY COUNTRY AND MY PEOPLE
THE IMPORTANCE OF LIVING
MOMENT IN PEKING
WITH LOVE AND IRONY
A LEAF IN THE STORM
BETWEEN TEARS AND LAUGHTER
THE VIGIL OF A NATION

LIN YUTANG

The VIGIL OF A NATION

ILLUSTRATED

THE JOHN DAY COMPANY · NEW YORK

Government wartime restrictions on materials have
made it essential that the amount of paper used in
each book be reduced to a minimum. This volume is
printed on lighter paper than would have been used
before material limitations became necessary, and the
number of words on each page has been substantially
increased. The smaller bulk in no way indicates that
the text has been shortened.

DEDICATED

to

The pilots and officers of the ATC
and the many men working now in the
Chinese Government and the Army
whose courtesy, efficiency, and hospitality
made wartime travel in China possible for me
all of whose names it is not possible to mention in this book
and to

MAJOR GENERAL CLAIRE L. CHENNAULT

who has unshaken faith in
the Chinese soldier

CONTENTS

*An eight-page section of illustrations appears
following page 118*

THE VIGIL OF A NATION

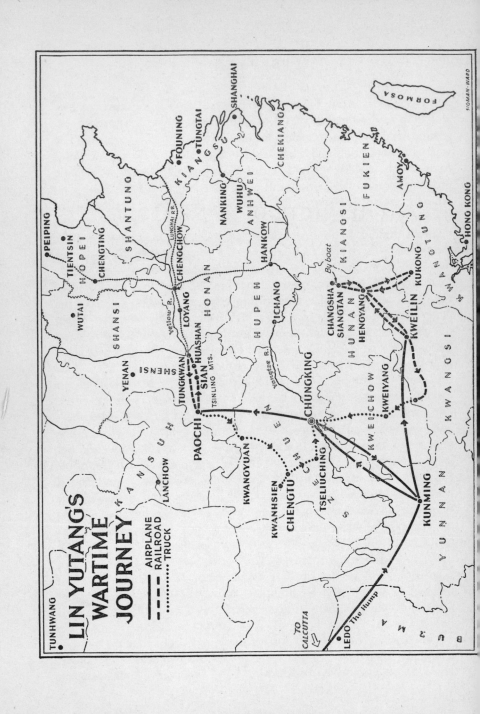

LIN YUTANG'S
WARTIME
JOURNEY

AIRPLANE
RAILROAD
TRUCK

TUNHWANG

PEIPING

TIENTSIN

HOPEI

CHENGTING

WUTAI

SHANSI

YENAN

SHENSI

KANSU

LANCHOW

PAOCHI

TUNGKWAN

SIAN

HUASHAN

TSINLING MTS.

KWANHSIEN

CHENGTU

KWANGYUAN

TSELIUCHING

SZECHUEN

Yangtze R.

CHUNGKING

KWEICHOW

KWEIYANG

KWEILIN

KUNMING

YUNNAN

KWANGSI

LEDO The Hump

TO
CALCUTTA

BURMA

SHANTUNG

FOUNING

TUNGTAI

KIANGSU

CHENGCHOW

LUNGHAI R.R.

LOYANG

HONAN

Yellow R.

HUPEH

HANKOW

ICHANG

WUHU

ANHWEI

NANKING

SHANGHAI

CHEKIANG

CHANGSHA

SIANGTAN

HUNAN

HENGYANG

By boat

KIANGSI

FUKIEN

AMOY

KWANGTUNG

KUKONG

HONG KONG

FORMOSA

SIGMAN-WARD

PREFACE

AT NO TIME in the history of Sino-American relationships has true and deep understanding of China's land and people, historical background, and present problems been more imperatively required. The war will come to an end soon, and China's role in Asia and in world co-operation will be newly determined. China will launch a gigantic program of industrialization and reconstruction, under the same government which had started the work with such good promise before the war broke out in 1937. American co-operation will be needed and intensely desired. Yet the American people as a whole know little about the people with whom they are expected to co-operate and to whom they will quite probably be lending money and material assistance. Unfortunately, too, this mutual understanding has been shadowed in the past year by a cloud of confusing criticism, tending to make the Americans worried about China and unnecessarily alarmed about the government, although deep sympathy and friendliness are always there. At no time has the situation been so tragic as now when we near the end of the war and Allied victory.

Having no faith in propaganda, but troubled by reports about the condition of my country, I went back for an extended journey, covering seven provinces. I am now writing this record of my experiences and impressions as a Chinese who saw the country from the inside after seven years of war. It is essentially a book about a journey, but it is my hope that such inside pictures, presented fairly, will contribute toward a better insight into the Chinese people and their problems. I believe the knowledge thus gained will be deeper and more intimate than from a volume of economic and political essays. One cannot begin to discuss the problems of a foreign country until one has some pictures of the land and its people. The problems of inflation, of the Army, of social and educational standards, and above all of the much heralded "civil war" will be described as I saw them, as a Chinese who is a member neither of the Kuomintang nor of the Chinese Communist party, but who sees them as problems of China's emerging unity as a nation.

This is what I saw and what I felt. Because I could have no illusions about any country after seven years of war and two years of blockade, I was not disillusioned. And because I had observed China's progress and problems for almost two decades, since the National Revolution of 1926-27, these problems and difficulties, largely social and psychological, were not new to me. The particular effects of the blockade were anticipated in the years when many people were complacent and thought nothing mattered on the China front until the European war was won. Now when the full blast of its effect is felt and the same people, caught by surprise or frightened, have begun to lose hope and turn against Chungking, I have not lost faith in the national leadership. Only a more intimate knowledge of the social and political background is needed. This is what I am trying to supply in this book.

What China wants is not maudlin sympathy, but faith and understanding from her Allies. I found on this trip that the Chinese do not mind criticism, if criticism is based on intelligent understanding and placed against the background of the larger purposes and greater objectives. Unthinking criticisms, however, based on superficial and extremely limited knowledge, or even directly on hostile partisan propaganda, will do more harm to the outside public by bringing confusion than to the Chinese themselves, since the latter have a lot on their hands and do not spend their time chewing apparently unintelligible gossip from far away. I think foreign prestige suffers when some of these perverse criticisms become known in China. If the East and West must meet, they should meet on some higher level of intelligence than the present. One basic background fact, for instance, is that the China war is now in its eighth year, and yet the morale and resilience of the nation are no worse than what American morale would be at the end of an eight-year war, or what English morale would be if England's Atlantic sea lanes had been cut off for two or three years. Taking account of this background, one would be able to understand quite a few things, and gain a better sense of balance.

There is no question that such faith in China will be justified. Soon the war will be ended, and the curtain of doubt will be lifted. Then we shall see the face of victory and of a China washing her wounds by the side of clear waters, resilient, confident, and hopefully rebuilding for the future, even as she was building in the years before the war. These moments of doubt shall pass away from the man who has faith. "For he shall be as a tree planted by the waters, and that spreadeth out her roots by the river, and shall not see when heat cometh, but its leaves shall be green."

2

À PROPOS OF THE MANNER AND MATTER
OF THE BOOK

I LEFT Miami on September 22, 1943, and arrived back in New York on March 22, 1944, covering the trip in exactly six months, more exactly than I had planned. As I sit down to write of my exciting experience in those six months, I do not feel China is so far away. Traveling from America to China used to take two or three weeks across the Pacific. This time, I flew back from Calcutta to New York in five days.

Going over to China seems almost like a visit to a neighbor's front porch. I believe the Age of the Open Door is over and the Age of the Front Porch has begun. For the Open Door was a misnomer. I suppose it meant that the door was to be kept open for anybody to go in any time of the day, like a house without an owner, and if there was an owner, it was not his business to inquire who were the visitors, what they came for, and what they did inside when they entered the door. Now the owner has returned, and a sign is hung outside the door reading, "Kindly knock."

Rather the good neighbors will come to sit on the front porch of an evening, and taking out their pipes, will chat and exchange gossip until the moon is high and then turn in for the night. The Age of the Front Porch began at Cairo, when the neighbors first met and exchanged their cards, with a promise to visit each other more often. The fear is not that the neighbors know too much about each other, but that they know too little, desperately too little. I feel sure that the rocking chairs on the front porch will be used more often after the war, and by that time the returned owner will probably be modern enough to offer a "coke" or a Manhattan, with ice. So let's begin.

China seems so far and yet so near. When the war is over, and the Alaskan air route is open, I am sure that a man can leave the United States on Friday evening and sup at Chungking or Shanghai Sunday evening and telephone to his secretary in New York Monday morning to say that the letter he wrote on Friday had better be held up until he gets back Wednesday afternoon at 3:45 P.M. The magic of shrinking space has been found. It is bound to work profound changes in the

3

minds and manners of living of the people of this age, as the invention of the railroad did. Perhaps our present notions of space and time are all wrong, even as the people eighty years ago who regarded New York and San Francisco as separated by a five months' covered wagon trip were all wrong. We have to take time to readjust these notions, and twenty years from now we will chuckle at the idea the people of the nineteen-forties had that China was a country far, far away. At that time, people will think mentally of the distance between China and America as they think now of the distance between New York and San Francisco.

Yet, as I reflect upon time, it seems even more incredible than space. We feel that space exists, as we can visibly measure it by the span between our thumb and fingers, but we do not know whether time exists or not. Some say they "spent" it, some say they "wasted" it, some passed it and some killed it, and some say they even "borrowed" it—but what is it? As I recall the experiences of those six months, I realize that they have vanished, and what remain are only pictures in my mind, and some perceptions, emotions, and memories.

It was the Seventh Year of the War. It was a period of time, like a river weighted with the driftwood of the past and rushing toward an unknown future. Such was a period of time; such was the Seventh Year. The Marco Polo Bridge incident seemed already long, long ago. People were living, dying, fighting, and hoping in 1937, and people were living, dying, fighting, and hoping in 1944. The sack of Nanking was only a memory, and so was the *Panay* incident. It was more than two years since Pearl Harbor, the first shock and the high hopes of the Chinese people, followed by disillusionment, with the fall of Singapore and Rangoon and loss of the South Pacific area. Burma was lost and China was blockaded. Help was not in sight, but the Chinese people still held on. Then came Stalingrad, and the reversal of the pattern of the war, and the victories of the African campaign. No one could have anticipated that such would be the course of the war; no one knew that it was going to happen that way. Time was a closed book; the past has been revealed; the future, as we say figuratively, only time will tell.

The events and people of those six months of travel were real. China holding on and the people fighting, hoping, living in the Seventh Year of the War, were all real. I was privileged to get a panoramic and kaleidoscopic view of these people during those days packed with excitement, but as I write of them now, I think of them as belonging to history, to the past. I know they have a mysterious meaning for the

4

future—I do not know how, but the secret pattern of time, though hidden from us, is certainly there.

So how shall I tell the story? How shall I tell it except in terms of my own perceptions, feelings, and the more memorable excitements of the moment? For how shall one tell an epoch, and say of it that it was so and so? The facile generalizations of historians, characterizing a period by a one-word label, have no place in reality. How shall one say that one decade was gray and another mauve, or that the period was romantic or realistic, and that people thought only in one way during a whole period? Any real stream of thought, in any period, will be found to have many crosscurrents, countercurrents, and eddies. It is also true that a few heroes or a mode of thinking may dominate a period, like Empress Eugénie's hat, but the day-to-day activities of the individuals are the mirror of the life of an era. The life of the nation during a period consists of the actions, thoughts, and domestic cares and troubles of individuals, acted upon by a thousand minute, transient influences, continually changing and shifting, like the dancing shadows upon the ground in a pine grove. The forest analogy is a good one; the forest is composed of trees, and all trees contribute to the character and smell and light and shade of the forest. Some spots in the forest are in deeper shade, and some in lighter, and there are open glades which permit the sun's rays to shoot down over the treetops directly upon the pine needles on the ground. The wind blows through the woods, causing the leaves to shiver and cast dancing circles of light on the ground, which are reflected again and caught up by other parts of the forest. At every moment, the forest's character is subject to a thousand changes. How, therefore, shall we speak of the dominant character and tone of a forest without studying the trees? The man who could shape the day-to-day thoughts and lives of the individuals of a nation would be more powerful than any dictator or the President of the United States.

So shall it be with my book. The writing of the life of a whole people during a period may be likened to the painting of a forest. I could not explore the entire forest. Every traveler is limited by what he sees, and two artists going together will paint the same forest in different fashions. Still one has to depend upon words, as the only means of bringing any moment back alive. For if one has a proper sense of the notion of time, one knows that there is nothing static in the life of a nation. Everything is in flux, and no two days are ever identical. Living from day to day, and going all the time, I was ready each morning to expose myself to the new sensory images and impressions from the happenings of the day. And so a day passed, and another, and yet another, as I traveled over mountains and rivers and cities and towns. Each day rose like an unchalked blackboard, and we did not know what it was going to bring forth, until the night had come and we said to ourselves it was an interesting man or woman we had seen on the highway. And so the "epoch" was made of days, filled with the impedimenta of life. But if we could recapture a day, a moment, and reveal its full meaning and hold it in true focus, we might be good historians of that epoch, as so mirrored in the way men and women eat and dress and live and think about the tomorrow.

It is inevitable that wayside lingerings over wild blossoms may be more important to me than the destination, and I shall fill the book with such wayside details and objects and persons. This may annoy some doctrinaire critics, who will seek in vain here for a grand formula three times removed from life, with which those who ideologically disagree with me can fight sham battles of shadow words. My opinions and feelings will be explicit enough, though not stated in forms convenient to any particular school of thought. Let those who like to indulge in pontifical truths and professorial formulas have them; let me have the colors and sounds and smells. Thus it may be found that I am more concerned in recording the little things on the avenue of life, as they seemed to me and as I felt them.

I am afraid the style will be much like that of a wayside chatter. There is something essentially idle about a journey book, not only because of enforced leisure on rainy days, but because the very act of travel suggests taking time off from the business routine of our slavery days. To be sure, the traveler is always moving on and doing something, and the reader of his book moves on with him, while his mind roves. But whatever the traveler does, it has not that authoritarian necessity or "sacredness" that we associate with office hours. Some idle comments will be inevitable, and perhaps some cracker-barrel wisdom.

I think that writing is only "chatter with the pen" (pit'an), as the Chinese call their essays. As I sit in my armchair and survey the tomes on my shelves, each volume seems to me only an effort at sealed eloquence. All are merely trying to talk and to say something, each in his best manner. Some talk better than others, some are pompous and very grave, and some take themselves too seriously. Some are hopelessly and congenitally inarticulate, and their efforts at self-expression must be a mental burden and something of a pain, but because they do have something important and profound to say, people are patient and willing to listen to them.

6

There is a class of ancient books which better illustrates my point about chattering. Wise men have lived before us; they came into life, thought and felt deeply, said some terribly wise things, and went away, seemingly curt and unobliging. What they said were eternal truths, yet they left us wondering why they said them. What we would have given if they had been more chatty and communicative and told us why they said those things! We are sure that their deepest observations of life and some of their profound convictions had trivial origins in the personal happenings of the moment. In a flash they perceived a truth, caught it, and casually mentioned it to someone standing by. Yet paper was so scarce and writing was so laborious a process that what these wise ones had said was inevitably reduced to a skeleton, stripped of the color of the moment, and the exigencies of the context and the tone of their voice were irretrievably lost for us. That is why these truths look so universal, and yet so impersonal. The best biographers and critics can at best reilluminate certain of these moments for us, as Boswell did with Johnson, with all his whims and crotchets. And we are pleased to hear from Plato that after talking everybody to sleep in an all-night sitting, Socrates went out and took a bath, fresh as ever.

I have never before written a book about a journey. It seems more difficult than writing fiction, for one cannot invent things. It must be like taking candid camera shots: either you catch *it* at the right moment or you don't, and some shots certainly must be destroyed. The writer of travel sketches is like the camera man in his dependence on his material, on what he sees, on the quickness of his finger, and on the large margin of selectivity at his disposal. He cannot invent objects and scenes that are not there. He has only the advantage of love and imagination and sentiment and can put his own thrills into the picture. Thus he often sees the unseen, being at liberty to dip into the past and peer into the future. He paints a picture in the fourth dimension of time, and necessarily in the fifth dimension of his own feelings. The fifth dimension is more important than all the rest. I only hope that my pictures may be as true and as candid as such pictures should be.

It follows then that my records as such will be subjective; for the railway-mileage kind of objectivity, the reader must go to yearbooks and Baedekers and those travel writers who aim at resembling them. All art is, I believe, subjective, and only to the extent to which the product is a comment by the artist on what he sees and not a mere objective reproduction and representation can it be called art at all. One must after all paint what one loves with his brush or with his

7

pen; to go against this rule would be to violate the first canon of art. The word "love" must be taken in its broadest and deepest sense, as a personal and deep and lively sense of the importance of the object before one. Unless one so loves, one cannot paint at all. The very selection of his subject is personal. It isn't that the Dutch painters didn't see the chateaux and the gentlemen and ladies of the court, but that they loved the barber and the interiors of the people's homes more. So it will be with painters of all periods. In the second place, the artist's comment is more important than the objective reality; the unseen is more important than the seen. And in the third place, no matter what the artist does, the technique is his own, the touches by which connoisseurs recognize and identify him. I am but a mortal man, with my personal likes and dislikes and inner excitements and responses all my own. I should not pretend that others would view the scene as I did; the truth about an epoch is hidden behind a thousand changing realities, and I hope that others will be as sincere with them as I will try to be. I must try to be fair, which is not absence of judgment but a good balance of it; but even the degree and quality of fairness achieved is necessarily a part of my own self.

O Travel, how many crimes have been committed in thy name! Some businessmen travel to attend a business conference; other wiser heads make a business conference the excuse for travel to their wives. Some pastors and priests have to go all the way to Rome or Moscow to serve God; that is the only way they can justify their leaving their sheep behind. In the Middle Ages, Christian knights and even kings had to travel to the Holy Land just in order to fight the Saracens in the name of serving God. I predict that in the years after the war, almost every American professor or publicist of any account will be going to Prague or Florence or the Riviera for some terribly important business under one of the general categories of investigation, strategic survey, conference of experts, or permanent observation post—so much so that if a professor of international credit or veterinary surgeon is seen anywhere in the U.S.A., everybody will ask him, "Why are you in your own country?" The clearest evidence of the approach of impending victory is that most professors of any account are already busily traveling to Washington. Flying over Jerusalem and seeing from the sky that Bethlehem was only a suburb of the Holy City, I realized that the hotel situation at Jerusalem in the days of Joseph and Mary must have been quite like the hotel situation at Washington. The finger of scorn is already pointed at the professor who is seen on his own college campus and who is subjected to the almost unanswerable question, "Why are you on your own college campus?" In the interim between the armistice and the signing of the peace treaty to come—i.e., during the cooling-off period—a sudden global-mindedness or Sense of International Solidarity will strike the people of account, and you will not hear one of them admit to so much as a smile at the prospect of touring Europe. May God forgive them!

The fact is, travel *per se* has become ungentlemanly. A professor from Kansas has to come to Washington, and President Roosevelt, being already in Washington, has to go to Alaska. There always is a mysterious, businesslike reason for it. This point of view is now affecting even the less important people. Even I had to tell people that I went to China to gather material for a book, since it would be impossible to explain to anybody that I went back to China because I was deeply concerned when I heard all sorts of reports about my country, and had to see it after two years of inflation and blockade. One English editor at Calcutta told an Indian friend that I had made a mess of things in America by writing *Between Tears and Laughter* and had to go back to China to prove to the Americans that I am a Chinese. I always like to hear speculations like that concerning myself. There are various theories of why and how I went to China and why and how I came out again, all except the theory that when my country was reported to be in trouble I had to see her. I must confess right here that I had a publisher's contract before I went, that I took in with me two big 150-page notebooks and came out again without writing a single line in them. People might think I had an armful of notes; I am afraid my whole diary runs under a thousand words.

There is an art of irresponsible traveling. Lest the phrase be misunderstood, I must explain that it is meant as a hopelessly inadequate English equivalent of the Chinese phrase *langyu,* or "splashing-about ramble." *Lang* originally meant "waves," which suggests "tossing" or "splashing about" (with money or gestures). Consequently in time it came to have the meaning of "extravagant," "uninhibited," "irresponsible," and "licentious." The Prodigal Son is *langtse,* and uninhibited talk is *langt'an,* while a licentious woman is *langfu*—she just tosses about. But it has finer, poetic uses. *Langt'an,* or casual, irresponsible, rambling conversation, in fact is supposed to be quite a scholar's occupation, and *langyu* is just gay, carefree, irresponsible traveling, with the sky as the limit, and even suggests that one enjoys one's travel. To borrow Irwin Edman's phrase, it is strictly a "philosopher's holiday."

9

The difficulty lies, it seems to me, in inducing the philosopher to go on a holiday.

The difficult thing, I am afraid, is to get a cultured vagabond. He is a bygone type. It doesn't do for a vagabond to talk of statistical averages and social security measures, yet that seems to be all that these modern roving correspondents are talking about, when they travel to gather material for a book. Vagabondia and economic statistics don't go well together. The decay of the art of traveling has brought in its train the decay of the books of travel. These intelligent observers on China come, with pad and pencil, to observe you like guinea pigs, with a scientific mind and judicial temper, and you are as afraid of their observation as you would be afraid of meeting and shaking hands with Dale Carnegie, for fear that this is merely his Strategem No. 7 to win your friendship or influence your opinion. You hang back a little and refuse to be observed in the one case, and to be won over in the other. That is now called sales resistance.

These press correspondents and other observers on China are horrifying; you cannot catch them on a single factual error. Brooks Atkinson, of the *New York Times,* is different; he has culture and I can never be sure of his facts; I am sure he loves his Aristophanes more than his facts. You get a kind of human warmth from him, but that is because he never went to a school of journalism. The Missouri School of Journalism, or any school of journalism, teaches you to report facts accurately, the Who, What, When, Where, How, and, if you are intelligent enough, the Why. The Why of all sociological phenomena is admittedly difficult, but anyway get the Who, What, When, Where, and, if you are clever enough, the How. Anyway, get the Who, What, When, and Where, which will make you a journalist. The journalist's concern is, I understand, just to get his facts straight, checked and rechecked. If he says an affair happened at 5:43 A.M., you are sure he is reliable; it could not be guesswork; he does not rely on hazy memories, he relies on notes. You see he is a trained professional. That is the journalistic technique they teach you at the schools. Any one of them has a trained and scientifically disciplined mind good enough to be detailed by Sherlock Holmes to observe the physical appearance, dress, fingernails, birthmarks, and movements of some unsuspecting person. You just add two and two and you see the result is four, and you just "report." But the deuce if he can deduce things without Sherlock Holmes's imaginative mind, whose inner processes are not strictly equated with mathematical additions and subtractions. With all due respect for the many intelligent travelers and roving writers who report on China, whose books show, in addition to all the journalistic merits of factual correctness of dates and figures, an avowed openness of mind, a striking judicial temper, and some analytical talent, I must say that some of them at least have successfully escaped a sense of wonder, and a good many of them missed the fun. They went to China in a very right frame of mind and came out of it with still a very right frame of mind, which is to say, they should not have traveled to China at all.

China, I understand, is assiduously training up modern journalists. I suppose there is some need of such things. One Chinese girl reporter came to interview me a few days after my arrival at Chungking. After I had spent an hour listening to her discourses on the merits of the second front, the political strategy of Winston Churchill, and other information she volunteered on the state of the country, over which she grew very eloquent, she did not burden me with any questions on my opinions or news from America, and I was completely refreshed when I said good-by to her. This, I said to myself, is the pleasantest and most relaxing interview I have ever had. There was another reporter at Hengyang who not only freely expressed in his published interview his own opinions and completely reported himself, but also during the interview offered to enlighten me on who Walter Lippmann was. His eyes twinkled when I could not catch his pronunciation of Li Po Men, and he thought, coming from America, I could not possibly have read Lippmann's *U. S. Foreign Policy*. He was seized with a desire to educate me on Walter Lippmann and ended up by enlightening me on John Steinbeck and Upton Sinclair. Some improvement in journalistic technique is evidently desirable in China. I commend Hollington K. Tong for his enterprise in starting a school of journalism. But there are some things in journalism, in fact the only important things in journalism, that such schools can never teach and are generally not to be found on the curriculum of a school of journalism, namely, Shakespeare and a Penetrating Mind. If you command a good English style and possess a penetrating mind, you don't need a course in journalism, and if you don't, the school can't help you.

But I was talking about the cultured vagabond. The vagabond is a different sort of being. He talks with people and does not interview them. His realm is irresponsible fancy, and his heart is warm. He has an eye for the trivial things of life and he loves to tell tales and hear them. He has a sense of history, a very vivid one, recalling anecdotes with ease, and his historical imagination sees things of the past and dreams dreams of the future. He fondles a tree or the burr on a bole, or an overhanging bough brushes his face and evokes a mood in him.

He sees more in a woman's face or a furtive smile than in a whole volume of statistics. He would see as much if he remained at home, but since he is traveling, he sees more of such smiles and faces, and strange landscapes and ancient battlegrounds and folkways are likely to excite him inwardly, and if the excitement is intense enough he breaks out into poetry. For then the subjective in him and the objective phenomena outside merge, the scene and the personal mood co-operate and emerge together as something new, something keen and exciting. There a moment is captured for eternity. That is the poetic moment. The poet but communicates that thrill, the thrill of a moment, but it is so intense that he feels and his readers feel that no one had felt such things before, and the moment is truly unique. It may be a feeling of beauty, of utter perfection of the moment, or it may be a feeling of sadness or forlornness, and it may be even casual, humorous, or resigned. But the moment lives thenceforth and becomes unforgettable. He does not report things any more; he transmutes them by the touch of his feeling.

Would that I had the tongue of the poet, the imagination of the historian and the vision of the prophet, and what I would see and be able to put down in this book! To go back to one's own land, to live with its people whose folkways have not much altered these thousands of years, to know their feelings for things, to know the sufferings which they have survived and the peace they have enjoyed, and to see them now in fighting war years, struggling with failures and mistakes, and yet with hope and determination to change themselves radically into a modern nation—this would be subject for an epic. One feels a thread of history and tradition, and a thread of change and progress, and these come together in the most weird and confused fashion, and one wishes to weave them into some clear pattern, if possible a beautiful pattern, of peace and justice and happiness. No land except China offers such a confusion and contrast of the extremely ancient and the ultramodern in thinking and feeling, such a tearing out from within. The young are impatient of the old and are fanatic and unbalanced, and call reactionaries those who try to harmonize the past and the future. Yet the past dominates them, with all its beauty and grandeur and pathos, and they cannot comprehend it.

I have captured some glorious moments, moments of grandeur and beauty and moments of sadness. I have stood above the ruins of a Tang palace and looked down the gulley to see women spinning and weaving wool in loess caves with hand looms. I have seen a peasant woman nursing her child in peace, sitting on the field outside the crumbled walls of the first Chou capital, and it seems to me the scene has not changed, has never changed these four thousand years. I have seen these and other things.

For the rest, I am strictly on the plebeian, prose level, the level of merely observing life and loving it. I can admire the heroes and forgive the sinners. But to the intellectual height of the true vagabond I shall not attain. The true vagabond carries pencil stubs only; I carried a German-made four-colored pencil. My vagabondage was good, quite good, and I prospered on it. I could walk longer and climb higher than I thought. My hunt for a can of coffee in Kweilin was a chapter of disgrace. I could not live without it; but the vagabond can, or can he? The vagabond is uncomfortable in a first-class railroad coach; I stuck to it, as Wendell Willkie did when he was in Sian. I felt compassion for an English lad riding third class, all alone. Quite a few Englishmen came inland when Hong Kong fell, joined the Chinese Army for training, could not go through with it, and dispersed God knows where. He, I said to myself, was really vagabonding, and I wondered deeply what was going on inside his soul and mind—such a young lad and lost, traveling all alone. If he was at all gifted mentally, and had a balanced mind, he would survive it and his mind would grow richer for the experience.

Such a mind a vagabond ought to have. There is that essential cheerfulness and animal faith in all true vagabonds. He is one of the crowd and yet always detached from it. That commingling of warmth and detachment makes a true vagabond. And then his mind's eye sees farther than the traveling businessman or the roving correspondent. I wondered, for instance, what that English lad's mind was able to see. Was his fancy free? Still the very motion of traveling, of going somewhere and seeing and meeting strange people, is bound to react on his mind and stimulate wonder. The most barren intellect, the most unimaginative mind, must, I think, start to wonder in times of travel.

A final word about myself. This is essential because I am in dire straits. For I find myself in the impossible position of a Chinese who is neither gloomy, nor war-weary, nor disloyal to the war leadership of the Chinese government. The sepulchral, lugubrious, and doleful tones that emanate from American sources in Chungking suggest that I should be, that I should share their hoarse, tomb-like echoes. Worse than that, it will be seen from the following pages that I am not even a Communist, and obviously all Chinese liberals today should be Communists and help to overthrow the Kuomintang government. I

13

went to Harvard, and there is still enough liberalism in me to dislike heartily all totalitarianism and suppression of individual liberty wherever they are found, even though it is a totalitarianism of the Russian type, which we feel constrained to admire today. In my literary battles with the Chinese "leftists" ten years ago, they used to sneer at me as a "liberal" who did not know that freedom of thought was outmoded and that the Lunacharskian thesis that literature should be the vehicle of party propaganda was the last word of western wisdom. It amuses me a little now to see them struggling to claim the label of "liberalism" because they are talking to Americans. The fact that all Marxists are claiming to be "democrats" and "liberals" and even procapitalists is one of the most astounding achievements of this war. The fact that I take a nonpartisan view and hit hard at internal disunity and suppression of the free press in Yenan, as well as in Chungking, will be exasperating in certain quarters.

I have to make my position clear, in justice to my readers. I am an independent writer, deriving my sole income from my books. I am not in the pay of the Chinese government. I am not responsible to it and do not make reports to it. I hold an "official visa," as a matter of convenience, because of the following American difficulties: Before 1940 I held a "tourist passport," which made it necessary for me to leave United States territory with my family every six months. I took the precaution also because, in 1931, when traveling as a League of Nations official, I was sent to Ellis Island and lost my liberty for forty-eight hours. Someone in uniform had to accompany me even when I went to a latrine. My Chinese passport was not recognized, so far as the immigration authorities were concerned, and the American visa had inadvertently classified me as a "tourist" without a "Section 6" paper. The official job, for which my present American official visa was granted, is "research on Sino-American cultural relations." My actual job, as I see it, is to help interpret China wherever I can. If I choose to support the forces of integration rather than the forces of disintegration in China, and if I choose to support the Chinese government where I think it deserves support and criticize its mistakes where it deserves criticism, that is my right as a citizen of China.

1

FLIGHT INTO CHINA

IT WAS the end of September, still hot like the tropics at Miami. My wife had accompanied me from New York to spend the last days together. We had two wonderful days, knowing that once the plane started, my journey would be shrouded in secrecy, as all travel in wartime is. While waiting for the plane, with an undisclosed time for departure, we visited the city. It was then that we caught for the first time the real atmosphere of war in the United States. There were some sixty thousand soldiers in training there. Early at six we would hear the bugle calls, and all day soldiers marched through the streets singing Army or Air Force songs, some dressed in full kit and some stripped to the waist and wearing shorts, suggesting practice for jungle warfare and endurance in tropical weather. In the afternoons we saw classes being held in unshaded wooden cabins, with the blazing sun beating down on them to keep up a perfect oven temperature. No wonder their faces were as red as turkeys. If it was a "toughening process" the Army was giving them, they were getting it.

A sense of the mystery of the journey and of the coming separation enveloped us. I did not know which route we were flying, but in any case this was my first airplane trip across Africa and India to China. Knowing that I would be flying across the tropics most of the time, I bought a sun helmet, two polo shirts, and a few extra gray shirts and told my wife not to worry about my laundry on the way. As an extra precaution, I bought two thermos bottles to fill with coffee and milk, and a bottle of Horlick's malted milk, in case I should miss my meals during the flight. Thus provided, I believed my frail frame, though long addicted to regular hours and sedentary habits, could stand the journey pretty well. A haircut and a visit to the dentist completed the preparations.

The inevitable morning came. I had gone through the briefing the previous day and was told to appear at the airfield at six. It was a cargo plane, and besides the crew there was a Chinese captain returning home with me. The spirit of good cheer had carried us to the end and made the parting not only easy but also an asset during the

15

journey. We had said good-by to each other at the line beyond which she was not allowed. When I had taken my luggage aboard the plane and was standing at the top of the ladder, what was my surprise and joy to see her sitting by the driver in a jeep coming right up to the ship, wearing a naughty and triumphant smile. How she bribed her way in and broke the Army regulations I was too happy to inquire. I suppose there are no fools like old fools. But parting of this kind was good and gave one something to cling to all through the journey.

The route I followed, I understand, is now no longer a military secret. We made ten easy hops to India, flying no more than six or seven hours a day. The ship stopped at Puerto Rico, Georgetown in British Guiana, Belem and Natal in Brazil, Ascension Island in mid-Atlantic, Accra, Fort Lamy and Khartoum in Central Africa, Aden in Arabia, Karachi and Calcutta in India. Thus we flew right across French Equatorial Africa. This was known as the southern route, while on my return I followed the northern route over North Africa. Flying from India to New York in three and a half days is now the common experience of many. Dr. H. H. Kung recently flew from Chungking to the United States in four days, or sixty-three flying hours. The matter is really very simple. One takes off from Calcutta at one or two o'clock in the afternoon, stops at Karachi, sleeps soundly, takes off and comes down at Cairo for the second night, at Casablanca for the third night, and the next midnight one stops at Newfoundland for a cup of coffee and lands in La Guardia airfield at six o'clock in the morning. The airplane has completely revolutionized our conceptions of travel time. One might as well wake up to it, as one of the most important by-products of this war and one of the permanent features of the postwar world. There is no question that after the war, Seattle to Shanghai in twenty-four hours will become not only a feasible but an accomplished fact. Again the matter is quite simple. A plane traveling 350 m.p.h. can, according to simple arithmetic, cover 3500 miles in ten hours. A change of crew would enable the ship to cover 7000 miles in twenty hours.

There is no need to dwell on this part of the journey as if one really saw the countries one passed in the air. All the way we were stopping in American barracks, and there was little chance to get an impression of the country or town one was passing through, even though it was the first time I had touched South American soil and the second time I had touched Africa. I could not even send letters with Latin American and African stamps from the American airfields, as I had promised a philatelic member of the family. But traveling in wartime, one could not have everything. There was some slight compensation in the sense of mystery surrounding the trip. You were either in danger or dangerous and either the Army was trying to protect you or you were trying to protect the Army and therefore yourself, by not revealing the military secret in your possession that on such and such a date your ship was at such and such a place. The satisfaction and minor moral triumph in keeping a secret compensated for the inability even to let one's family know one had or had not safely crossed the Atlantic. One chafed at the little restrictions and inconveniences, but no more than any civilized being. It is like paying the income tax, going through that agony of mathematical involutions and fine metaphysical differentiations between total income and victory tax income, and net income subject to normal tax and surtax net income, and victory tax deduction and personal exemption and earned income credit, never knowing which to deduct first and which later. You get madder and madder as you come to the end and then someone says, "After all, it goes to build battleships to knock out the Japs," and your heart skips a jump and you smile and say, "Of course."

The age of commercial flying is only beginning, and some of our inveterate prejudices have to be gradually worn off. A kind of adult education is required here. There is a story of a Chinese gentleman making his will before going on his first airplane journey, in the first months of the war in 1937. He was in Hankow and was commanded to appear at Nanking the following day. As an official of a ministry, he had no choice but to take a plane provided for him. The evening before his departure, he called his wife and sons and daughters-in-law and nephews together, and lighted some red candles, and after what was considered a last supper, gravely announced his will and gave his dying instructions. Holding his youngest child's hand, he said, "If anything should happen to your old man . . ." and broke down and could not go on. His wife was sure that his old bones would not be able to survive his expected crash. There were prayers and assurances in the condolent mood that after all not *every* plane crashed and there was hope they might see each other in this life again. The family sat up with him through the small hours of the morning in sighs and tears, followed by courageous efforts at smiles, as if nothing was *really* going to happen, but living intensely every precious minute of their father's bodily presence upon the earth. Finally, the old man made bold to mention the matter of coffins and began a furtive discussion as to how much of one's body would remain after sustaining a fall of five thousand, nay, of perhaps seven thousand feet, and what one was to do in case there was no corpse to be found. This is a true story.

Some of our contemporaries still may not have got over this attitude about a flying journey, the same attitude that we had about ocean and railway and motor travel. There are undeniably ships sunk on the ocean, but we do not make our wills before crossing the Atlantic, and friends or relatives sending one off on the wharf smile without a thought that their dear one is going necessarily, or even possibly, to a watery grave. I went through a bad railroad wreck, but still maintain that, objectively speaking, railroad travel is safe. Stories of airplane crashes no doubt make good news and create an impression on the public's mind entirely out of proportion to the standard of safety achieved. The routine maintenance service of checking a plane after every fifty hours of flight, and the developments of the engine, have brought flying to a state when there is no more reason why an airplane should develop trouble on the way than a town bus. After a few flights one gets familiar with the sensations of landing and taking off as one is familiar with the sounds of a street bus stopping and starting every few blocks. The difference is that the air bus lands one after a few hours in a different country, and one steps out, not in a neighboring town twenty miles away, but in Morocco or Algiers. I was so inured by the time I was on my return journey that when our plane was returning to the airfield at Cairo and I heard in my sleep that "Number three engine has caught fire," I dozed off and did not know when we landed and took off again. The next morning the pilots referred to me kindly as "a sleeping bag." They did not realize how much confidence I was reposing in the ATC pilots.

I have seen the movie—*The Memphis Belle*—telling the story of a bombing mission to Germany. It gives, I think, the most fascinating sensation of a flight and of what one sees from the air. It presents a clear, straight story with a reality that grips, without any contrivance of melodrama. You mentally go up ten thousand feet and get a vantage point to look at the globe, with its blue waters and shore outlines and green pastures and deep forests and cities and towns and highways and rivers. You see the globe and it is round, and in twenty minutes you get a sense of its roundness, through perceiving its advancing and receding horizons, almost as if you were looking at a school globe. As the earth below you shrinks in space, you feel like a genie in the *Arabian Nights,* looking down on a toy globe, unbelievably beautiful in colors. As one ought to see Manhattan by going out at sea on a steamer, so one ought to look at the earth, reduced to the encompassable size of the eye's vision. One sees the sun setting behind a sea of clouds or watches a rainfall fifty miles away, or dashes through a rainstorm for only five minutes and comes out in the sunshine and gets a better physical sense of the earth we are living upon.

I insist upon the colors, too, as suggested by the picture *The Memphis Belle*. There is as yet no method of reproducing the colors of the sea except by technicolor aerial films designed for the purpose. Flying over the Caribbean Sea, one's senses are struck by the display of colors where the water is of different depths. As the contours of the shore line shrink into miniature proportions, one also sees a beautiful pattern of colors in that brilliant tropic sunlight, from deep navy blue to purple, lavender, turquoise, aquamarine, shading off into bluish and cabbage green and defined by the buff of the sand beaches against a fringe of bubbly white where the surf is—all on a miniature scale so that the whole seems like a moving, living toy or a jeweled palace made by some cunning artist. The string of islands, with water inlets and creeks and bays and crossings, becomes a connected pattern as the bottoms of the bays become visible, their relative depths indicated by the delicate shading of blues and greens. Where the land rises, it becomes an island, and where it slopes beneath the water, it becomes a strait, or an inlet, or a shallow crossing, and you see the accidents of topography interrelated, intelligible as a mass, as you see them on a model. A fishing craft or a tramp steamer appears like a speck or an infinitesimal leaf, crawling at an almost imperceptible pace, and then you realize that the strait which seems like a shallow rivulet from where you sit may be miles wide. Then you have to imagine that inside that tiny speck there is a miniature toy steam engine, perfectly fashioned with pistons and boilers and shafts and all, in a miniature ship provided with cabins and decks and saloons, all complete. Along these decks walk microscopic creatures who have made that ship and designed that clever engine to make it go, and these creatures themselves are provided with liver and heart and lungs and facial features. You marvel at such a living miniature and feel like a god looking down upon the human beings that inhabit the earth and toil and love and fight till they die.

As there were only two passengers, we were permitted inside the crew's quarters, being taken as adult democratic individuals who knew what might and what might not be done. They were a good, hardy lot, these American boys of the crew and those I saw on the ground, breezy and strong and cheerful, griping and jeering and cussing in that inimitable Private Hargrove manner, with not a speck of malice in their souls. They ate, they swore, they worked hard, they sweated and were personally clean, and didn't mind the grease, loving their work and their engine gadgets, yet most living the moment when their work was through. They teased and kidded and clowned and you couldn't believe a word of what they said. Woe to the mollycoddle who has just left his mother for the first time and takes their words too literally. Yet all this kidding and clowning did not interfere with their discipline and co-operation where work and ministering to the ship were concerned.

The captain was a blond. There was something about his accent and voice, the American voice, milk-fed and strong at the source and somewhat lazily rolled into articulate speech like that of a Harvard student. I suppose there is such a thing as an American voice, which is so distinctive and so good to hear when in a foreign country. The accent has a characteristic laziness, that goes through all the stages from mumbling and rolling of tongues to the slightly more careful enunciation of orating Senators. The English accent is lazy, too, when one compares it with the even distinctiveness of the French, or the muscular exertions of German *"ach"* and *"ich"* and *"Schlacht"* and *"fünfzig."* But the English counteract that effect of laziness in slurring over their vowels by affecting the muscular tenseness about the throat of a man on the point of strangulation. The American completely lets go.

The rather bizarre and inimitable mixture of cussing and slang which forms army speech, so successfully reproduced by "Private Hargrove," gave you confidence in the pilot's knowledge of his machine. Evidently he had been playing with switches all his life since he could call switches disrespectfully bitches. Then he looked out into the sky behind his sun glasses, his clean blond hair fluffing in the wind, while you heard the twin motors purring smoothly along—oh, it was beautiful to see! Simple like children, with few wants but a hankering for cigarettes, contented with coffee and sandwiches for their meals, with an utter contempt for boiled eggs, and delighted like children with the discovery of a can of mayonnaise, these boys sailed through the clouds! At night they rolled in bunks or on the ground, or on top of any level mass formed by the coincidental leaning together of some packages of cargo, and rested their heads on their bent arms and fell asleep. Such was the manner of living and sleeping with the army in wartime.

I was never more American-conscious than when I was on the journey, and never more so than when I was on the way back to America, after an absence of six months. Here in the United States where almost everybody is an American, you are not conscious of American traits. Traveling in distant countries, the American is at once recognized. He is on the whole more carefree and wears his part more easily than the sons of other countries. "Breeziness" is the word. Compared with the average Chinese and with other foreigners in China, he is distinguished by a trait of boyishness. There is a youthful jollity and Mark Twainian fun and folly implied in this quality, suggested even by the way obviously grown-up soldiers are called "boys" and office women of thirty are delighted at being referred to as "girls." The American is at once familiar and easygoing and has a natural pride in himself and his country. You have the feeling that he can't be taken advantage of easily and won't take advantage of anybody. He stands for his rights and respects the rights of others and loves getting into a fight any time, verbal or physical. He blasphemes and swears when things displease him, and half believes in God, but more in an instinctive hillbilly sense than in the church sense. He is also a spendthrift with a good business sense. His social dealings are simple and direct, coming from a society where everybody is everybody else's equal, and where if he does not like a place it is relatively easy for him to cut his ties and move about until he finds what he wants, and where if a man honestly tries to do his job well, he gets a fair deal. He clowns and loves a good time, but only the most fantastically shallow observer can deceive himself that he is "soft" or "effeminate." How did that notion ever get into the head of the deep and profound metaphysical German observers? He submits to discipline but only when that discipline squares up with his sense of justice. He stands for no red tape and innately hates rituals, and has more respect for puppies and horses than for aristocracy and kings. All these tie together into a pattern of quiet efficiency and simple courtesy and good-neighborliness that struck me vividly when I saw the officers and men of the ATC on the way to this country after a period of absence.

My reading of *See Here, Private Hargrove* gave me an insight into the character of the average American, in particular the G.I. I saw on the journey, the inner man as exposed in army life, stripped of his social armor. I believe the characterization is accurate and true. That soldier who jiggled his toe in the small of his buddy's back by way of waking him up in the morning is a funny but enormously effective creature. To be sure, this is a humorous book, portraying only the affectionately familiar and comical side of the G.I., and it says not a word about the other side—his serious side when he gets to work. But even without any profound knowledge of human psychology, the reader easily senses that he has got the stuff that makes a good soldier, ready to scare away the Devil himself with a good mouthful of slang, and when the Devil sasses back with quotations from hell, he can take it, too.

I lament the fact that the book isn't easily translatable into Chinese, for it would help enormously in a better appreciation by the Chinese of the American G.I. in China. To a Chinese crowd, and even to an educated Chinese circle, the G.I. in China certainly seems strange. Yet in spite of the necessary strangeness to each other, between the average American who knows nothing about China and the average Chinese who knows nothing about America, who are now, however, brought together by the war, I know the barrier is no deeper than that of language and superficial customs. The average American officer or enlisted man is forthright and fairly tolerant; sometimes his manners when he is displeased amount to brusqueness, and the Chinese, not knowing the American frankness, or not familiar with American profanity, are a little taken aback. I knew a Chinese flyer who was greatly offended when he heard a Chinese fellow-pilot referred to as a "son-of-a-bitch"; he knew enough English to know what that phrase means but not enough to know how many people share that common honor in army barracks. Without direct evidence, I know every G.I. has been at one time or another affectionately and politely called a "monkey" by his sergeant or by his buddies. The Chinese officer cares more for dignity, even for literary expressions, and if he does not know American manners, he is apt to take the American's addressing him familiarly with a "Hullo, Joe," as an evidence of disrespect. The moment the Chinese and the American talk fluently a common language, however, whether in English or in Chinese, all barriers vanish, and the Chinese say he is frank and natural like themselves. If the Americans are sometimes brusque, the Chinese discover that they have the compensating virtue of saying what they think and telling you honestly to your face; on the other hand, they can be quite thoughtless at times and tend not to face realities until they come up against them smack in the face. In international politics, I have never seen the American people play a "deep" game, and I don't think they can. The thing the Chinese have yet to learn is that when an American soldier swears, they need not take it in the dictionary sense. Someone ought to publish a historical study of swear words used by English and American generals and sea captains, and explain to the Chinese people that they mean, in the army and at sea, only something slightly less affectionate than "I love you," and then all will be well. On the whole, the impression the Americans give in China apart from their huskiness and their mechanical ingenuity and business efficiency, is that they are frank and direct and easy to deal with. The Americans, when they come really to know the Chinese, also find the Chinese easygoing and frank like themselves. The two peoples can remain just as they are and do not have to change a bit to be friends.

Throughout my journey, seeing American camps and airfields, I was impressed by the prodigal wealth and mechanical advances of America. I doubt that Americans at home quite know it that way, but the G.I.'s overseas are feeling it, I am sure, by the benefit of contrast. The Americans really don't even know how powerful their nation is, like rich men's sons who don't know exactly how rich they are. It is probably better that nobody tells them, not too much, so that as a nation they will behave only as just one of the several powerful nations, and enjoy a sincere feeling of the common equality of nations. It is not only that the American G.I. is better fed and better cared for than the soldiers of other nations. The transports, the supplies, the products of American machinery and American labor are literally pouring over the surface of the earth. In airfields and camps for American soldiers, the SOS has spent millions. The American Army just does not reckon in pennies and apparently never has an occasion to stint. The American Army may complain that it is short of this and short of that and has never enough to supply all, but by all non-American standards and the standards of other armies, that army is a spendthrift and a prodigal. What is needed by the Army is built in a short time. Camps at Natal, at Accra, at Kunming and Kweilin were expanded speedily, though they cost millions. One sees the shining silver bodies of the C-54's, and the brilliant airplane workshop, lighted by neon vapor at night and visible for miles, at a station in Cairo. A factory lighted by mercury vapor in Trenton or the outskirts of Philadelphia attracts no attention, but in Cairo it does. In native eyes, it is simply burning away quicksilver.

Going at an easy, comfortable pace, we arrived at Calcutta in ten days. Dr. Pao Chünchien, the consul-general, and his wife, whom I had known in Peiping years ago, were extremely kind to me and put me up in their home. They and other Chinese friends helped me with the booking of a flight to Chungking and other preparations.

I was all set to fly "over the hump." Our plane was supposed to leave from the airfield ten miles away outside the city at seven in the morning, and the passengers were notified to assemble at the Great Eastern

Hotel at 4:30 A.M. to clear the customs. I was therefore to get up at 3:30. I urged Dr. and Mme. Pao not to get up for me, for I would steal out of the house in the silence of the night. They had a perfect Peking servant who had been staying with them for over a dozen years. All Peking servants are perfect, and more dependable than an alarm clock. After finishing some letters at one o'clock, I went off into a sound sleep. I had laid out my Chinese gown, which I had brought from New York. I wanted to leave all my foreign clothes in a suitcase in India, being anxious to get into the comfortable gowns at the first opportunity. I was waked at 2:30, and had coffee and a bowl of hot noodles. Dr. Pao was an old friend of mine, but I felt guilty when I saw him up in his pajamas.

The car was ready, and I sped through the dark streets of Calcutta. The passengers assembled at the customs office looked like sleepy ghosts, and this effect was enhanced by the dead silence of the yard and the street outside. One by one we went up to the desk while others dozed in chairs. The customs officers were like the customs officers of any country, men who asked you the most personal questions, including the maiden name of your mother, with a most impersonal outlook, interested only in scribbling notes on paper.

As far as the flying operations are concerned, flying over the Himalayas is like flying anywhere. You expect to go through the routine sensations, the eardrums crushing outward as you go up and crushing inward as you go down. Sometimes there is a squeak in the ear canals as if a baby eel had rushed into them and landed flat against the tympanum. Sometimes there isn't. A few puffs with the nose held between fingers usually equalize the pressure, and relieve the chest. We were to go up without oxygen masks, this being a passenger plane of the CNAC. We might go as high as twenty thousand feet, and this might be an inconvenience.

The engine was warmed up. As usual, the plane taxied down a runway and turned ninety degrees at the end, and there the pilot ran first one engine, then the other, to top speed, for routine tests. The whole ship vibrated and chafed like a horse ready to break into a gallop but held back by the rider. Then the engine slowed down again and you knew you were ready to taxi the runway at a dazzling speed until the ship lifted itself in the air. She turned back into the runway and the whole earth seemed to turn round, and as one heard the steady mounting beat of the engine, packing more and more power and jabbing the air with a sharp, metallic swish like cutting a thin tin plate, the objects of the airfield swept past in a whirl. At this moment, one always had a feeling of suspense, that the miracle might not happen this time and this heavier-than-air machine might not lift itself from the ground before the strip ended. But it always did. Without one's knowing, its toes silently left the ground, and only when one looked at the houses and trees a few hundred feet below did one realize one was now floating, air-borne. Then the plane banked to change direction, and one side of the earth went up and the other side went down. The passenger felt he and the plane were erect, but the earth seemed to poise itself on one leg, about to keel over.

Were we circling the airfield or not? We were definitely coming down and heading back toward the operations building. One of the meters did not register, owing to some defective wiring. Most of the passengers got off while the mechanic was repairing and testing the meter.

A second time we took off, and a second time we came back. At eight, the plane finally started on its journey, and the engine soon settled down to a steady, pulsating whir. Nothing is more comforting and reassuring than the smooth, steady hum of the engine when one is up in the air. This was a Douglas C-47 and was provided with very comfortable, adjustable lounge seats. There were more than a dozen passengers in all, some Chinese and some Americans, including the very grave and reticent Gunther Stein, correspondent for the *Christian Science Monitor*, who had just come back from New Delhi, and an American missionary returning to her station in Fukien. The stewardess, a slim Chinese woman in foreign dress, came and gave each passenger a lunch box and a blanket to wrap around his legs. She was Mrs. Ma and told me her husband was also working with the CNAC. I asked her if she knew the CNAC stewardess who was killed by the Japs, and she said she had heard of her. I do not remember that stewardess' name, but she was a wonderful modern Chinese girl, college-educated, bright and independent. Flying in from Hong Kong to Chungking in 1940, I had met her, and my children all remember her vivid personality. She had graduated from Yenching and had contributed articles to a magazine which I edited. Her fluent English, Mandarin, and Cantonese and her slender size qualified her for the job on the Hong Kong–Chungking run. Small and dark-complexioned, she had a remarkably intelligent, cheerful and alert face, typical of many young college women in China. Talking with her, I learned that she was a lover of modern literature and had read much. The story of her death, as told me by the CNAC people, was as follows: Their plane had left Chungking for Kweilin. Midway they learned there was an alert at Kweilin and turned back to a field somewhere in Kweichow, pursued by Japanese fighters. Just as they landed, the Japanese planes swooped down upon the airfield and fired at the passenger plane. A number of passengers were wounded or killed. The stewardess helped the wounded to get out on the ground, where all cowered under the wing and the fuselage for protection. As the Japanese plane returned to fire again, she decided to dash across the field and was hit by machine-gun bullets in the abdomen and died in a few hours. Who would have thought that such a young girl should lose her life so abruptly, as so many of her sisters have done in the war?

The "hump" did not begin till we had stopped and refueled at a certain station in the province of Assam. The main range of the Himalayas was to our left on the north side, but from here on we were to climb higher and higher and remain at a high altitude for over an hour. In bad weather the plane might fly as high as twenty thousand feet, and on clear days as low as eleven or twelve thousand. I understand the crew also were not provided with parachutes because the passengers weren't, although they were so equipped when piloting freight planes. The CNAC had only about thirty or forty planes for carrying freight into China, working as a team with the American ATC planes, and only four planes in all were available for passenger service into and inside China. Day and night, in good *and bad* weather, these Chinese pilots flew, together with the American planes manned by American soldier-pilots, to bring in supplies for the U. S. Air Force in China and some essential supplies for China. It is one of the most hazardous trips in the world, comparable in its risks to the Murmansk voyage. The U. S. Army had set a goal for 10,000 tons a month, and had to reach that goal, no matter what happened. When I flew in in October, they had not reached the mark yet, but by the time I came out in February, they had exceeded that goal and were flying 15,000 tons a month, at great risk and sacrifice.

It was a cold, gray day, but not too cold for October. The period was in fact ideal, escaping the monsoons of summer and the ice formations of deep winter. Up higher and higher we went; one could feel the climbing sometimes by the pressure of the seat against the pants. The trip was bumpy, but only mildly so. For a moment we would sail right through a mountain of vapor, and the purr of the engine would change in fiber, like the sound of a skiff hitting the waves at sea, and water drops would swim aft in horizontal streams on the cellophane windows. Then there would be a sudden drop and

26

your viscera went up and the ship slumped down, and you saw you had emerged out of the tower of vapor into a clear sky. While flying through a fog, you had the uncomfortable feeling that perhaps you were running head on into a peak or an oncoming plane, but the feeling was relieved when it was learned that the planes traveled in opposite directions at different designated levels, the odd thousands for one and even thousands for the other.

Then the clouds appeared before and below you and you felt you were near to heaven and were afraid to whisper lest the gods might hear you. It was a strange land upon which angels and sprites might dance, but humans would sink when they stepped on it. The clouds appeared in the distance almost solid, luring one with a sense of security. The sun would be shining upon the mass, transforming it into an ocean of snow-white fleece, through whose gaps one could peep down into the abyss of the shaded nether world. When the sunlight was bright and intense, the clouds looked like crumpled silver, oceans of it, beaten and drawn out and spun into fine, fluffy skeins and clusters of thread, too fragile for touch, but the work of beating out that ocean of silver wool must have required millions of silversmiths, so vast and extravagant was everything in the scale of nature. You would say to yourself, Nature is beauty and beauty is as beauty does. Yet you knew all the time that this phantasmagoria of glory was held in suspense and borrowed a temporary, ephemeral existence from a subtle and delicate balance of heat and air pressure, and that, at one breath, that balance would be upset and the whole world of crumpled silver would change color and disperse and be destroyed.

You told yourself you were now sitting on top of the world, sailing by a magic craft that had mastered the mystic powers of wind and rain. Man had unlocked the secrets of the elements and made slaves of them; he had discovered the open-sesame of nature and surpassed the dreams of the teller of the tales of the *Arabian Nights,* or the wildest hopes of the medieval alchemists and ancient magicians. You saw more columns of vapory towers ahead, and you wondered whether this time the captain was going to slice through it or go around it. Sometimes he plunged right into it and came out of it in a few minutes.

In ten or twenty minutes the cloud formations had been left behind and we were sailing through the clear air, with nothing to obstruct our view of the earth and its rugged peaks. But the earth was uninhabited and untouched by human skill or intelligence, being worked on only by the wind and rain and the misty atmosphere of the mountaintops. The snow would melt from the rocky peaks and run into cataracts and mountain torrents unseen and unobserved of men. On the lower stretches vegetation would grow and multiply for centuries in silence, following merely the instinct for survival. Ages must have gone by since the Himalayas first stood there alone with God. Down below, somewhere in the thick jungles, forest sages have debated since millenniums ago on why there are mountains and jungles and lambs and ewes, and have given up, knowing only there must be God and deciding to say nothing more about it. Some of them have written fifty thousand words on the mystic syllable OM and still have not done with it, while others have lived and fought and died, like the beasts of the jungle, asking no questions and perplexed by no doubts. This human world lay now below me at my feet, shrunk in size, and its human beings were no bigger than little ants, leading Homeric campaigns against one another, stirred by Homeric passions and mauling one another in battles and close combats as bloody and ferocious as any ant battles could be. It had its demagogues and mountebanks, working on the passions and ambitions of races, dreaming of the glories of conquest and leading men to slaughter, but it had also its heroes and poets and soldiers, but all no more than the size of ants. What cruelty, what cheating, and what sacrifices were going on down there!

The passengers were told that since there was no oxygen tank, we would feel sleepy and probably the best thing was to sit perfectly still and go into sleep, thus requiring and consuming less oxygen. But I was not willing to sleep over this stretch, and tried my best to keep awake. I turned round and saw that many of my neighbors were perfectly still, eyes closed, apparently in sleep. There was not a sound except the steady drone of the machine and the sweet purr of the propellers. It was ghostly; we were sailing at an altitude that was unearthly, if not celestial. The stewardess was sitting in her seat, reading a paper. I turned the ventilation socket above my seat and directed the jet of cold air toward my face. My theory was that a continuous stream of fresh air carrying a little oxygen content would give me a greater total amount of oxygen than the still air. I asked the stewardess whether my theory was plausible, and she didn't know; she had no theories of her own. I asked about the altitude, because I had lost my altimeter in a handbag, and was told we were flying at seventeen thousand. I arranged myself comfortably in my seat, wrapping the blanket around my legs, and a feeling of drowsiness crept over me.

I don't know what I was thinking. A verse of my mother's came back to my mind, one she often used to tell me when I was a child. She said it in the classical pronunciation, not in our dialect, and it used to amuse me. It told of a Taoist saint who went up to heaven and returned to earth after centuries had passed, and then repeated the verse which said that "one day in heaven is a thousand years on earth." I had been told that the day before my mother died, while I was away, she had a dream, and after waking, had happily told her grandchildren the dream and repeated this verse again. What if it were true, and after a few hours in heaven I should come down to earth and find China in 1964 or 1974? What would I see? I saw a long, long bridge across Shanghai and Pootung supported by strong steel cables, and another beautiful bridge spanning the Chientang and another long one across the Yangtse at Wuhu, and most glorious of all, the Triborough Bridge, connecting Hankow, Hanyang, and Wuchang. There were many, many bridges all over China, all very beautiful and all made of steel. But there were other things, too—drinking fountains at squares, and parks for children and four-lane parkways and wonderfully clean and fast buses speeding along to the foot of Huangshan, the Yellow Mountain. And the gold and silver and copper and manganese and all the treasures of the earth would pour forth, and China would be a rich and prosperous and peaceful country and all farmers' children would go to school. These people of China, the men and women, would be sure of themselves, and say of the present generation, "It was a good job they did. It must have been an exciting period, when there was so much to do, a whole country to transform into such a modern, industrial nation. But they were brave men and women, and they did it."

These thoughts, it seemed, came to me in the flash of a few seconds. Only a mood remained. Had I fallen asleep? The air was cold and I shut off the ventilation socket. A crew member came out to see if everybody was all right, and stood for a moment at the door and went in again. I turned around and saw two American officers wrapped in their sky jackets, soundly asleep. A lady was shifting in her seat. The stewardess was reading. Nothing had changed, and I must have gone to sleep and been dreaming only a few minutes. The purr of the engine was smooth and steady. All was well.

In about an hour we passed over the hump. Now we were in China, flying over Chinese territory. Five thousand feet below us, I could recognize Chinese farmland and village houses. The familiar terraced rice fields were everywhere. After flying over Tali, with its tall, majestic peaks and blue mountain lakes resembling a Swiss landscape, we would be in Kunming in half an hour.

China lay at my feet. I remembered that I was returning by the back door. I would soon be seeing Kunming for the first time, but Kunming would be China, too, with a Chinese landscape, peopled by Chinese men and women. I felt a strange glow of excitement, not the keen excitement of youth at fresh discoveries, but one rich in memories. It was good to be home, to be lost in the land and its people and its customs and traditions and become an unrecognizable part of it. It would be like returning to a house where the trees, the backyard, the kitchen and threshold and doorsteps would be all familiar. It was like a part returning to the whole, where everything would be taken for granted, and one would feel safe and secure in a corporate entity bigger than our individual selves. I would be just one Chinese among millions of Chinese, and could talk of trivial things and accept certain customs without questioning and meet old friends and call up old memories.

I was returning to China for the second time during the war, after three very hard years had passed, and was intensely anxious to find out how she had changed. I was sure of one thing, that no matter how hard the circumstances, her fighting spirit could not change. There might be a few added wrinkles on her old face, but she would still say to me, with immense pride, "Son, we have kept the colors flying!"

It was half past two when our plane landed at the Kunming airfield. I wanted to shut my eyes and then look and I hoped to see China exactly as I wanted to find her, not too happy, but not too sad. The passengers landed and stood around; a few new passengers were going on to Chungking. I strolled about. Some sixty feet away I saw a group of peasant girls and women working to fill up a small shell hole in the airfield, and I went toward them. The girls, dressed in black and each holding an empty bamboo basket, were pummeling and pushing and chasing each other with romping laughter, and their mirth was irresistible. Silently I said to myself, "This is just right. So long as our people have not forgotten to laugh, China is all right." I could not have prayed for a better reception.

After about an hour our plane took off again for Chungking. A tail wind helped us, and in two hours and twenty minutes, we were circling over the city of Chungking.

It was half past five when we landed, but the sky was already gray. I stood looking at the rocky city from the airfield on the islet in the middle of the Yangtse. It looked so peaceful now, that symbol and citadel of China's resistance.

Three years ago, as I was coming out to do my writing, I was standing upon the same islet waiting for the plane to take off. It was a late August morning, near the end of the bombing season, and I was sorry to leave. The closing of the Indo-China railway after my arrival and the holding up of some essential reference books had shattered my plan for doing some writing inside China. The decision to leave China again was made after consultation with, and with the approval of, the Generalissimo. It was felt I should do my part in helping to interpret China abroad, a field in which there were singularly few laborers. An air-raid alarm had just sounded; the enemy planes would take two hours to arrive. But I could see a long stream of people walking on the road up the high bank, going into the shelter in the yet cool hours of the morning to sit out the air raid—hundreds of them, men and women in an endless stream, carrying stools and bundles and leading young children by the hand, going into the dark caves cut into the cliff, a whole city disappearing underground beneath the protective shelter of the rocks. It seemed like a picture of the Chinese people at their heroic best, a profoundly moving spectacle. They had been doing that almost every day for three summers already. There had been a severe bombing the previous day, and wisps of smoke from yesterday's fires were still curling idly in the sky. Someone ought to have painted a picture of that moment; it would be a great picture, a historic testament to the true spirit of Chungking, sad and gallant.

Now, as I stood on the same spot, the enemy planes came no more, and the people could work and sleep in peace. Three more years of war had passed, the fifth, the sixth, and then the seventh. The Marco Polo Bridge incident and the fall of Nanking seemed now so long ago; for seven long years China had fought single-handed. Who could have predicted that China would fight so long and so stubbornly? That was what Chungking meant to me and to the hearts of the Chinese people. There was Chungking, tattered and bruised and rather friendless, under siege for two years and still holding out, with rescue still far off, alone refusing surrender in an Asia that otherwise would have become a solid Japanese continental empire. It would be interesting to speculate about what Allied strategy would be against such a solid continental empire, cushioned in Thibet and the Himalayas on the west and the southwest and the Mongolian desert on the north.

Chungking stood there, waiting, waiting, waiting patiently, pathetically for the materials with which to start the counteroffensive and liberate her land and her people from the invader. It was the vigil of a nation, keeping watch in the hours before the dawn of victory, no less tense and inwardly exciting, however dark and calm the night out-

31

side. Outwardly, it was not so dramatic any more, like Chungking under the air raids, but the spirit of resistance was still there, latent and not given effective implement. The Burma Road had been cut off two years ago; there was an effective blockade, and prices were skyrocketing. The front had been stabilized. The story of China's resistance had been told. There was no more news of dramatic nature. And idleness was bad for the critics. There they sat, wasting their pity on China, and there sat China, wasting her hope.

I had arrived at the dead end of the world's war front, isolated, blockaded, and still holding out, never giving up until the supreme purpose was accomplished. I had arrived at Chungking, the stepchild of the United Nations, and like all stepchildren, heaped with ridicule.

But in my mind's eye, there stood Chungking, the Eternal City, rising like the phoenix out of the ashes of destruction, with feathers scorched and shaggy. But the spring would come, and new and resplendent plumes would grow, I knew. There stood Chungking, of which our children and grandchildren will tell legendary tales, about that remote era called "The Birth of a Nation," with its decrepit huts and hovels on the bank and its thousands of labyrinthine catacombs which future tourists will visit with curiosity and point to with pride— altogether an incredible story. And there will grow around it a halo of old glory, such as we of the present generation can neither see nor appreciate, being too immersed in the warring present.

2

CHUNGKING

IT WAS GOOD to be home. I had no intimate knowledge of the city, as on my previous return to China I had lived at Peipei, some forty miles away. But it was home for me because it was China. I promised myself I would know it really well this time. I wanted to lose myself in it, to become a part of it, to talk with its leaders and rub shoulders with its common citizenry, to eat at its restaurants and stroll along its streets, read its newspapers and share in its gossip. Here, if anywhere, I could find the soul of China, the particular quality of men guiding the destinies of the nation in its travail, and the attitudes of the rank and file, intellectuals, government employees, and businessmen, who

32

had sweated and suffered and hung on for seven years, despite the war and the blockade. I wanted to find that subtle, indefinable quality of the Chinese psychology, that daredevil, nonchalant endurance of hardships, and also that remodeling of the same mind through an awakened national consciousness and a keen, impatient desire for progress, modernization, and reform. Both would have to exist side by side; otherwise it would not be China, and I was happy to find both. Neither of these qualities was new to me, nor the frailties of the nation. I thought of the last years of China before the war, when the nation was rapidly building for the future, when there was a sense of hope and of the birth of a new nation, when the country had at long last pulled itself together under the then Nanking government and, despite mistakes, was making rapid progress—and then Japan struck. It was as if before a clay vessel was perfectly fashioned to the potter's satisfaction, it had to be sent to the kiln. This nascent nationhood was destined to be submitted to the ordeal of fire before it was quite ready. Would it crack, or would it be hardened by the fire and emerge, perhaps a little wobbly, but whole and unscathed? It was an unusually hard test, but the nation had stood up for seven years and my mind was at ease. But I also did not expect to find a perfect vessel, beautifully fashioned and artistically finished. Its turnings would be uneven, its dashes of enamel hastily put on, and in spots it might have an eggshell thinness. But one would for that reason marvel all the more and, holding it in one's hand, say, "It's a miracle," and prize it the more.

Here was Chungking in the seventh year of the war and one of the most bombed cities of the world, conscious of its achievements and of its tasks yet undone. I wanted and expected to see, not a Chungking dressed up for parade, but one in war attire, a little shabby at the elbows for the seven years of hard service. It would be a Chungking tattered and heroic, beloved and familiar as life itself. Three years ago, when I had left, two-thirds of the city had been bombed out. Now the bombings had ceased and the city had had time to rebuild itself. Yet the Far Eastern situation had worsened for China in the last two years, and there was an acute inflation. Would I find the people starved and weary, as the reports said? To my surprise, the people in the streets were no less well dressed and certainly no less gay than they had been. Instead of the hectic tempo of 1940, when office workers sat at their desks until the third alarm and came back and started working again while the fallen plaster was still being cleared out of the room, I saw a different life. There was an air of placidity on the faces of the men in the streets, as if the war had been driven back several hundred miles to

33

the front, a sense of temporary security and eased tension and dependable office and meal hours and, despite living and transport hardships, a happy and certain assurance of the approaching victory. No doubt the placidity was deceiving in a sense, for the people of Chungking were ready to take it again should the bombings be resumed.

But a hundred American planes for the defense of Chungking had made all the difference; the bombings did not come, and there was a breathing spell. Streets had been widened and new buildings had gone up. Contrary to my expectations, shops were overflowing with goods and the restaurants and theaters were full of people. A virile movement for the modern drama was going on, and people were discussing the current plays in parlors and restaurants. One might complain of physical discomforts, the absence of grand buildings such as should grace a nation's capital; but one should not ask too much. The wonder was that Chungking was still there, still holding out and leading the country in war. Bless Chungking for its courageous leadership, its staunch spirit of resistance, its underground factories and air shelters, its educational programs and colonization programs for Sikang and Sinkiang, its preparations for local self-government; for its fine determination and hopes for the future and its miraculous achievement in saving China from the fate of France. But bless Chungking also with its blunders, its muddy roads and leaky roofs and cracked washbasins and drafty theaters, and its doleful, uncertain electric lights.

I was met by General Hsiung Shih-fei, and we climbed the well-known three hundred odd steps up the bank and drove to his home. General Mountbatten was coming, and the Chialing House had been booked for his staff. Housing remained the greatest single problem for travelers to Chungking, and Chinese always stayed with their friends when they came to the city. I threw myself upon General Hsiung's hospitality. The house at Buffalo's Horn stood on the top of the Chialing bank, reached by a long flight of stone steps. Mrs. Hsiung was a young, charming lady, a student of McTyeire's at Shanghai, and she was particular about the bath and food hygiene and clean bed sheets, and there were children in the house. I was given a room of my own and provided with a chest of drawers and a desk to work on, and candles to supplement the treacherous and in any case too dim electric light. I was happy and thankful.

There was the problem of tobacco. In 1940, when I was at Peipei, I had bought tobacco leaves in the market and cut them with scissors and had got along fairly well. An addict of "Half-and-Half" for these past three years, I had thought of the problem before I went into China. The way I smoked I could never carry enough to last me six months, on account of limitation on air luggage. Now the good thing about tobacco was simply tobacco. Just as I later stooped to a filthy coffee made out of bottled coffee powder, so I decided I would smoke anything that was made of the fragrant weed. But I didn't want to smoke paper fumes in cigarettes. Szechuen has many brands of cigarettes and quite good cigars, but these were not for me. There was a brand of pipe tobacco called *Hwa Fo Lin*. I smoked that in Szechuen, and I smoked Yünnan tobacco when I was in Yünnan, Kukong tobacco when I was in Kweilin, and Kweiyang tobacco when I was in Kweiyang. It was all kind to my throat and it all satisfied. That is the mark of a true smoker. There are times when the thirst that rises from the soul cannot be satisfied by anything else.

At General Hsiung's house his youngest daughter, a little four-year-old child, as the hostess, wanted me to feel perfectly at home. She would rush in and out of my room with her cat, and would come and whisper to me when a visitor was waiting to see me in the parlor. What a little woman! We christened her the "Budding Socialite." There were week ends when the two older girls and a boy of seventeen would come home from their school and college at Shapingpa, and the table talk at dinner would be very lively, and I would feel the atmosphere of a happy home. Mrs. Hsiung would have knitted a new sweater for one of them, and they would eat all they could to make up for the poor food they ate at school. Having daughters of the same age, I felt very close to these girls. This was Young China, and I knew exactly how they felt and thought. But I could not get any one of them to say English words. Like all children of this age, they were being pestered with algebra, and taking it stoically—young, intelligent and hopeful.

Life in Chungking, capital of a warring nation, was not all war. Free China alone is half a continent, and without daily bombings, the front seemed far away. The bad aspect was the business-as-usual attitude. But it is just this ability to carry on, war or no war, that gives one confidence that China can endure, and that morale will not break. I could not decide exactly what that attitude was. After seven years of war, about the time for a young bride to become a mother of three children, anything but a war-as-usual attitude would be very unusual indeed.

Whereas Chungking was bombed in 1940, one could hardly see a trace of the scars now. The air shelters stood with their entrances barred and locked, and some were being used by commercial firms for storage. The bustle of Chungking was terrific. It teemed with human beings. One saw Cantonese and people from Shanghai and the North, besides all the natives of Szechuen, whirling and milling about on the sidewalks. If one got into a bus and sat next to a modern-dressed lady, more likely than not one would hear her talking the Shanghai dialect. As the buses were few, passengers lined up single file at the station, with a guard to keep order. Sometimes the line was fifty or sixty feet long. One got a feeling of despair as one watched that long line of waiting passengers ahead. But a bus would come along, and, amazingly, the line would be shortened by some thirty or forty persons. The bus was about half the length of a New York street bus, but it held thirty, one-third sitting on the side benches and two-thirds standing, packed tight. The door closed, and the bus started jogging and panting and throbbing along the winding ups and downs of the streets, and the tightly packed crowd swung and swayed with it. The boy conductor had the duty of collecting fares and giving tickets and change to passengers he could not see and could barely reach with his hands, over the shoulders or under the armpits of four or five other passengers, and all that in a perpetual earthquake. No boy conductor after such a month's training could ever be seasick, I was convinced. Yet the bus went amazingly fast; the express dumped you in the center of the city from the outskirts in about ten or twelve minutes.

You get down at Tuyukai, which is Szechuen pronunciation of Tuyuchieh (named in honor of Chang Fei, the black-bearded, loud-swearing hero warrior of the *Three Kingdoms,* very popular in Szechuen). Here is the busiest part of the city. You inevitably come upon the Spiritual Fortress, standing in the center of a square, hideous as a name and as a piece of architecture—a concrete pole that resembles a magnified chopstick. The architecture isn't Chinese, nor is the nomenclature, which as a phrase is in line with the affectations of modernism in contemporary Chinese writing.

Near here there is an electric clock with a story behind it, which the citizens of Chungking love to tell with chuckles. The clock stands in a square, with four faces in four directions. On the day when it was installed, people gathered round to watch it. In the course of the day the crowd grew bigger and bigger, and the policemen's efforts to disperse it were without avail. What had happened was that the man had forgotten to set the hands on the different faces of the clock so that they should indicate the same time. So the crowd would start from the north and see that it was 5:58 and go east and find the time 6:05

36

and on reaching the south find it was close to midnight. And the crowd kept going round and round, until they were quite convinced that whatever time they had on their own watches was incorrect, and they laughed and went off and were replaced by newcomers. It became a perpetual merry-go-round. The clock was a great success in the eyes of the idlers seeking for something to talk about. It was rectified the next day, of course, and by that time all Chungking knew that now there was a standard clock, THE clock, to set their watches by, which otherwise most of them would have stolidly ignored.

Standing at the Spiritual Fortress, you see the thoroughfares branch out in all directions, with concrete buildings, chiefly of two stories, and feel that it is a busy and prosperous city. As you wander along, you suddenly discover the famous shop names you knew elsewhere in China: the silver and silk shops of Shanghai, the scissors shop of Hangchow and the old medicine shop of Peiping, all transplanted. So are the newspaper offices of Shanghai and of Hong Kong, not in their former grandeur, but all bearing the familiar names. You find the Tasanyuan and the Kuanshengyuan Cantonese restaurants of Shanghai, reopened here, and in fact as you start looking for restaurants, you find there are more Shanghai and Canton restaurants than restaurants of Szechuen. There is a tremendous number of small eating places on every street, with medium-priced meals for that big class of office workers whose families are elsewhere in Free or even Occupied China. A popular name for many of these small restaurants is "456," because the word for "7" is a pun for "to eat," and when one reads "4-5-6," one thinks of food and is tempted to go in. There is a price ceiling for meals, but every variety of food is to be had; you can go into almost any regular restaurant and be sure of good food, and you come out feeling life is still beautiful and your labors for the day are not in vain. And you walk into a sweetmeat shop and find exactly what you would find in a Shanghai *Taohsiangchun,* cakes and pastry, lichee, *kweiyuan,* sugared plums, dates and Foochow shredded meat and Yünnan ham and sesame candies and "ox-hide gum." And you find that the Commercial Press, Ltd., and Chung Hwa and Kaiming and World Book Companies have all moved here, holding on and waiting to go down the river after the war is over. In a word, you find all the different cities telescoped into Chungking, and you wonder no longer that Chungking is jammed.

Chungking is, so far as my travels go, *the* city in Free China, with the greatest commercial, political, and literary activities going on, and that is what a "city" really means. But Chungking is a boom town, by

37

American standards. One could not ask for too much, when one realized the cost of building materials and the urgent job of putting up a roof over one's head after the thorough bombings. The city was not planned, not built as the nation's capital, but converted out of a second-class *hsien* town. Chosen for its fog, its rocky cliffs, and its location, where the Chialing and the Yangtse meet, it simply grew with the war. Streets have been widened since the bombings, but old parts of the town still remain. Here and there one saw fairly stable stucco buildings, or three-storied brick structures, or an even row of shops, not too bad to look at, but really built with a bare skeleton of thin timber to support the roof, with hollow walls made of woven split bamboo plastered with a coat of mud and whitewash, in expectation of more bombings. A few five- or six-storied concrete bank buildings only set in greater contrast the shabbiness of the others. The main streets, varying from twenty to forty feet wide, were a *tour de force* that the war capital had recaptured, as it were, and re-created from the bombed ruins left by the enemy. The people's homes spilled off from the main arteries and sprung out where no houses should be, up the steep flanks of rocky cliffs and down the mud gulleys of some ancient hillsides. Roads crisscrossed where no roads had the right to be, and led between shanties unexpectedly to modern concrete buildings, entirely at odds with the rest. It was neither town nor country, neither city nor suburb, it was just guerrilla architecture born out of this war.

Sometimes I would stroll in the neighborhood of the Buffalo's Horn and stand with the crowd, reading the morning papers pasted on the walls along the streets. Many stood there to read, sometimes for half an hour. Or I would go into a tea shop and from the back window overlooking a mud depression, watch the back side of Chungking. The tea shop was situated round a bend, and from the window one could see the backs of the row of houses on another street, standing at different levels on the slope, surrounded by mud. They had several floors, with porches overlooking the gulley, and were inhabited by a host of families, each, I suppose, occupying a room. The congestion was terrific. But this was war, and each family considered itself living in exile, ready to go down the river as soon as the enemy could be pushed into the sea. To keep the rooms clean of mud was a problem for every housewife. I used to watch in those morning hours how the housewives, their hair usually bobbed, came out to brush and air the clothing on the verandas where no sun ever shone in those October days, and swept their floors, with the sure knowledge that the next comer would inevitably bring in cakes of mud and scatter them about. How they must have longed for the sunshine of the lower valleys and for a few more rooms, and yards of their own!

In Chungking one learns to use one's legs. My body got more exercise in one month there than it ever got in six months in New York. When the sidewalks were not too muddy, I learned to pick my way fairly fast. But there were many ups and downs, flights of steps and slippery bypaths, and going down one of those on rainy days could do more for a man than a whole morning's calisthenic drill. It was a balancing act and a dance combined. The residents of Chungking took the mud in their stride, and one learned to laugh at a fellow passenger's fall. The people used the umbrella for two purposes, one against the rain, and the other as a portable mudguard to hold low over the legs and ankles when a motorcar was seen coming on, splashing and squirting jets of mud three to five feet away. It was not till I came back in December that I realized how clean and dry and comfortable for walking the streets of Chungking could be. Rickshaws were few and nine times out of ten refused a fare; sedan chairs were forbidden except where there were no highways or for invalids; people would take the bus or go on foot, or if the distance was really too great, would not go at all. There was always a way out, or *yu pan fa,* as war-harassed China says.

Trying to feel the life of the city as its citizens do, I would stand in line at a station and hear the gossip of the passengers waiting for the bus. Once a well-dressed woman approached the crowd and in a low, embarrassed tone asked for help. She showed her identification card, such as every resident of Chungking had to have, and said that her husband was a government employee, but had been sick for months. When the history of the war is written, I am sure her husband's name will not be in it. Yet if I had gone to that man's home and asked if he would have China lay down arms and patch up a peace with Japan, he would have said, "No." There are millions of them, unsung and unheard of, silently suffering for the sake of victory and not even thinking of it as deserving mention. Their contribution to the war is no less great than the names we shall read on the pages of history.

I used to see a woman selling oranges on the bend near Lianglukou. She had a child on her lap and another child of five picking up the orange peels that the customers threw about. On the face of that woman were written the strength and endurance of fighting China. It was the face of a normal peasant woman, eyes dark and lips thick, not really handsome, but it was Chinese, and her shoulders were strong and could carry the basket of oranges. Her husband was in the war, and she had not heard from him for three years. There is a chance that he will turn up alive when the war is over. Meanwhile she is carrying on, and she will bring up her children to be good men, self-respecting men, by herself alone if necessary. The mothers of China have done it often; and she has her sense of honor.

People said she was thriving, but I doubted it. If she had grown the oranges on her farm, that might be true. But she had more probably bought them wholesale and was retailing them. The oranges cost two to three dollars apiece, and she had rolls of banknotes, including some hundreds and fifties. That sounded like a lot of money. But that only meant that she made enough to cover her expenses. I don't believe she is living better than she used to.

I have heard that the laborers are prospering. Again I doubt it. Certainly they don't look so, not the rickshaw pullers and sedan-chair carriers. The rickshaw puller would get fifteen dollars for running a short stretch of ten minutes. But what is fifteen dollars? It buys a bowl of noodles. The managers of the factories must see to it that the workers and their families do not starve. But to say that they are thriving is a travesty. The farmers who are selling their own produce, vegetables and fruits and meat, no doubt have more money to spend than they did formerly. A few could sport brand new long-gowns. But remembering the level they had been living on, one can say only that they are feeling less the pinch of poverty, and that now they are getting a tolerable living that they should get anyway.

The gaiety and unconcern and the stolid endurance of what to Western eyes were really deplorable conditions were outstanding and mystifying. Apparently, in nature's scheme, there is not a blessing in this life without its concomitant evils, and not an evil without its compensatory blessings. The weakness of China is also her strength. The Chinese people might fight better if they were a little less nonchalant and better disciplined, but also they might endure less well. If the Chinese people were psychologically like the Germans or the Japanese, they would, even with their social and economic backwardness, organize themselves in a different manner; but they would also crack quicker. The ideal would be, of course, the individualistic, voluntary, and democratic approach which China has, plus the organized democracy based on social, educational, and industrial advances of the United States, which China hasn't.

Since China was in that stage of progress toward modernization when the war broke out, she had to fare the best she could. Yet from their past of grim economic struggles, the Chinese people have developed certain basic racial qualities, not the least of which is nonchalance. A British journalist who had just arrived, a very intelligent man, made a remark that would surprise the Chinese public. He had been through the streets and watched the people strolling placidly along, refusing to give others the right of way. "The Chinese people are great democratic individuals," he said to me. "They don't give a damn for anybody." In a way that is true; but the Chinese, taught by tradition that it is the civilized thing to be polite, not only would be surprised if they heard that remark, but I doubt if they would understand it. Placid and unconcerned, talkative and ready to laugh at others' mishaps as well as their own, they went their way. The faces of the passengers on the bus, whatever else they might be, were certainly not gloomy, and least of all obsequious. They crowded each other, they yielded, they rolled and rocked in their seats, but they did not "give a a damn for anybody." If the weather did not behave, they would criticize God himself. Order was very well preserved at the bus stations. But I maintain that public courtesy with strangers, submission to discipline and regimentation are not racial characteristics of the Chinese people.

That was how China carried on the war, each man fending for himself, each family fending for itself and for its friends. That was how the Chinese solved the vast problem of the migration of millions. That was how they had been carrying on for the last seven years. And that was how they were facing the inflation. Chinese good cheer and unconcern under distressing conditions must now be admitted as one of China's greatest assets in the war.

Everyone is feeling the pinch of war. My figures are never good, and I write from memory. Prices change, too, from week to week. But I can write out the following prices current in October, 1943, in Chungking:

A candle	$7
An imported candle	$30
A box of matches	$2.50-$4
A package of ten cigarettes	$15-$50
A package of twenty Chesterfields, Luckies, Camels	$160-$180
A cake of toilet soap	$20-$50
A cake of Lux or Palmolive	$150-$200
A book	$30-$150
A magazine	$10-$20
A newspaper	$2
A cotton gown	$1,200

A silk gown	$4,000-$5,000
A pair of leather shoes	$700
A foreign suit	$10,000
An automobile tire	$100,000
A satisfactory restaurant meal	$50-$100
A bus ride	$7.50-$15
An army officer's monthly salary	$1,200-$3,000
A college professor's salary	$2,500-$4,000
A government employee's salary	$4,000
A bank employee's salary	$4,000-$6,000

The average rise of prices, compared with the price index of 1937, was two hundred times. If one takes this as the average decrease of purchasing power of the Chinese dollar, it means that an employee whose monthly salary is $4,000 is actually earning $20. On the other hand, the government provides rice for him and his family at a nominal rate.

A Chinese stage and movie star rehearses all afternoon, and performs at the theater in the evening. Then sometimes she has to go to work at the movie studio for the rest of the night, because only during the night is the electric power sufficient for the lighting needed. Then she goes to bed at dawn and sleeps through the morning. Yet when I saw her she was as fresh as a daisy. For this work, she gets the so-called $4,000.

Medicine is expensive, and one just cannot afford to be ill. Life is reduced to its essentials of food and clothing. It has been going on like this for the last three years. They all know that inflation is part of the war, and since everyone wants to carry the war to the bitter end, they do not see how the inflation can be avoided. It is amazing how people learn to adapt themselves happily, some even comfortably. The human power to adjust to new circumstances is always greater than we suspect, and than outsiders who are not subject to the circumstances can imagine.

So the war has been brought to the rear; it is brought home to the people in their food, their dwelling, their transportation, and their habits of living. The Chinese people do not grumble, but are more likely to smile at their misfortunes. They are talkative and love to criticize the government's measures for price control—that is in their blood. It is hard to see how certain foreigners in Chungking can get the impression that the people are sullen, or can go so far as to suggest that they are "war-weary." How the people would hoot at such an insult! Suffering, yes, but sullen never. It is curious how one can live in a land and completely fail to see the inner spirit of its people. Foreigners in China are peculiarly allergic to physical discomforts, being used to so much better transportation and living conditions. Not only that, they are in the democratic habit of howling against things that seem wrong in Washington, and there is no reason why they should stop that useful, healthy democratic habit in Chungking. The Communists, capitalizing on the effects of the blockade and the inflation, are able to paint a fairly somber picture of the administration. Hearing this, and hearing the way Chinese in general freely criticize and joke about their government (which is an inveterate Chinese habit), some smart Americans believe that, as wise and penetrating observers, they have a "hunch" that the people are inwardly disloyal, discontented, and war-weary. The censorship further helps them to disbelieve everything printed in newspapers, and good Americans propose to think for themselves, which is another true index of a democratic people. The Chinese people must joke about their government, even as the American G.I. must "gripe" if he is any good for military action. Chinese are extraordinarily frank about official measures and people's private lives; they gossip and they laugh in parlors and public restaurants; they criticize the government everywhere except in public speeches. Further inference, however, would lead to the realm of national psychology, and here foreigners are apt to go astray. Chinese patience with evil and with unbelievable hardships is a national characteristic and must be understood; Chinese soldiers put up with conditions of food and care for the wounded under which American G.I.'s would certainly refuse to fight. The psychological reactions do not register in quite the same manner because the background is different. If by "war-weariness" is meant that the Chinese people from top to bottom are hoping for the early end of the war, that is so as it is in Russia, England, and the United States. If, however, by the term is meant that the Chinese are ready to lay down their arms and would rather not go through with the war, I must say that I did not find a man or woman, in any part of China, who is thinking that way, or who is disloyal to Chungking, except the Communists.

Apart from the human capacity for adjustment, the Chinese society goes about fighting the inflation in its peculiar Chinese individualistic way. This is something difficult to explain. The answer to the problem of inflation in China can be only through the individualistic, and not through the collectivistic approach. The Chinese are either not educated enough, or not regimented enough, to submit to price control;

43

besides, printing ration books for the three hundred million people would use up all the available paper in Free China. Things are just not done that way, and the Chinese would resent it. In Communistic areas the rigid control of the people, with commissars penetrating the countryside and controlling the women's organizations and farmer's unions, enables the Communist régime to know the exact number of chickens and pigs and crop produce in every household. The Chinese national government cannot do that. It does not know that farmer Li has three pigs, or that farmer Chang has four chickens. Perhaps the regimentation of the people's lives ought to be more rigid in times of war. I do not know. All I know is, that has not been the Chinese way, the traditional way of *laissez faire,* and I believe in the long run it will not work while China is China.

The total result of the inflation is less alarming than economists might imagine. When sugar control was established, sugar prices went up. When the pork price was fixed, pork disappeared, because it did not pay the farmers to bring the pigs to the city. When the price control on pork failed and pork was forbidden, the restaurants served it and the people ate it. Now pork is in the stage of being both banned and eaten. This is due to the social and economic backwardness and the low educational standards, but I believe that was how the Chinese survived. Each individual must find his own way, and each organization must make certain adjustments to retain the services of its staff. Official rules have to be broken. Some government organizations make advances to their employees for hospital expenses on the birth or death of a child, in that old-Cathay, undefined manner, in total disregard of regulations, and following the basic human consideration that when a man is in dire extremity, it's only good sense to break the law and help him. When the director of the organization is questioned for exceeding his budget, he explains the reasons and the Minister of Finance understands and winks an eye. If a college president is short of funds, he goes to his friend the banker; somehow it is arranged. Personal relationship counts for everything. That is China. Of course, all this makes for confusion. It means that many officials are unable to keep within their budgets; but since budgets can never catch up with rising prices, they do not see how it can, or should be, avoided.

The businessmen and the farmers do not suffer from the inflation, because they have the goods; many of them in fact prosper by profiteering. Salaried men who have any savings at all try to join the ranks of businessmen by investing in some small shops run by their friends. More often their wives do it for them, or they do it in the name of their

44

wives. Some borrow from their friends, some fall back on their parents, and some sponge on their relatives. Some sell all they have. I went to a restaurant owned and run and served by students of the Southwest University of Kunming. I remember seeing the waiter sitting at an empty table working on a physics formula and then getting up to serve customers when they came in.

Many needed goods are smuggled in from the occupied areas, with somebody running the risks and making the profits, and so the shops are full of goods for all who have money to buy. You may or may not like it, but that is the way, probably the only way, China can fight off economic disaster.

3

PANDAS, WIDOWS AND THE LITERARY FAMINE

THE climate of Chungking was disliked as universally as the enemy. The city was soaked in damp. Colds last for months in the winter. The October weather here is best described as suddenly clear, suddenly rainy, and neither clear nor rainy, and both clear and rainy at the same time. It was impossible to draw the line between the two. There is an old saying in China, probably two thousand years old, that "a Szechuen dog barks at a sun," because the sun so seldom appears, and when it does, it shows its sickly, pallid face from behind a veil of clouds like a thief.

But this wartime capital was deliberately chosen for its fog in winter, and the weather was worse for the enemy than for the people, who breathed fog and security. As between the fog and the bombings, they certainly would choose the former. Why have a clear sky and see the city in flames? And so the people took the climate of Chungking also as a contribution to the war. They cursed it and were grateful to it, even as they used to curse the moon in the summer nights of three years ago, and would rather have had a dark moonless night that they might sleep in peace.

The Szechuen weather is crazy. It seems that God wanted to give the people of Szechuen every variety of fruit and flower, tropic, subtropic and antarctic, but decided, in compensation for the variety, to give them a less noble species of each. I saw with my own eyes a butterfly perched on a chrysanthemum, which was like finding a sun helmet on an Eskimo. This is a strictly botanical and zoological fact. There are butterflies in Szechuen in deep winter fluttering among chrysanthemums and plum flowers. Nowhere else would this be possible. The pride of Szechuen in her oranges is unassailable; in color, texture, and taste the Szechuen orange is exactly like a California orange; some claim it was the father of the latter. But once that is admitted (to prevent quarrel with the Szechuen people) we must go on and state fearlessly that the province has some medium quality of every kind of fruit in which other provinces are bound to excel. It has dates of Peking, but not so good as the dates of Peking, and lichee of Canton, not so good as the lichee of Canton, and pumelo of Kweilin, not so good as the pumelo of Kweilin. It has cherries, *pipa, lungyen* (dragon-eye, a subtropical fruit), big olives, sugar cane (good), peaches, and horrible sandy pears. Strangest of all, it has dwarf palm trees, never growing higher than ten or twelve feet. What brought these palm trees there that I have not seen elsewhere in China? Everything shrinks to a subnormal size in Szechuen. As you wander in the outskirts, you think you see donkey carts, pulled by donkeys. You are sure they are donkeys, until you come up and swear that you see ponies. They are just Szechuen ponies, so different from the tall thoroughbreds grazing on the loose in the wheatfields of Sian, even as the men of Szechuen are shorter than the men of Sian. Is it the rocky soil or the inadequacy of cosmic rays? I am now convinced that the panda is only an Arctic bear who has wandered from his habitat and become lost in Szechuen, where he shrunk for the lack of vitamins A and B. I shall not be surprised now if I find one day a three-inch lizard in a pool on top of Mt. Omei and he should tell me that his great ancestor was an alligator from South America, who simply fell upon bad days and decided to shrink himself to his present size. Even Szechuen shrimps shrink. If you were willing to pay an enormous price and order a dish of fried shrimp in Chungking, you would be able to discover them only with a microscope. But, in honesty and fairness, one must confess that Szechuen has good flowers, very good flowers and every variety.

"God is unkind to you. He seems to give you the poorer kind of everything," an outsider from "down the river" would say.

"God is unkind to you," a Szechuen native would reply. "He would give you lichee and snatch away your dates, or give you dates and snatch away your lichee."

There is a kind of gentle raillery without malice going on between

46

the Szechuenese and the people who have come up from the different provinces. The Szechuenese lump them all together as "down-the-river people" *(hsia chiang jen),* including people from Kansuh who have never had anything to do with the Yangtse River. Another term for the outsiders is "antipodes," or "people beneath your feet" *(chiao hsia jen).* Having grown up under harsh surroundings from their pioneer days, the natives are tough and well able to defend themselves. As Szechuen was practically a separate world, buttressed against the outside by high, impassable mountains and accessible only through the treacherous Yangtse Gorges, the people never saw so many foreigners before. Now as they see these indolent and soft people from Shanghai, who bite into their territory, a kind of sly battle goes on whenever the natives and the antipodes meet. The Szechuen people call the outsiders "robbers," and the outsiders call them "rats." At a restaurant, an outsider will say to the waiter, "Give me a package of cigarettes—Szechuen brand." "What Szechuen brand?" asks the waiter. "The Golden Rat, of course," says the man from down the river. His Szechuen friend will then call for the waiter and say, "Give me a package of cigarettes —Shanghai brand." "What Shanghai brand?" And the Szechuen man says, "Pirates, of course."

In the suburb where the better residences were, a winding road was cut through the steep sides of a village hill. On your right below, huts and houses and vegetable patches and old cemetery grounds ran down the gulley, tumbled and straggled, as if on their way somewhere, like pioneers, or exiles merely pausing for rest. On your left rose more steep hillsides. Who would have expected to see fields of corn and vegetables up there sloping at such an angle? But there they were. Here the view was the prettiest. The congestion of traffic and shops disappeared. One got a glorious glimpse of the Chialing, five hundred feet below, and the mountains of Kiangpei beyond. Below on the right were the Chialing House and the homes of Dr. Sun Fo and General Stilwell and General Ho Yingchin, Wu Tieh-cheng and K. P. Chen at different levels of the five-hundred-foot ascent, reached by zigzag motor roads. Far below near the riverbank, barely visible, was the bus road leading out to Shapingpa.

At night this road was excitingly beautiful. Thousands of electric lights dotted the landscape where Chungking's war factories were. (The enemy knows them very well.) Out of the dark one would hear bugle calls or the explosions of dynamite. They were good to hear, for they were the sounds of China building for the war. Strolling in the dark, I would meet lovers, sometimes the boy and sometimes the girl singing a modern ditty. Once I heard a couple singing "Dixie Land" and "The Old Oaken Bucket."

Higher up was the Futukuan, now renamed Fushingkuan (because *"futu"* in Chinese sounds like *"hutu"* which happens to have almost exactly the same meaning as the American word "hoodoo"). This was where the Central Training Institute was. I was told by Dr. Sun Fo that one of the Americans about to leave China told him about concentration camps. "There is one right here, a short distance from your house," said the American. "Where?" asked Dr. Sun Fo, greatly surprised. "Farther up this road," the other said. "You mean at Fushingkuan? Why, that is the Central Training Institute," answered Dr. Sun Fo. I suppose the Central Training Institute does stand for a "fascist" camp in the minds of the Communists. But this shows that the least dependable report may be from one "who has just come back from China." . . . Late in the afternoon, one would meet professors coming down with brief cases in their hands, and sometimes soldiers or students in uniform.

At one point which commanded a wonderful view of Chungking and its environs a stone monument commemorated the lives of Thirty-Seven Widows. There was a large stone panel, with the names of the illustrious widows inscribed. On close scrutiny, I found that the horizontal tablet was wide enough for fifty names but approximately one-quarter of the space was left blank. What had happened? Had the thirty-eighth widow failed to turn up and earn her way to immortality? Or had some war put a stop to this some centuries ago? These, I found, were all wives of college graduates, and it reminded one of the past when heroic courage was so much appreciated in women by the ancient Confucian scholars. But these were not Widows Heroic *(liehfu)* who had made the supreme sacrifice or done some deed extraordinary; a Widow Heroic would get a monument all to herself. These were merely Widows Chaste and Faithful *(chiehfu),* about whose chastity the scholars entertained an inordinate degree of concern. This, I am sure, was a kind of collective bargaining for immortality, entered into by the village scholars. I rather hated the husbands as I read the names; the inscription always read Madame So-and-So, Scholar So-and-So's wife. They were a class by themselves; a peasant's widow might remarry, but no widow of a Confucian scholar of any rank would think of so dishonoring her husband's name. And so the scholars slept peacefully underground, knowing for certain that their widows would be faithful to them. That was why they took the trouble

48

of joining together and erecting a common monument, with a stone panel broad enough to hold fifty of the Widows-Chaste-and-Faithful-to-be. But somehow only thirty-seven made their hopes materialize and now breathe an odor of chastity for posterity. Anyway, they were there and nobody paid any attention to them. *Pax vobiscum!*

At the Thirty-Seven Widows, then, one got a glorious view. The Yangtse River flows beneath your feet on one side, and the Chialing River flows on the other side, and down where they meet, the busiest part of the city stands. The promontory turns and twists and is now covered with human structures and caverns bored into its hillsides by the hands of men. It is like standing at the top of the Spanish Cloisters looking down at Manhattan, with the Hudson on one side and the East River on the other, with the exception that Manhattan is practically level, while the Chungking promontory thickens and heaves up like the head of a turtle. Below and across lay the fair fields of Szechuen, incredibly green in sun or rain, and beyond on all sides ran ranges of mountains.

Standing up there I tried to locate on the river the U.S. gunboat *Tortilla* and the French gunboat, but I couldn't. "Tortilla," I imagine, is Spanish for "turtle," although I know no Spanish. (I turn up the dictionary, and it says a tortilla is a flat, round Mexican cake, but I am sure the dictionary is wrong; it is so unromantic to name a gunboat *Pancake.*) These gunboats have been there for seven years and are there for the duration of the war, like fish caught in a shallow pool. Three years ago in Chungking I read a sad story about the French gunboat. The French sailors had been living there for years and had fraternized with the village children. But in 1940 France had just fallen. The children were cruel, although they didn't mean to be. "France has fallen! You *wangkuonu!*" (meaning "slaves without a country"), they shouted and jeered at a lonely sailor. The sailor evidently understood, for he went back to the boat, saluted his flag silently and disappeared below the deck. I wish the kids had had sense enough to apologize to him the next day. Village children and great presidents can be very cruel.

Chungking swarmed with hundreds of bookshops, and the people stood, jamming the bookshops and reading for hours, especially in the afternoon, in the hours before supper. These shops were a kind of reading room, without chairs. People read standing, as hungry people eat. It was a literary famine. Books were scarce, and the readers had enormous appetites. They were interested in the outside modern world, but there was, and is still, practically an embargo on books into China. I suppose this is unintentional, but it is an embargo all the same. It was difficult for magazines to get articles on the outside world. Two or three outstanding English books, such as Wendell Willkie's *One World,* and John Steinbeck's *The Moon Is Down,* or Ernest Hemingway's *For Whom the Bell Tolls* and Captain Lawson's *Thirty Seconds Over Tokyo,* would be smuggled in and several Chinese translations would be published and sell 5,000 to 10,000 copies. My own English books could be found only in pirated editions or in Chinese translations. At present, there is not one copy in the whole of China of *The Wisdom of China and India,* published in 1942 in New York. None of my friends had heard of it. A copy of *Life* was regarded as a treasure and passed from household to household. Only the *Reader's Digest* has an authorized English edition, reprinted in Chungking. In a few organizations the overseas edition of *Time Magazine* could be seen.

There were usually thirty or forty Chinese magazines in the bookshops, weeklies and monthlies containing articles on literary, economic, and political topics. All pictorial magazines have gone out of existence, owing to the prohibitive cost of plates; there is just one pictorial, published by the American OWI. Of the Chinese magazines, *Time and Tide* is probably enjoying the best circulation, selling, I was told, about 30,000 copies. On the shelves of these shops stood Chinese volumes, chiefly dealing with the war, economic planning, national projects, accounts of battles, interpretations of the Sanmin Chuyi, and collections of President Chiang Kai-shek's speeches. But there were also travel sketches, collections of short stories by modern authors, and plays, of which about twenty are produced in a year, because of the rise of the modern drama.

There were always secondhand copies of books printed before the war and sold by starving students or professors to make ends meet in times of family crisis. And once in a while one would come across a volume, beautifully printed in wood block. The cost of printing was such that sometimes a well-to-do author would rather go back to the old-fashioned wood block, since it was hand-printed and one could "brush" a few copies off the press as desired at any time. Chinese handmade paper was never designed for the machine press. When it is used for newspapers, the printing is a strain on the reader's eyes, but when printed with the large characters of the wood block, it is as beautiful as any volume published centuries ago.

This is merely an illustration of the disharmonies which the transition age is imposing upon us. I believe every custom, every social habit, was established and developed to perfection through centuries of social experience, whether it is the women's hairdo or writing utensils. The imposing and borrowing of foreign customs immediately produces a conflict and disharmony. The Chinese ink was developed to perfection; at its best it has a fragrance and an incomparable luster lasting for ages. So with the red ink pad for seals; it keeps for years and never gets dry or leaves an oily blur on the paper. Whatever was considered desirable was bound to be perfected after centuries. So with the Chinese paper; its best kind responds to the touch of the artist with the sensitivity of a photographic plate and records all the caperings and light tappings and swift turnings and onward rushes and final triumphant pauses of the artist's pen. To attempt to write good calligraphy on foreign paper would be hopeless. Chinese paper was made to absorb the Chinese ink, which dries quickly. But to write on its soft, thin, and tenuous tissue with a pencil would tear it, and to write with the foreign pen and ink would both break and blot it. The triple harmony of brush, paper, and ink (including the ink slab) is the achievement of centuries of Chinese technical development, upon which were bestowed naturally the greatest love and care and ingenuity. But you just cannot make newsprint out of it or run it through the modern press.

Another related illustration is the development of Chinese paste, instead of glue. The paste enters into the texture of the Chinese paper and becomes a part of it, and a Chinese envelope sealed with paste is practically impossible to reopen without injuring the paper. Glue would thicken and harden and disfigure the paper. The paste and Chinese paper go together, but the paper and glue don't. You cannot change an element of the technique without disturbing the harmony of the whole. Now the fountain pen is superseding the Chinese brush among Chinese students, which involves of course also the change to machine-made paper of a harder texture, and brings in its wake the degeneration of Chinese penmanship. Meanwhile, it will be decades before Chinese can manufacture good fountain pens and quantities of newsprint and linotype, which the West has taken decades to develop, and for the next decades we must put up with bad print, bad paper, and bad calligraphy.

These are but some of the side aspects of the ugliness and pain of a changing China. Our articles, our faiths, our ideas must pass through a period of shabby pseudomodernism before they can mature into a new and fruitful culture.

51

4

THE NATION'S LEADERS

DURING the month of my first stay in Chungking I was well occupied. I had the opportunity to renew old acquaintances and form new friendships, to talk with the leaders and, in chats in parlors, offices, and over dinner tables, share in their respective plans for China and the aspect of things as they saw them. Staying at General Hsiung's home, I was fortunately able to share in the discussion of China's postwar plans and problems in the evenings, when conversation was more casual and topics were turned idly about, sometimes revealing new intimate angles, and a happy but immature idea might suddenly strike someone in the party, to be laughed off or flayed by the others. General Hsiung was, and is, the Secretary-General of the Central Planning Board, of which Chiang Kai-shek is the President. A general in the campaigns of the National Revolution of 1926-27, he had suffered an injury in his foot and could no longer serve at the front. He had been garrison commander of the Shanghai-Woosung area and governor of Kiangsi before he came to the United States as head of the Chinese Military Mission. His mind and interests were more those of a civil administrator than of a military general. He had a deliberate manner of expression and a subtle, almost meditative frame of mind more appropriate for the conference room than for a military camp. In fact, his dominant interest was in the problems of industrial development, begun when he was governor of Kiangsi. When he was asked by President Chiang Kai-shek to serve as executive chief of the Central Planning Board, he advised either shutting it up or going into it in a big way, with the idea of working out a unified national plan for postwar reconstruction. He asked for an enormous budget and got it. He gathered around himself a large group of economists and industrialists, and although no expert in economics, he kept his mind open, receptive, searching, and alive.

Therefore in the evenings a number of such friends gathered to continue their discussion of China's industrial problems, with digressions into the philosophy of Laotse, of which General Hsiung had a deep understanding. Laotse's doctrine of "inaction" or *laissez faire* was in fact, according to Hsiung, the ordering of action so that great and lasting results were obtained with the least effort, by making an ally of the natural sentiments and instincts of men, or more mystically, by acting in accordance with the principles of nature. One of his favorite illustrations was the disposal of refuse in Peking under the Manchu régime. The Manchu government did not hire a fleet of street-cleaning trucks to carry the refuse to the outskirts of the city, which would be "action." It simply issued an order forbidding carts carrying vegetables and food into the city from going out of the city gates empty, which was "inaction." It made refuse carry itself away!

Among the more frequent visitors in General Hsiung's home were Ho Lien, the Nankai professor of economics, K. P. Chen, the modern-minded and extremely wide-awake founder and president of the Shanghai Commercial and Savings Bank, and the joke-loving and astute political strategist, General Wu Tieh-cheng, one-time mayor of Shanghai, who was responsible for bringing the Manchuria of the "Young Marshal" and certain Kwangtung factions into the Kuomintang fold.

There were two especially interesting figures, who almost made a pair in size. One was Weng Wen-hao, educated in Belgium, and Minister of Economics, who had made an outstanding record in recent years and was a man of great humor. Given a cabinet post, he remained essentially a scholar. Small and thin, he had a deep depression in the middle of his forehead just between and above the eyes, caused by a motorcar accident in which I believe he was the only survivor. Dressed in his simple cotton Chungshan uniform, he might have been taken for a small government clerk. Once before an air raid he came to the entrance of the special air shelter of his own ministry. He had not brought the air-shelter identification card with him, as he had come from an appointment elsewhere, and he stood with imperturbable humor for a quarter of an hour waiting for rescue. Finally someone who knew him approached and said with surprise, "Why, Minister, what are you waiting for? Why don't you go in?"

"I was not admitted," said Weng. "I told the guard I was the Minister, but he would not believe me." The other official passed a remark about the stupid guard, who was of course a little frightened. "Forget about it," said Weng with a smile; "do I look like a minister?"

When he was in the company, the conversation would be punctuated and illuminated with his laughter. The other member of the pair was another extraordinary man, Lu Tsofu, the president of the Minsheng Steamship Company, who had a drier kind of humor. We shall come to him later. And there was Dr. Sun Fo, of course, the great Kuomintang liberal and social thinker.

53

Of particular importance were my conversations with Dr. Sun Fo. While living at Dr. Sun Fo's home at Chungking after my return from the Northwest and from the Southwest, altogether for about five weeks, I had the privilege not only of enjoying Dr. and Mme. Sun Fo's hospitality but also of hearing his views in long talks over the breakfast table, after lunch, at tea, and after supper. There were often Chinese and foreign guests dropping in for lunch or tea, and I had a leisurely opportunity to absorb their views, particularly those of Dr. Sun himself. Mme. Sun Fo had a knack of making people feel perfectly at home, and she was liked by people. Their own children were away studying in the United States, but many young visitors were constantly in the house, which gave it a lively, youthful atmosphere.

As his recent book *China Looks Forward* indicates clearly, Dr. Sun is a great liberal social thinker, widely read in Western social and economic theories, a great admirer of Russia, and a sincere critic within the Kuomintang. His hobby was to tune in the broadcasts from San Francisco, London, Moscow, and Berlin after supper. The short-wave reception was perfect, and it was his fastest, though not his only, way of keeping up with the latest news. When some obscure Pacific islands were mentioned, I was amazed at the accuracy of his knowledge of their distances and positions. He had a few American magazines and a complete file of about a dozen daily newspapers published in Chungking. On his shelves stood some of the latest volumes published in England and the United States.

He had a capacity for wading through heavy volumes and for remembering statistical facts and figures. Severe and dignified in public, he was genial and human at home and loved little jokes and stories. When the conversation bored him, he retired to his radio, or worked on various drafts of the new laws in China. Many mornings and afternoons he would be giving lectures. At the time when I was there he was busily engaged in daily conferences of the Council for the Enforcement of Constitutional Rule, at which he usually presided with Tai Chitao. This council was established by government order after the government's resolution to introduce constitutional government one year after the cessation of the war, and at these meetings all political parties, including the Chinese Communist party, were represented. As this subject lay very close to his heart, I often had the benefit of sharing at home the overflow of his enthusiasm from the conferences.

It was characteristic of Dr. Sun that he talked sometimes with a cool objectivity about facts and figures, and sometimes with a deep conviction on ideas and emphatic viewpoints, when he would rise to a passionate outflow, or to a tone of indignant disapproval of things that seemed utter stupidity to him. One such stupidity, he believed, was the neglect of a quick understanding with Soviet Russia, in view of the many war and peace problems that were sure to arise. At such times he talked like a fiery revolutionist, and his eyes grew very big.

I remember my first close meeting with him a dozen years ago in Shanghai. We were on a spring outing to a country club, and he suddenly asked me, "Who do you think is the greatest man in Europe?" I had no idea. "De Valera," he said, and I caught then the first glimpse of a revolutionary thinker. In 1940, when I was sharing his air-raid shelter one day and we were playing quiz games during the air raid, he came out with the question, "Who is the woman author who is also a diplomat?" It was Mme. Kollontay. He had mastered Sidney and Beatrice Webb's work on Russia, and quite a few others. During his visits to Moscow, when he was negotiating personally with Stalin for the three big loans to help China with war supplies during the first years of the war, he was greatly impressed with the efficiency of the Russian experiment. Long before the siege of Stalingrad, he predicted as certain a Russian victory and foresaw the whole Russian strategy, as Max Werner almost alone did in the United States. China will need him when she is ready for a policy of cordial co-operation with Soviet Russia.

These discussions helped to give me a better-rounded view of the future of China. The most important points are two. First, Dr. Sun was emphatic about the possibility of a peaceful settlement of the Communist dispute. One day he talked with complete frankness on this problem to the foreign press correspondents, and I saw a note to him the next day from Brooks Atkinson, their informal dean, expressing their deep appreciation of his frank and convincing talk, and wishing for more of that kind. The second point was his great optimism about the future of China after the victory. He was cocksure of the rapid advance of the American Navy along the Pacific and of early victory. And then he pictured after victory a great era for doing great things, an era filled with hope and splendid opportunity for China to rise rapidly into a first-class nation. Then he talked like a dreamer, like his great father, and smiled a very broad, contented smile, seeing the realization of an old dream. It was as if he saw the day of victory already. He told me that all this petty grumbling and criticism will be forgotten at the time of the Allied victory, and we will see the people of China in a spell of "high jinks." It was so good to hear that note in this time of blockade.

I had time to feel the pulse of Chungking and get a first-hand impression of the problems and the mental currents of the people, and a general idea of what they were thinking and feeling. I had a chance to gather, discuss, and exchange their ideas about the war, plans for the future, and also the more immediate problems of current local interest. I had good talks with the genial, placid Vice-Premier, Dr. H. H. Kung, and I had the chance to talk with men like K. C. Wu, Chen Pulei, Yu Tawei, Chu Chiahwa, Hollington K. Tong, Liang Han-chao, Chang Taofan, Yu Yujen, Tseng Yangfu, Ku Yuhsiu, and with editors, bankers, professors, students, writers, actresses, painters, and housewives. Often I was asked questions which I could not answer, not having a prophetic gift: When will the war end? Who will win the next American presidential election? When are we going to get the tanks and artillery for the counteroffensive?

Sometimes they were puzzled and concerned over the current criticisms of Chungking: Why this sudden wave of hostile criticism? Why this suspicion and distrust that we are not fighting Japan? Who is behind it? Their attitude was one of bewilderment rather than of resentment. Most of these men faced tasks yet undone and were more concerned in doing them and going ahead with them than with what foreign countries said about them. When the criticism was fair, they admitted it and said, "But it is true"; and when it was untrue and silly, as many were fantastically silly and grotesque, they laughed it off and were amused. In China people thought principally of China, and there were a great many problems of immediate interest to them, like the colds that last for months in Chungking, or the movement for college student volunteers to Burma that was starting in that winter.

Then there were more purely intellectual and deeper problems concerning the opposing ideologies with regard to China's continuity or break with the past. I had a three-hour-long talk with Chen Lifu (M.A., Pittsburgh), the Minister of Education, on the conflict of ideologies between the Kuomintang and the Chinese Communist party with regard to preservation of China's national and racial tradition, manners, and morals.

Chen Lifu was a man of extraordinary intelligence, whose mind had a sharp, cutting quality and who had always something special to say in the matter of ideas. His hair was grayish, and his face well-modeled, with fine features resembling his uncle's. In the three-hour-long talk we never left the realm of ideas. He does not believe that a nation can exist without faith in ideas and its past, and is in general a believer in the national tradition, with a special philosophy of his own on the idea of "living" as the motive power and goal of human life. He is strictly a Kuomintang man, and as an arch anti-Communist is probably the man most execrated in the Communist camps. We talked about this Kuomintang-Communist conflict in the sphere of ideologies. Besides the political conflict, there is a great battle of ideas, a rift, basic and sharp, suggesting a deep and unbridgeable chasm, which seems to me more fundamental. It is rooted in the fundamental opposing attitudes of the Kuomintang and the Communist party on the question whether the traditional Chinese culture must be saved and salvaged, or whether it should be uprooted and discarded completely.

This intellectual conflict is not generally known abroad, but is a large and seething current invading the minds of men in present-day China, and it will affect the character of the coming age. This controversy between nationalist and anti-nationalist ideologies is naturally a live issue and is an important feature of newspaper debates. When it is known that the radical extremes state in all seriousness that "Chinese youth should not study Chinese ancient books" and that "all Chinese books contain poison," *i.e.* feudalistic ideas, it can be understood that the discussions are at times both maddened and maddening. Chinese scholars, like Ku Chikang, Feng Yulan, Chu Tseching, and others, who suggest that the past national culture or the Chinese philosophy of life is worth defending and that all Chinese history is not just a stinking pot of corruption and exploitation of the masses, have been under constant attack by the *Hsin Hwa Jih Pao,* the Communist daily published in Chungking. I myself have been the subject of very lively attacks in at least half a dozen articles in this paper, including the charge that I write only "pidgin English" and that I know nothing about Chinese or Western culture. On the other hand, the history of Chinese rebellions has been interpreted from the Marxist line. The lawless Taiping rebels, noted for wanton loot and massacre of whole city populations (nine-tenths of the population of my home town, Changchow, were slaughtered in my grandfather's days), and even the notorious bandit gang of Li Tsecheng in the seventeenth century, whom nobody would think of defending, were upheld as "revolutionists" standing for mass struggle. One criticism of my *Moment in Peking* was that I completely failed to mention the "economic causes of the Boxer uprising" as a revolutionary mass agrarian movement. I always thought the Boxer uprising was rooted in deep, racial anti-foreign *ideas,* and that ideas had as much reality as potatoes. This was from a non-Communist youth, but the fact only shows the prevalent Marxian fashion and influence among the contemporary youth of

China. One of the most acrid criticisms of Chiang Kai-shek's book, *China's Destiny,* is against his stand for old moral ideas and old culture, which was pointed out as evidence of his "feudalistic reactionism." His laudatory mention of the upright, unimpeachable Confucian scholar and statesman Tseng Kuofan, almost a model of Confucian virtues, drew an entirely senseless and virulent comment which has nothing to do with a fair, critical appraisal of this historical character in an atmosphere of academic freedom. Tseng Kuofan was a Confucianist and therefore must be discredited. Defense of Tseng Kuofan's moral character was defense of counterrevolutionary habits and ideas. It was as simple as that.

There is a bout going on now inside China between Master Kung and Karl Marx, and my bet is that Master Kung will win. The people in the grandstand are sharply divided and hoot at each other. The Marxian fans would like to see Master Kung's whiskers plucked, and the Kuomintang fans would like to see Confucius claw Karl's bushy beard. Any fair discussion of ideas is impossible when the discussion of such important questions of ideas becomes a party issue. So far the participants in the controversy are not even aware that the issue involved is between the fundamental humanism of Confucius and the economic and deterministic materialism of Marx. This wholesale challenge to China's past and negation of all historic values except mass revolution explains the Communist appeal to China's youth as a fundamentally revolutionary doctrine. In what country does not youth like to be thought of as "progressive" and take a hand in upsetting something or other? But this also explains its fundamental weakness as a national doctrine. If Marxism is an adequate way of life, it will work; if not, it will leave a vacuum of moral ideas in which the instincts of men for family and social living are unsatisfied. Time will settle that, not words, and I can imagine that twenty years from now, the ardent Communist advocates will become as pro-Confucian and as desirous of having roots in one's own racial and historical tradition as the Kuomintang minister of education, Chen Lifu.

The temper, or distemper, of such discussions is interesting as showing the moods and tempo of contemporary Chinese thinking. Speaking at the Central University, I suggested that the *Book of Changes,* one of the Five Classics of Confucianism containing the deepest principles of the Confucian philosophy of human events but usually neglected, should be studied by scholars interested in understanding Confucianism. In any normal country, such an academic point should pass unnoticed, or at best arouse a slight ripple among a few scholars. The hue and cry was raised in *Hsin Hwa Jih Pao* that I was urging that "all youth should study the *Book of Changes.*" It was as much criminal heresy, as dastardly and dangerous to the morals of youth from the Communist point of view, as if someone should suggest putting *Moll Flanders* in the hands of American schoolchildren. That was the general level of such criticisms. If I had chosen to talk about Plato or Petronius or Sappho, they would think me "progressive" and possibly even "revolutionary," since I would be talking of foreign things.

On the whole, it is a good sign; it means that China is in a mood for change, a mood that must precede a more balanced and saner appreciation of one's own national ideals, which will come perhaps ten years from now.

I saw President and Mme. Chiang Kai-shek six times on this trip. When I went for lunch or dinner at their home without other guests, we could talk and relax and be at ease. Sometimes we had the opportunity to talk for hours after lunch. When the President left for his official duties, I carried on the conversation alone with one of the most fascinating women in the world. I think the President was kinder to me than I deserved, but I suppose he liked to hear the opinions of a man who is outside the government circles and who, as they both know, would never go into a political post. The greatest benefit to me personally was that I learned a calm patience and tolerance and a large view of things from one of the most amazing figures in China's history. That man thinks in terms of decades.

The President's home was a foreign-style two-storied building on an elevated position at Tsengchiayai, in the city. One approached it through a broad, clean, and slightly curving alley, and just before coming to the gate, the alley turned off to the right where the President's secretariat was situated. The guards were always previously notified of the President's appointments and would admit the guests without more than a routine, courteous question. Going up a few flights of steps, one reached the vestibule, deposited one's hat, and went into a quiet, carpeted parlor. I am not a man to tremble in the presence of the mighty, but I did feel a faint thrill in that room. It was decorated with Chinese scrolls and flower vases, two sofas and two armchairs arranged around a fireplace, besides Chinese hardwood chairs in other parts of the room. Many historic conferences have taken place in this room. I liked the good taste and dignity of it, as befitting the residence of the head of a state. Usually Mme. Chiang came in first, and we would have some chat around the fireplace before the President appeared. She put me at ease, in that warm, homey atmosphere, so that even when she looked at the hole in the sole of my only pair of leather shoes, I did not feel embarrassed.

The President would come in with a courteous, soft-voiced greeting. His enormous eyes gave you a direct look, softened by his reassuring smile. In his Chinese jacket and gown, he was very good to look at. He has a Chekiang forehead, high and full, and always holds his head erect. I especially liked the way he scratched his close-cropped head or gently rolled his fingers over it, because scratching one's own head means thinking, and gently rolling one's fingers over it means the mind is roving over ideas. I felt I was seeing his mind visibly in operation. It was like seeing Albert Einstein clutching his bushy hair with his stout fingers. Men are thinking animals, but the only way we can actually see the thinking of brilliant statesmen, poets, and scientists is by that outer movement of the fingers roving from the front of the head to the back and from the back to the front, caressing the thoughts, as it were, and halting at an important clue or judgment or decision. Chiang's mind has always a perfectly calm and leisurely quality, as of one who has successfully solved many brain-cracking problems and is ready and confident to solve many more to come.

Once, when other visitors were present and the discussion was on a serious topic, I saw his face change and there was a sharp, full glow in the light of his big eyes, and his lips were compressed. When he looked serious, he looked very serious. But otherwise it was a face soft-skinned and firm and without a wrinkle at the age of fifty-seven, with a gentleness and refinement totally unexpected in a man who had been leading strenuous campaigns for the last eighteen years. That was the first impression I had had when I had seen him in 1940. In spite of these hard years he had not aged a bit. This is related to the second and equally striking impression, his perfect calm. He appears not like a man in the hustle and bustle of war, but like a chess player who knows in his mental calculations that he has already won the game, and that no matter what move the opponent may make, he has a countermove and is only leisurely waiting for the moment when the opponent will say, "I give up." People who had seen him during the feverish retreat from Nanking told me that one afternoon when some twenty callers were waiting in his room to see him, all about important business, he gave clear, brief, definite instructions, this man was to do this and that man was to do that, with not a tremor in his voice. That, we must conclude, was how he was able to conduct such a calm, steady unswerving course of the war and of diplomacy, when all the odds on earth were against him and against China.

The third impression I had of him, and this was the most important, was of a man influenced by the humanistic culture of the past, a Confucian in outlook and personal living, matured with experience and grown broader and more tolerant than in his younger years. The influence of Tseng Kuofan was deep upon him; he made his children study Tseng's family letters very carefully, and he gave his sons the type of education and breeding exemplified by Tseng's letters, with emphasis on hard work, self-discipline, regular schedules, thrift, frugality, and humility in social relationships. All this came out in his appearance and in the ordering of his personal life. I think the influence of Tseng Kuofan was bad upon him only in one respect; I refer to his habit of personally attending to all details, which may be fine in a military general, but perhaps not the best quality in the civil head of a state. The best rider should hold his reins as if he didn't, following Laotse. He should find completely able assistants, like the "Little Tiger," General Hsueh Yueh, delegate to them complete authority, and expect only the highest results from them. But more important in Chiang are the largeness of understanding, the Chinese subtlety and historic outlook, the tolerant and mature philosophy of living, based on ancient Chinese culture, that I see as characteristic of his mind and policy. Those qualities are going to be the most valuable in the days to come, as China works out her problem of internal unity, as China must. The bitterness and harshness of his early campaigning years are gone. One can no longer think of him only as an able general and strategist, though he has united China by superior force and strategy. One has to think of him now as a ruler of a transforming state, a pacifier of all factions, standing over all, devoted to carrying out the necessarily slow process of building a modern nation out of feudal and semifeudal human material.

This is a point difficult to appreciate apart from the contemporary Chinese background. Sometimes he is called a "dictator," and there is no question that he and nobody else rules in China, and that he stands for no nonsense. Yet when one looks back upon the past seventeen years, it is surprising that, with the exception of the "purge" of Communists after 1927, it is a régime devoid of "political murders" or wholesale "purges" of the Russian and German type. He never turned against his revolutionary comrades and did not kill one of them. He shut up, on occasions, his political opponents like Hu Hanmin and Chen Mingshu, placed them under surveillance, and later released them. He fought Generals Feng Yuhsiang, Yen Hsishan, Pai Tsunghsi, Li Tsungjen, Tang Shengchih, Tsai Tingkai, and then was able to win them over and work with them. It had to be so in China, and it was so, and credit must go both to Chiang and to his opponents like the Kwangsi generals. He had to contend with a number of semi-independent warlords; toward these he worked with tact and tolerance; he always absorbed them, but only by an enormous patience and a gifted sense of timing.

At lunch or dinner, we had good but simple meals. Having grown up from a poor family, the President still loves his rice congee, and there were usually two small dishes for him, like Foochow shredded meat, pickled bean-curd, or salted turnips, to go with it. Mme. Chiang ate little anyway, and the President, being a military man, finished his meal very fast. They urged me to eat, but what could I do? My mind was not on the food, but was focused to catch everything they said. Chiang's habit is to ask questions and to listen. He would ask what I had seen on my way and would add his comments, suggesting this or that, with an air of ease and casualness.

After lunch we would go over to the parlor, the Madame and he walking close together. He would sit in an armchair by the fire, while Mme. Chiang would often stand up and pace about when the conversation grew lively, and her words and feelings were emphatic. It was in such moments that I formed the impression of a man "dignified but not severe, courteous and poised and at ease with himself." I felt that he was a happy man, in full possession of himself.

He neither smokes nor drinks. He likes water. His personal habits are those of a self-disciplinarian, bordering on Spartan asceticism. At Cairo the Allied representatives were surprised at his early rising hours. Daily, winter or summer, he gets up at five or half past five, has his hour of reading and meditation and his simple breakfast; then from eight o'clock on he goes through memoranda and official documents, prepared in order for him by his secretary, Chen Pulei. He works on these at his desk or in his chair, reading them, okaying them, or "initialing" them with comments. This he does till about eleven, when he may have short conferences. He has his lunch at about one or half past twelve, and he utilizes the hour to talk with more officials or visitors who have come from the provinces. Then he retires, has a rest, and reads or practices his calligraphy, which is sharp and square and with full concentration on every stroke, like his character. At five he sees visitors again, and sometimes he has guests for dinner. He always retires at about ten, and all his guests know this and take care to leave on time.

Some of his officers try to live up to his standard. General Hsueh Yueh, the "Little Tiger" and defender of Changsha, gets up at half past three every morning. What Chiang cannot stand is lack of punctuality. At the Monday memorial meetings, he is always punctual himself, and few if any Chungking officials dare to show up late. This must be accounted for by his military training. In all the summer camps for officers' training before the war and in the Chungking Central Training Institute, punctuality, cleanliness, and endurance of the hardships of the army life were vigorously enforced. At Kuling, where I spent the summer in 1934 and where an officers' training class was going on, the Generalissimo used to stand in the open two hours lecturing under the blazing sun. Once Wang Ching-wei was caught at one of these army lectures and had to stand immobile in the sun with the rest. He was miserable and groaning at the end. At the memorial meetings in Chungking, where all stand throughout the meeting, the Generalissimo used to stand too. Only after he had become President and people reminded him that the late President Lin Sen had been allowed to sit, did he consent to sit down as a matter of state form. He has an innate sense of decorum and carries easily the dignity of his position.

He cannot stand dirt, sloppiness, or lack of order. Before the war, at the Aviation Academy to which he gave his personal attention, he used to go about inspecting the rooms, and would run his fingers over the window sills or even the tops of doors, and woe to the cadet whose room was found with a speck of dust!

But his alert, youthful appearance is, I believe, more a matter of moral culture than of physical regimen. He knew that he had unified China by force and superior strategy before the war, but since the war was declared he has achieved a different kind of loyalty, a loyalty in the common people's hearts. For instance, the wild, spontaneous, nation-wide celebration of his rescue from Sian must have reacted on him and made him kinder and more tolerant. After he has led his people to victory, his prestige will be so high that anyone who challenges him will have little support from the people. This thing has gone pretty deep. Once in 1940 I was talking with a sedan-chair carrier on my way up Tsinyun Mountain when there came an air-raid alarm. "Hah!" said the sedan-chair carrier, "the Japs can never outfight our Chairman." He used the word *tou,* denoting medieval tournament or the single combat of celestial spirits in high heaven.

63

Is he ever angry? Yes, he is. There are occasions when he loses his temper. He doesn't swear, and he doesn't have to; his anger is enough. When he was kidnaped and held in captivity at Sian in 1936, he was as much infuriated as offended at the insult and indignity. He fumed and thundered at his captor, the "Young Marshal," and then refused to talk to him. If Chiang has any fault, it is his stubbornness. They could kill him, but he wouldn't negotiate terms. His release had to be unconditional.

But he gets angry at other things. He is impatient to put things through, and in the army he always did. Not so with civil affairs. He wanted to create a modern nation, and when he heard of abuses and corruption and official indolence and public lethargy, they made him mad. He would harangue the students at the Central Training Institute for hours, trying to create a new mind, a new enthusiasm, and train up a class of men and women disciplined and alert and ready to get into the job with whole heart. He took the Central Training Institute seriously and frequently gave long speeches there. In many speeches he publicly flayed the nation for abuses, for laziness of mind and body and slowness to wake up. Many went away inspired, and some slipped back gradually, and went about cynical and wise and indolent as ever. In his speeches he often used the moral whip, which is characteristically Chinese.

I have often thought of the contrasts between this moralistic approach, the totalitarian approach, and the democratic-constitutional rule-of-the-law. Growing out of a missionary college and a Chinese Confucian society, I have lost faith in the power of the sermon. And I believe sermonizing is being overdone in China today. Certainly there is no way of speeding up China's progress without some change in the prevalent social psychology of the people. The Chinese people are a great people, patient, cheerful, hard-working, courageous, deserving of sympathy and all that. They also have defects—not the least of which is a congenital and incurable sense of humor in politics, for example the supreme gift of "openly obeying the law and discreetly breaking it," or "obeying on the *yang* side and disobeying on the *yin* side." After all, the government is made by the people; the Chinese government is made of and by the Chinese people. When you say the Chinese government is good or bad, or the Chinese people is good or bad, you think not only of the high government leaders or of the common people; you think also of the rank and file bureaucrats, the town and village civil employees and the policemen, who are the "people" themselves. No government can rise above its civil employees, made up of its own people. The malpractices of conscription offer the best example. And no national health program can be better than the quality of its doctors, nurses, and health officers.

As China approaches her period of national reconstruction, I wonder how she is going to do it. Russia has succeeded, but she has succeeded by the totalitarian technique, by liquidating or exiling or shooting a mayor or a factory manager who fails to produce the quota of thirty thousand tons of wheat or steel decreed by the state. Obviously this totalitarian approach cannot be applied in China, if I read Chinese temperament and Chinese history correctly. You just can't go about shooting people right and left in China. It cannot be done. The only alternative seems to be moral persuasion, infecting and injecting a class of young men and women with an artificial fever and a spirit of enthusiasm, inspiring them with a vision that this nation shall be put right and on a sound, modern basis within this generation, by a total "mobilization of the spirit" *(tsingshen chichung)* as the slogans at the training institutes say. Yet moral persuasion must fail unless the insidious example of corruption is removed from the minds and experience of enthusiastic young men and women. This can be done only by freedom of the press under the protection of the law. First and last, and apart from all paper constitutions, only when civil liberties are secured can the people have the power and the spirit and the released energy to protect themselves, and to weed out corruption and public abuses by the democratic process of newspaper exposures and fearless attacks. No amount of strengthening doses of moral vitamins will prevail unless the purgative of a free press is there to purge the body politic of parasitic poison. The health of the state depends on "colon hygiene," much as one may dislike the metaphor, and the guarantee of the proper purgative action is the constitutional liberty to howl at our public officials. The cornerstone of democracy is the willingness of the officials to be howled at. Then they can do either of two things, defend themselves in the free and untrammeled forum of public opinion, or take the case to court and justify themselves there.

5

SHIPS AND MACHINES

SUDDENLY, with no background whatsoever, I became interested in China's industries. I had caught the fever of industrialization talk in China. Never had I visited so many factories and seen so many machines in a single month as during this trip. I visited iron and steel works, cotton and woolen factories, machine shops, power plants, a shipyard, and an arsenal. I also had my lighter moments and had a beautiful outing to Peipei, where I own a house, in the company of Mr. Ku Yuhsiu, the Vice-Minister of Education, and his brothers and their wives. I am afraid I must forego describing a spouting basin, an ancient relic in the museum of Peipei, from which one can make the water spray up in a fine shower four inches high by just running one's wet fingers along the brim, or describing a half-starved French-returned engineer, deserted by his wife, trying to revolutionize motor and steam engine by constructing a wooden model, and being fed by a devoted carpenter, who made and sold cabinets to keep him alive.

The managers of the different plants, thinking that coming from America I probably had seen the Pittsburgh blast furnaces, which I haven't, would apologize for the size of their unpretentious plants. But that was not the point: like Dr. Johnson's remark about women preaching, I marveled at the thing being done at all. The moving and transplanting of China's machinery, like the building of the Burma Road with human hands, was a marvel in itself. I greatly marveled at the building of a steamship out of a salvaged keel, the making of boilers without new steel plates, the removal of a four-thousand-pound generator over mountain paths without power transport, the taking down and setting up of a cast-iron furnace, standing forty or fifty feet high in the open, with all its complicated tubes and funnels. And I took an intense interest and great pride in seeing lathes turning, looms working, especially those that were made by Chinese. Whether these plants measured up to the American standard was not the point.

The story of Chinese matches is illustrative. Using a box of matches in Chungking, I usually found that three out of four or five would not light. Quite a few in every box were only matchsticks with no tip at all. A confirmed pipe smoker should be annoyed after striking three matches that didn't light to find a fourth one without a tip, and should curse silently in his heart and call this a Godforsaken land. But all depends on how one looks at it. In my childhood I saw only Japanese or Swedish matches. Now China can make her own matches and one out of four is certain to light. That is no small national triumph, and I have the right to be immensely pleased.

So I was proud of all the things a blockaded China was compelled by necessity to make for herself. I was proud of China-made pencils and dry batteries and dental creams and toothbrushes; I was proud of Kukong-made telephones and Kweilin-made radio sets and Kunming-made gear cutters and Shensi sweaters and Chungking leather shoes and ladies' handbags and Chinese woolens, coarse as they might be, and of Yumen gasoline, though imperfectly refined. I was proud of all China's baby industries, not because of what they were and what they produced, but because of what they were able to accomplish during the war and the promise they held out for the future.

Factories were spread out in greater Chungking as far as forty or fifty miles up and down the Yangtse. Early during my stay I went to Peipei for a visit, and there I met the mayor, Mr. Lu Tsoying, brother of Mr. Lu Tsofu who had pioneered in the industrial development of Szechuen. Mr. Lu Tsoying accompanied me to Chungking on one of their own Minsheng steamers and introduced me to his brother. The elder brother then arranged for me to see the different wartime factories, including his own Minsheng Shipyard and Machine Shop. While sailing down the Chialing back to Chungking, Mayor Lu told me the whole story of the Minsheng Steamship Company and of his great brother, for whom he had a prodigious respect.

The Minsheng had a phenomenal history. Starting with eight thousand dollars paid-up capital, with which it bought a hundred-foot steamer to run between Chungking and Hochuan on the Chialing, it had a unique development, until now it has a fleet of ninety-eight ships. It played a great part in the war of resistance from the very start. It was the story of a business genius with a modern mind. Without any proper education, Mr. Lu struggled in poverty and taught himself until he became a mathematics teacher and then editor of a paper. When the company was formed, he was practically unknown. But he was a man who loved the machine for its own sake and who had a modern, mathematical, analytical mind for scientific business management. On the steamer, his brother pointed out to me a railway line from the coal mines at Paimiaotse, running along the mountaintop probably a thousand feet above the river, and I saw the only system of cable-drawn trolley cars in China running up and down the slopes carrying

67

coal to the river edge. It was Lu Tsofu's work. He had developed Peipei before the war and has given it a scientific research institute, a park, a museum, a hospital, and different schools. The development was not exactly simple. For Peipei was the meeting point of several county districts and was infested with lawless bandits. He was given the job of suppressing the bandits in the area between Peipei and Hochuan. That was, I believe, after he had made a name for himself with the first steamship operating in these waters.

At the time the company was formed, back in 1925, all Yangtse shipping was practically in the hands of foreign firms. The China Steamship Navigation Company, dating back to Manchu days, was still a moribund organization; some heroic efforts were made to rouse it from its slumber, but it was like rousing a huge, sprawling drunken giant fallen asleep on the street. With enormous wharf properties all along the coastal ports and a fleet of steamers, its profits were eaten up by inefficient management and the comprador system. So while the Japanese Nippon Yusen Kaisha ocean liners were calling at Hamburg and Liverpool, the Chinese dragon, the Chaoshangchü, still slumbered, and its reform was not effective till the nineteen-thirties under the Nanking government. The Yangtse shipping was run for freight, and although the human traffic was great, it was strictly regarded as part of the cargo. The conditions of "deck passengers" on the coastal steamers, foreign or Chinese-owned, remain among the horrible memories of my school days. Besides, there were constant civil wars in the first years of the Republic, and what Chinese shipping there was, preferred to register with foreign consulates and fly foreign flags. There were therefore British, American, Japanese, Norwegian, Danish, Portuguese ships, all except Chinese ships, sailing on that big inland Chinese river. Moreover, these Chinese companies owned only one, two, or three ships each, competing among themselves for cargo, human and otherwise, and they had a cutthroat competition with the big Jardine, Matheson ("Ewo"), and American and Japanese firms. Also the small companies operating within Szechuen were liable to be commandeered for transporting soldiers without pay, and all the companies were losing money.

Mr. Lu looked into the situation and decided it was all a matter of business organization and management. He had already bought more steamers and made them run on schedule on the Szechuen section of the Yangtse. He saw the immense possibilities of passenger traffic on the only line of communications between Shanghai and the inland provinces of central and western China. He abolished the comprador system, centralized control in the ship's offices, instituted a passenger service, established a schedule of periodic sailings, looked to the comfort of passengers, set up men's and ladies' toilets, trained up a new staff of stewards, put in ventilation systems for steerage passengers, installed radio communication on each ship, published radio news for passengers and tourist information and pictures, changed the porter situation, established hotel information service at the wharves—in other words, reformed the passenger service from top to bottom and made travel a matter of comparative pleasure and convenience, instead of the uncertainty and hardships of the ancient ways. He had put an end to the competition with the foreign-owned boats which ran principally for freight, and catered to only a small number of saloon passengers. And he convinced the Szechuen warlords of the necessity of paying for transportation of soldiers.

Soon after the first steamers were found to be a success, he set up a machine shop for repairs instead of sending a damaged engine thirteen hundred miles down the river to a Shanghai dockyard. This was a success, too, and grew into the present shipyard, scattered over miles and partly hidden in underground caves, which has already built twenty-one vessels, constructing its own boilers and engines. When the war broke out, the Minsheng Steamship Company already had a fleet operating on the Yangtse down to Shanghai, successfully competing with British and Japanese boats, while up the Gorges, in Szechuen waters, it had developed a system of river transportation that was the basis of the opening up of the Szechuen interior. When the capital was moved to Chungking, it found a small but efficient power and water-supply system and machine shops, without which the maintenance of the wartime industries would be impossible. In fact, without the Minsheng Company there would have been no river transportation except rowboats and barges for the soldiers of Chungking, during the retreat from Nanking and after.

The real drama of the company began when the war came on. With Shanghai fallen to the enemy, everybody said the Yangtse was blocked at the lower point and the days of the Minsheng Company were numbered. Instead, it threw its entire service and resources into the war, though unlike American private companies, it helped the government and the people without being helped by the government in return. During the dramatic retreat first from Nanking, and later from Hankow, it provided almost the sole means of rescuing Chinese factory equipment and arsenals from down the river. During this retreat there were a few foreign-owned ships still operating, but these kept religiously to their technically correct "neutral" position. They accepted only commercial freight, and refused to ship anything that had to do with the war. The Minsheng ships, as a contribution toward the war, accepted only about thirty dollars per ton for army equipment and arsenal material, and forty dollars for government goods and property, while charging sixty to eighty dollars per ton for private cargo. The foreign-owned boats were able to charge three to four hundred dollars per ton for commercial goods, while maintaining their strictly neutral character.

Somebody ought to write the story of the Chinese Dunkirk, the retreat of personnel and equipment up the Yangtse Gorges in the last days of the Hankow campaign. The industrial skeleton of China, her arsenals, steel plants, aviation plants, heavy and light machinery—in other words, the whole industrial life of China that was to be saved for the prolonged struggle—besides the museum pieces, the libraries, the entire government personnel, and a great part of the school and college staff and students, were concentrated at Ichang, waiting to go up the Gorges into the safe hinterland. After the fall of Hankow there were still thirty thousand government personnel and ninety thousand tons of material awaiting transportation at the bottleneck.

The scene was one of indescribable confusion. Men's hearts were flurried and afraid, and their nerves were taut. The streets were jammed with people, and machinery parts were lying on the ground everywhere, choking every foot of the shore. All were waiting for salvation to come from the Minsheng ships. China's industrial lifeblood depended upon it. The Minsheng office was packed tight from the outer gate into every corridor and hallway with officers and officials, each pressing for priority for his particular charge. Each and every one was important, was vital to the nation.

Into this scene of confusion, Mr. Lu descended from an airplane. He observed that his men's time was all occupied with interviewing and negotiating with the officials, and no time was left for running ships. The officials were noisily registering their displeasure with the Minsheng staff, and the impatient claimants for shipping space were arguing and fighting among themselves. It threatened to be like a panic when all are lost because all are pressing toward the exit, blocking everybody, including themselves.

Mr. Lu called a conference with all the transport authorities of the Army and other public and private agencies. He pleaded for putting an end to piecemeal negotiations and giving his staff time for running the ships. He told them that there were still forty days of good sailing up the Gorges for the bigger steamers, that there was a maximum tonnage that could be transported within that period, which would be apportioned to the different organizations, and asked each organization to make up its own unit of first essentials in accordance with the given quota for immediate evacuation, leaving the rest to be transported by river barges, to await further plans after the forty-day period, or, if necessary, to be abandoned. As to what batch of material was to go by which boat, they were to leave it entirely to him. The eminently reasonable proposal was agreed upon by all. The company was once more able to plan its schedules undisturbed. In forty days the mountain of goods and machinery that had cluttered the shores had vanished, and the thirty thousand personnel had disappeared, leaving Ichang a desolate, forsaken city.

As there were many treacherous rapids through the Gorges and beyond, the boats could sail only by day. Hence time could be saved by utilizing the night for loading and unloading. The voyage from Ichang to Chungking took four days up and two days down, and in order to make as many trips as possible, it was necessary to rearrange schedules. Only the heaviest machinery, difficult to unload, was transported up to Chungking; other goods were deposited hastily at Wanhsien, and still others dumped at Fengchieh and Wushan, and even at Patung. The more powerful ships were made to tow barges behind. Not an hour or an ounce of power was lost. It was all mathematics, according to Mr. Lu. Every day five or six or seven ships would leave Ichang, and a few would return in the late afternoon. Before the ship approached the wharf, the hatch would be opened and the cranes made ready, while the cargo on the wharf would already be put in barges and tenders. As soon as the boat anchored, the loading began. All night, under the blazing lamps on the shore and on the ship, the longshoremen would work, carrying a wheel or a steel rod or part of a truck engine, singing the carriers' eternal song to the rhythm of their steps and to the accompaniment of whistles from the tenders and the rattle of the cranes—a symphony of retreat and human struggle, so brave and so sad, while the swift night torrents of the Yangtse lapped the ship's sides and impatiently rushed on.

On the basis of such a record, an American public would probably decide the next presidential campaign and shout, "Vote Lu Tsofu for president!" In China, let us shout, "Lu Tsofu for premier!" It is my conviction that what China needs is a business government. China needs a business cabinet of Lu Tsofus, a government with men chosen solely for their proved ability to get things done.

I am telling this story, not only as an account of Minsheng's heroic part in the war, but also as an introduction to the man whom I was about to meet. Mr. Lu had been vice-minister of communications for several years (in recognition of his ability) and had resigned about a year ago. I was eager to meet him after hearing about him for so many years, and also because in the last ten or fifteen years there had grown up a new class of Chinese, older Chinese business and industrial leaders with a modern outlook, men like K. P. Chen, Y. T. Tsur, Chang Kiangau, Wu Ting-chang, Wong Yun-wu, and others. This was something new, a gift of time itself. It represented a cleavage in the Chinese social fabric, and a social phenomenon of almost the greatest significance. Chinese businessmen only fifteen or twenty years ago were not modern in mind and method, and the Chinese progressives were generally "intellectuals." But it was inevitable that with the passage of time China should have a group of men in their fifties who are thoroughly modern industrial leaders. Most of these men seem to prefer the Western dress, and most of them are from the southeast coast. They have shown great organizational ability, are wide-awake and progressive and have a knack of getting things done. Intellectually, too, they deserve great respect; they read and keep abreast of the march of events. There was a Shanghai banker, now deceased, who read Anatole France at night. In the course of the war many of them have been drafted into important government positions, but essentially they are business heads, rebellious against official red tape and concerned only with efficiency, with getting results. The ability to get things done on the part of this elder generation of industrialists is the best promise of a China emerging successfully into the industrial age under the system of free enterprise. Moreover, I am convinced that what China needs in the coming period of industrialization and reconstruction is a government run by business leaders of proved ability—less politics, but more "pep."

Mr. Lu is about fifty and is from Szechuen. Unlike the Shanghai industrialists, he is thin and small, and physically almost frail-looking. He has small, rather dreamy, meditative eyes and talked in a thin, hard, somewhat metallic Szechuen voice, with a dry smile constantly hanging around his lips. His manners were direct and businesslike. When I saw him for the first time at his home, he wore a Chungshan cotton suit of mottled gray, clean, but unpressed, resembling a neat, simple working man. (The Chungshan suit, named after Sun Yat-sen, alias Chungshan, is the official dress of government employees, cut like a foreign suit but worn with the coat collar buttoned around the neck without a tie.) It seemed to me he preferred to wear pants just because he could walk faster in them. I could not imagine him dressed in a long gown and shambling in the leisurely mandarin gait, although his thin frame and his low voice suggested more a scholar than a prosperous businessman. At his home he served a foreign lunch, another sign of his modernity. I am sure he had thought everything out scientifically and had decided that foreign meals were more efficient. His mathematical mind must have derived satisfaction from the thought that he was getting the maximum of food values from the smallest quantity of food, and he would be impatient with the culinary extravaganza and antics that we call a Chinese feast. We had a luscious steak and raw tomatoes, and toast with native jam.

In our conversations, on this and later occasions, I had ample opportunity to verify his mathematical mind. He talked rapidly, but clearly and precisely. He did not talk of the economic development of Szechuen in broad and general terms, but said the production of tung oil could be increased so many per cent, of rapeseed oil so many per cent, of rice and cotton and beans so many per cent; he could at a wink convert English mileage into kilometers. I used to watch a matching of like minds between him and Weng Wen-hao, the Minister of Economics. Physically, as I have said, they almost make a pair; both have humor, and both have accomplished great things for their weight.

I wanted to visit the Minsheng shipyard and the factories, and Mr. Lu arranged it for me. On the day before the trip, I was surprised to have Mr. Lu tell me over the telephone that the car would come for me at a certain hour *and minute*. That was the way he ran things. There were two other visitors, Mr. S. A. Trone, an American working with the China Defense Supplies, in Washington, and Mr. S. C. Wong, director of the Central Machine Works at Kunming. So before I knew it, I found myself in the company of industrial experts, taking a hitherto unsuspected interest in factories. We gathered in the narrow alley of the National Resources Commission at Buffalo's Horn and packed into the car that came on the exact moment.

After driving for half an hour, we reached the bank of the river. It was a clear October day with an occasional drizzle which bathed the foliage just sufficiently to brighten the green of the hills and fields across the river. The scene was like a painting just from the hand of a master painter, who had succeeded in giving it the final touches of subtle shades and delicate harmony. One was almost afraid the mist might thicken and the hues might change. Some military trucks were standing on the cement pavement leading down to the ferry, and besides the soldiers, a number of men and women were perched on top of the truckloads, some fifteen feet above the ground. This was a privileged form of travel, for the military trucks could use gasoline, while the buses ran on charcoal gas or alcohol; it was therefore faster to ride with the soldiers, and one could be sure of reaching one's destination. There the women sat, huddled on top and completely in the open, exposed to the October wind and sun and rain, to start a journey of days, probably to Kweiyang, and thought themselves lucky. This was to be a common sight to me later.

Picking our way across the pebble beach we went to a small boat which took us to the steamship in mid-river. Across the river, high rocky cliffs stood out above a stretch of houses nestling by the riverside. Mr. Trone, the American, was a perfect traveling companion. He was a power expert of Russian extraction and had helped to build the Dnieper dam. During the trip he provided all the talk, and I could sit quietly and just listen. He was middle-aged and had a well-mellowed look, but he talked with an intense energy, punctuating it with a warm, full-throated "Yah, yah!" As we sat on the deck of the steamer, admiring the beautiful scenery of the Yangtse, where the river and sailing boats merged into a delightful, changing autumn picture, he talked with an energy completely "foreign" in the Chinese atmosphere, and yet with a meditative quality and understanding that made him completely belong there. He had traveled in distant parts of China, and the Chinese countryside and towns and architecture seemed to possess a fascination for him. It was not quaintness, but the human qualities of the civilization that struck him, the blending of nature and art, and the toil and thrift and patience and good humor of the Chinese people.

Mr. Wong comes from an extraordinary ancient Soochow family, with many distinguished literary talents, but having studied in America, his talent was shown now in making Diesel fuel pumps and spiral bevel gear-cutters, manufactured at the Kunming Machine Works, requiring the accuracy of a thousandth of an inch.

When we arrived at the Ch'ienchien Steel and Iron Works and went up the high steps on the bank, we were met by the commanding officer in uniform. He had studied engineering in Germany, and talked fluent German with a Chinese accent. Mr. Trone and the Chinese officer rattled on in German incessantly for two hours, Mr. Trone asking questions but still doing most of the talking. The commander warned me by saying with a laugh, "This is no Pittsburgh." But I would not judge Chinese industries by American standards or any standards at all, except the standards of war necessity. I cared only whether China was producing enough steel and iron for the needs of her arsenals. She was. I did not expect to see the steel plant housed in mile-long concrete buildings illuminated by mercury lights as at Detroit. The surprise was that the whole Hanyang Steel and Iron Works had been moved here at all, some seven hundred miles from Hankow. Not that it did not have rows of machine lathes driven by power, and thousands of workers living in a separate village near by. To look at the fifty-foot blast furnace, camouflaged with gigantic nets and leaves, and to realize that all the complicated tubes and pipes surrounding it had been taken down, piece by piece, and put together again in working order by Chinese engineers gave me a kind of mystic delight. I was still more staggered, and Mr. Trone was staggered with me, a few days later when we saw a 4500-kilowatt Vickers electric generator, moved twice up and down hills after Japanese bombings, and now housed very securely inside majestic solid granite.

The name of that steel plant is "Ch'ienchien," which means "Migration and Reconstruction," but it could be better translated as "The Reconstruction Steel and Iron Works in Exile." The plant is government-owned and spreads above the riverside over a thousand acres. The Japanese had come several times to bomb it, and had bombed out a building, but had never done serious damage to the machinery. The workers lived in a primitive colony by themselves, cut off from any town because of poor and difficult transportation, and the government was providing for them and their families less in cash than in supplies of food and clothing and shelter. It was at the same time a shame and a glory, but it had to be so. One wished the men could be as well paid as American war workers, and admired them for carrying on all these fighting years.

There was a shop where workmen hammered out crude bars in the old blacksmith fashion. I watched men, stripped to the waist, their faces blackened with soot and backs wet with sweat, hammering away at red-hot iron. As they swung their hammers overhead and brought them down with so much force and strength, each blow seemed to be struck at the enemy. The song of the anvil, as their hammers descended in a perfectly timed rhythm, was a Song of Resistance, not in words, but in the regular metallic hammer blows, in the intent, focused eyes of the workers and the movements of their muscles. In their pauses for breath they seemed to ask, as they looked at the blackening iron,

"When will the war end?" Then they would spit on the hammer handles and start striking again. The steam presses were impressive, but no less those men at the old-fashioned anvils. When the war ends, these men will have their pay in better living conditions, in the liberation of China and in the knowledge of having done their part in it. But hard times are ahead, and their hammers shall continue to strike in a fury until China is secure in arms.

We visited the Minsheng Shipyard in the afternoon. After a trip along the river, we went into a new Minsheng boat nearing completion, and my eyes first lighted upon a steam engine constructed entirely by Chinese. I had not believed it possible. One might as well imagine China building a Flying Fortress or a Buick limousine. The development of machines in China was one of the things that most impressed me on this trip. The steam engine has always had a fascination for me since I first saw it as a child of ten on my first trip to Amoy, and even now I never miss an opportunity to stare at two crankshafts turning two discs at an angle to the main shaft in a steady, kissing, grinding motion, apparently actuated by superhuman powers. In my childhood, the steam engine was a beautiful toy, but unalterably foreign, associated with the foreigners. China imported such foreign things from abroad; foreigners thought of them, designed them, and made them. That made me admire the Western civilization from my childhood. But now the beautiful toy stood before me, made by Chinese. When the Detroit age comes to China, someone ought to collect these pieces and place the first Chinese-made steam engine, the first Chinese-made locomotive, and the first Chinese-made motorcar in a historical museum. They will symbolize a wrenching and a renovating of the Chinese soul, whose consequences we dare not imagine.

But the most interesting thing we saw was the wartime underground factory. Man's inventiveness is always equal to the demands of necessity. Chinese had retreated far from the coast, and when they decided not to retreat further, they bored underground. I am sure if Americans were presented with the same necessity, they would have done the same. A stretch of sand beach led to the machine shops where stood piles of material from salvaged ships—pipes and tubes and boilers, from which new engines were made and fitted to new ships. For the only source of steel plates was salvage, and what they were able to scour from the country in the first years of the war. In one building a big staff of draftsmen was working on blueprints in a very well lighted room. The machine shops led directly into dugouts in the cliffs, where the finer machinery was installed. These underground machine shops were in the form of long tunnels, as all Chungking air-raid shelters are, to insure against collapse of the roof. These tunnels were fifteen to twenty feet wide and were electrically lighted, and in them about eighty lathes were working, lined end to end along the walls. There the work could go on without interruption, secure against air raids. In the following days I saw a great number of such underground factories, some of them fitted with wooden floors and leading by winding turns from one side of a cliff to another. At Paochi I was to see the biggest of them all, the Shen Hsin Textile Mill, with twenty-six exits, the tunnels reaching a total length of about three miles, a city inside a mountain.

I told Mr. Lu later an idea of mine, which was to make boats with propellers driven by manpower. For a long time, motor power will be either too expensive or unavailable in China. Tens of thousands of miles of inland rivers are navigated by boats worked by oars, punting poles, and lorchas, with five or six men jiggling a big, heavy oar placed at the stern. Even before engines or even outboard motors become available for inland river transportation, the man-driven boats ought to be improved. It is a characteristically Chinese problem, and ought to be solved in a Chinese way, by improving the efficiency of human power. One sees daily, on the Yangtse, boats manned by teams of eight to twelve oarsmen, representing a tremendous waste of human power, and making a snail's progress. Up the Gorges a small boat sometimes requires a team of a hundred boatmen with ropes slung across their shoulders and straining their backs, treading the pebble beaches to pull it upstream. Manpower is cheap and abundant in China, but we ought to invent a more efficient and more comfortable use of it. A simple device, working on the propeller shaft from a treadle, would enable the boatmen to drive a propeller as a bicyclist treads his wheels in a more comfortable position and with far greater speed. A man working on a punting pole wastes two thirds of his energy walking back and forth along the side of the boat, and the back-and-forth motion of the oar means that half of the time it is out of the water. The propeller insures a continuous motion, while less energy is wasted. Two to a dozen men could work on the same system, and the shifting of gears, for adjustment of manpower and speed, could be done simply by switching a leather belt from one disc to another. I am sure that if a boat employed eight to ten men to work on a propeller shaft by hand or by foot, it would make twice the speed that is made by the same number of men working on oars, and it should be possible to achieve a speed of ten miles per hour. Mr. Lu said he was worried about how, when the war was over and millions would be going down the river, they were going to meet the problem with so few boats. A large fleet of such propeller-driven junks might help to solve the problem.

There is a story of some Australian sheep which seems a fitting parable of China's road to industrialization. It was told me by an old gentleman, Mr. Chou, owner of the Hengshun Machine Works, affiliated with the Minsheng Company. Some months before Pearl Harbor, Chinese authorities negotiated with the Australian government for a few sheep of the fine Australian breed to be brought to China to propagate for wool-raising. Forty or fifty sheep were shipped to Rangoon under the charge of two Chinese experts. While they were halfway there by sea, the Japanese pushed into Burma from the east and were threatening Rangoon, and so the ship landed in Calcutta. Here were the two young hopefuls, faced with the problem of getting the sheep into China, after Burma was cut off. They therefore went up to Darjeeling, herded the sheep on foot across the Himalayas and into Thibet. Their destination was somewhere in China's Northwest. When last heard of, they were still somewhere in Thibet with their Australian sheep, and it was said that the sheep had multiplied into over a thousand. This is a true tale, and what a tale! So China must plod along in all her modernization-democratization problems, surmounting with a heart difficulties as big as the Himalayas. And China will do it.

There is another anecdote that I must record here. While at Peipei, visiting the Camp for Disabled Soldiers (called "Honored Soldiers" in Chinese), I learned that old Mrs. Chao, the "Grandmother of the Guerrillas," was there too. She was living near Peipei, and people honored her wherever she went. On my previous visit to China, I had just barely missed meeting her. I had known about her work with the guerrillas, and had written about her and reproduced one of her speeches in *A Leaf in the Storm*. Now I went to see her. She was from one of the Manchurian provinces and must be in her sixties. Like any Chinese grandmother from the country, she talked with the natural dignity of old age. Her son was with the Central guerrillas, not the Communists; in the American public's mind there is an entirely incorrect idea that all guerrilla fighting is done by the Communists, because of the propaganda in the first years of the war. I had heard of the death of her son, serving as an officer in central Hopei, and wished to hear the story. Without a tear in her eyes or a tremble in her voice, she told me how, in 1939, when her son was retreating from the Japs with his men in a riverboat, the Communists waylaid them and shot them by machine guns from the bank. "It was a death trap," she said. "The boatman was their man." I was so sick at heart that I didn't want to hear more. But that woman was made of steel, with a heart of gold. I had to go Northwest and find out the truth.

6

TO THE NORTHWEST

OUR PLANE for the Northwest was to leave early in the morning, and the passengers assembled at seven at the Sanhupa airfield, on an islet in mid-river. About two hundred people, the passengers and those who had come to see them off and others who had come to meet the incoming plane, were jostling each other in the waiting room, which was a half-open mat shed about seventy feet long. The morning was cool, and I was well provided with a gown padded with silk wool, incomparable for lightness and warmth. A dense fog enveloped the city and one could see silhouettes of people emerging from the whitish gray vapor, bathed in a sort of twilight. Above that mass of ponderous, murky fog was heard, at half-hour intervals, the drone of a plane, like the footsteps of someone upstairs whom one has never seen and who has no means of coming down.

Another problem developed. It appeared that there were two full loads of passengers, one going to Paochi, and the other farther north to Lanchow. The plane, which had started from Kweilin during the night, was supposed to make the two separate trips during the day. If it flew to Lanchow first, the passengers for Paochi would have to wait till it came back in late afternoon, after a round trip of at least six hours. If it flew first to Paochi, the passengers destined for Lanchow would have to wait four or five hours. So there was a Lanchow party and a Paochi party, each pressing its own arguments for taking off first. As I was going to Paochi, I was quite convinced of the rightness of the plane's making Paochi first, since that was a shorter distance, and the plane should really stop over at Lanchow for the night. It would be too much work for the pilot to return a second time to Chungking. The CNAC officer at the airfield dared not decide. The telephone was kept busy. At one time, the news came through that the Lanchow party had won; fifteen minutes later the news was reversed. The final word was that it was up to the pilot to decide. The CNAC had Chinese pilots, but this plane happened to be run by an American pilot, and the American pilots were amenable to control only by American officers of the company, which is jointly owned. Meanwhile the people were milling round or sitting, blanketed in that November pea-soup fog, and sharing in the miracle that one could reach the remote Northwest across the formidable Tsinling Mountains in a few hours.

About half past ten we learned that the plane was detained at a military airfield some fifteen miles away. After circling for hours over Chungking in the fog, unable to come down, the pilot found it possible to locate another airfield. It was a military airfield and the plane had landed without permission. Negotiations must go on with the military authorities before the plane could be released. We decided that the plane would have time to make only one trip that day, either to Paochi, or to Lanchow. Like all air passengers, we were utterly dependent on the pilot's judgment.

At half past eleven the plane landed and began unloading passengers and parcels. Out stepped the pilot and walked toward the office. We were all keyed up to learn what his verdict would be. It was that he would not fly any more that day. He had got up in the middle of the night and needed sleep. We agreed with him, as we did not wish to go into a plane with a sleepy pilot at the wheel. Neither the Paochi party nor the Lanchow party won. It was a draw.

Sadly I walked up the famous flight of steps on the steep bank, along with some two hundred other people who had got up at five o'clock and squandered a whole morning and wished now they had lain in bed. A very sick man, Mr. Chiao Yitang, who was a well-known doctor and official and who was returning to his Shensi home after an attack of malignant malaria, was carried back up the steps. The people dispersed aimlessly. Some complained that they had given up their hotel rooms and didn't know where to put up for the night. I turned up at General Hsiung's home, to the amazement of his family.

The next morning we gathered again at the airfield. The same faces were there. A young foreign woman with a pleasant face had attracted my attention the previous day, because she wore Chinese dress. All morning she sat in the waiting room, warm and comfortable and seeming at home, but talking with nobody, and I didn't have the courage to go up and speak to her. What we miss by these reticences! Only children can masterfully surmount the barriers between strangers.

80

Grownups have a hundred inhibitions, but to children, what nonsense this retiring each into his own shell!

A young woman came up to me and said she was my niece, and indeed she was. She was from Amoy and, having studied in Shanghai, was now married and her husband was working in Szechuen. That is the way people of all provinces are mixing up now, and that is the way nieces grow up and get married and have children without our knowing about it. I had not been back to my home town for more than twelve years.

The sick old Mr. Chiao was there again, lying on a couch, attended by his wife and daughter and two sons. He was a Chinese doctor, but plasmo-quinine had cured him of his malaria. He was returning to the sunny plains of Shensi for recuperation, and his wife was going with him. Both of his sons were students of engineering, and one of them was planning to go to Cornell as soon as he could pass the examinations.

Everywhere I went, young boys and girls were inquiring about study in America. An unknown girl had written me the most touching letter, asking for my help and saying she would be glad to scrub floors and work in the kitchen if she could stay with my family. I wrote to tell her why it was impossible, but she wrote again and again, each time a more touching letter. Really if I had seen her, my will power might have broken down, and I might have entered into a conspiracy to smuggle her abroad. But I was moving all the time, and I had lost track of her. The last time she wrote she did not put down her address, assuming that I had it; but I didn't, and there the matter stopped. These things aren't right. So many things aren't right. If I were God, I would make it possible for all these young people yearning for modern knowledge to come to the shores of America.

Mr. Chiao was head of the Association of National Medicine (which means Chinese medicine). We discussed this topic, which is entirely misunderstood. Chinese medicine has been dismissed by Western doctors as a compound of quackery, superstition, and magic. That the scientific technique of Western medicine is the only reliable method to arrive at sure knowledge cannot be disputed. But I still maintain that there are no physicians who understand at the same time both Western and Chinese medicine. Chinese doctors never are able to explain the therapeutic functions of their medicines in terms that Western doctors can understand, and Chinese doctors of Western medicine do not know enough Chinese, as a rule. I have not met one Western-trained doctor who can explain the English meaning of Chinese medical and physiological terms. These terms describing pathological conditions and therapeutic functions mean something very definite in the practice of Chinese physicians, and we ought to take the trouble to find out what they mean in the terms of modern physiology. Anyway, the principle of Chinese medicine, regarding the body as functioning as a whole, maintained and affected by a delicate system of compensating circulating fluids, is fundamentally sound. A man whose nerves are jumpy is described as suffering from a "too hot liver fire." It may be that, and it may not be, and it may be that the trouble is not even in the liver. But by that term the experienced Chinese physician refers to the recognized pathological condition of a jumpy pulse and treats it by certain drugs. Whatever the true nature of the disease, the correlation of diagnosis and treatment is there, and the disease is often cured. It may be like a porter telling a passenger the wrong name of the train he is to get into and then by sound intuition and experience putting him in the right train. You argue with the porter that the name of the train is incorrect, but he says dogmatically, "You sure get there. You're going to Washington, ain't yuh? You calls it Congressional, and I calls it Congo. I's been workin' here twenty-five years, and I knows it's the right train if that's whar you want to go." The Chinese doctor talks an incomprehensible language. Until we know his language, we have no right to judge Chinese medicine at all.

In the *Private History of Queen Feiyen (Wisdom of China and India,* p. 959), it is recorded that in the first century B.C., the Queen and her sister took a gland from the male musk deer to restore their vitality, but that if too much was taken, the monthly flow would become too thin. I am sure that this is the first recorded instance of taking male hormones by women, about which Western doctors are just beginning to make intensive studies.

A "hundred-day cough" is a hundred-day cough no matter by what name you call it, and digitalis is digitalis, quickening and strengthening the heart, even if the Chinese doctor says merely it is "hot and dry medicine." But suppose it is not digitalis, but an unknown drug, like the famous *paiyo,* reputed to be of extreme efficacy in stopping bleeding, healing wounds, and facilitating the growth of cell tissues. One ought to have the generosity and open-mindedness to investigate. Some of its claims will be found to be false and some will be found to be true, and all ought to be brought within the framework of established evidence, checked by the standards of Western medicine and made amenable to chemical analysis and understanding. This *paiyo,* in particular, had achieved a national reputation and was used by the

82

Kwangsi generals in their army for treatment of wounds. The old man, Mr. Chü Huan-chang, of Kunming, who alone knew the secret of manufacture, was brought to Chungking by the Chinese government, and negotiations were going on for buying his secret. But he died during the negotiations, and now some one of his sons or daughters alone possesses the secret. This is unfair. If it is good, it ought to be shared by the whole world. The government should commandeer the secret for its army. And if it is bad, or makes false pretenses, the medicine should be banned.

The Chinese physicians, too, are incompetent to advance the cause of Chinese medicine, having no sound knowledge of Western science. The thing to do is not to go through the Chinese pharmacopœia and subject the drugs to chemical analysis, item by item. This would only add to Western egotism. The thing to do is for a Western-trained doctor with some imagination to attach himself as an apprentice to a really first-class Chinese doctor and watch for three years, observing how he recognizes symptoms and cures people in the course of a treatment. Then the story of Chinese medicine may be told with some understanding. Without humility, we can learn nothing.

An officer at the field introduced me to a very impressive old man in a military cap and cape, Lu Hsin-keng, and committed me to his care, for he was director of the Lunghai Railway, by which I was going to travel to Sian. He was of the Chekiang industrialist type, short, with a full forehead and a bright, brisk look and the ruddy complexion that comes to some successful men of middle age. When you see a man with such a face and look, you know he is the executive type. The way he accepted charge of me, in a few clear distinct syllables, assured me that I didn't have to worry.

Some twenty-five passengers boarded the plane, shortly before twelve o'clock. The sick Mr. Chiao was put in a special chair at the rear, and I took one of the last bucket seats.

Shortly before we arrived at Paochi, at two o'clock, Mr. Lu stood up in the plane and invited all the passengers to take a special train for Sian which had been prepared for us. It is difficult to describe my first feelings when the plane landed. The air was crisp and invigorating, and the sweep of the bare, sun-lit plains of Shensi liberated one's spirit. The airfield was a "natural," situated in a vast expanse of grass and sod, and while standing there we did not realize that we were on a flat plateau rising some five hundred feet above the plain below. We could see the peaks of the famous Tsinling Range across which we had just flown. This mountain range acts as a sharp climatic frontier: north of it the sun changes, the air changes, the geologic structure changes, the plants and animals change, and the people and their customs change. Here was the true North, with the sunshine and vitality of the North. The taller stature of the northern people and a certain gay simplicity about them opened my heart as if I had found something I had long needed. I saw a horse, a true horse, that was something of a vision after the donkey-sized varieties of Szechuen. I cannot forget the picture of the tall, noble horses let loose to roam freely and frisk over the green fields about Sian. This was the true, the ancient China, the cradle of the Chinese civilization.

The plateau on which we were standing was formed of loess, and on the sides of the sharp descent into the valley people were living in loess caves. I must explain here two words denoting the Shensi topography: *yuan,* a plateau, and *ch'uan,* a low plain. The country exists on two sharply differentiated levels, with villages and fields on both. Even the Chinese don't understand the meanings of these two words, frequently met with in place names, until they have seen these formations. The *yuan* are not mounds or hills: they are simply plains on the upper level, corresponding to the tops of canyons. But the *ch'uan* are not canyons either: they are simply plains on a lower level. Which is the original level, seems a geologic mystery. Have the *yuan* gone up, through the accumulation of loess, or have the *ch'uan* gone down, washed by floods? Neither theory seems quite satisfactory. But anyway the loess is a very fine, sticky soil, free of rocks, ready to be sculptured or modeled into any shape, sufficiently resistant to wind and rain to form the walls and ceilings of shelters, while it is also rich soil for cotton and wheat.

As our car zigzagged downward we saw Paochi city below. It lies in a long, narrow strip between the plateau and the turbulent, unnavigable Wei River, within the shadow of the towering Tsinling. The name of the Wei River is as old as the *Book of Poetry* and the House of Chou, stretching back to the twelfth century B.C. Coming upon it is like coming upon the Euphrates or the Nile for a Western historian. For it was here that the Chou house rose to power. The name is so classical that one's mind automatically associates it with historic legends, and one hardly expects to see it running still today. From here to Sian and onward along the Yellow River, in the stretch covered by the Lunghai railway, one might stop at any point and find that ancient kings and queens had died or were buried there. The route of the Lunghai railway was in fact the route followed by Tang Ming-huang when he escaped from Sian to Szechuen, and it was at Maweipo that his favorite queen, Yang Kweifei, was handed over to the rebellious army and "granted suicide." It was here, too, that the poet Tu Fu, in the terrible war years, wandered, tattered and hungry, back to his home.

Here in the Northwest, ancient China, as I like to imagine it, still exists in the life and customs of the people, and the enormous weight of their historic past is still upon them. It is a country agricultural and primitive, wide and expansive, and the people are children of nature, eternally cheerful under the sunshine. It is difficult to imagine the people breathing that air and living in that country as mean-hearted or degenerate. The palaces have vanished, times have been hard, there have been famines; but the population is essentially agricultural, and there is a ruggedness about the peasantry that makes them survive hardships, fight wars, and turn bandits if necessary; but there are no more honest, cheerful, and peace-loving people on earth.

In the streets of Paochi and the scenes along the railway, the houses, the yards, the costumes of men and women with their trousers tied round the ankles to keep out dust, the shop fronts, the peddlers, the horse carts, the peasants riding on donkeybacks, and above all the gay chatter of the bedraggled populace, all resembled those of Peking. I was instinctively happy with these common people of the North. The South has cunning and intelligence. The North has no cunning, but it has a character all its own; it can hate and kill and laugh and forgive. These children of the North are untouched and really untouchable by the West; in them lies the true strength of China.

In that countryside I could see in the distance a girl dressed in striking scarlet contrasting bravely with the green of the fields, a boldness that would scare the South. That country maiden, while she knows all the old etiquette, is perfectly able to take care of herself and is not afraid of men. It is because the etiquettes are established and the customs are old that she knows both what she may not do and what she may do. One can hardly imagine someone trying to convert these people to Western ideas, like Christianity, without taking care that the Western ideas are first converted to them. A sense of the ridiculous, coming in the shape of the Doubting Satan, must have often struck the minds of some of the proselytizing evangelists, at least the more intelligent ones. The ideas of the peasantry are those of Confucius and follow from his moral code, but this is so inseparably a part of themselves, of their society and customs, that it is now indubitably their own. I am sure they would change the faces of all Western gods and remake them in their own image. Their virtues will be their chains, but their vices will also be their virtues. They symbolize the inertia but also the strength of peasant China: they will be slow to change and will resist progress until progress finds a way to humor them and their keen realism and good sense. For they are attuned to their way of living, to the land and to the universe.

Riding in a train—the fact that the railway was kept running—seemed a luxury in the seventh year of war in China. But this was more; we rode in well-appointed first-class cars with compartments of one or two berths, like the American roomettes. Of the trains running on this line, there was one called Green Express, or in Chinese "Green Steel-Body Train," and our train was made up of two such cars. The other people in the party were mostly passengers from the plane, and all had more or less important positions. Several were representatives of the Provincial Assembly of Shensi, which was a new institution, being the provincial counterpart of the National People's Political Council. I stretched out in my berth for an hour's sleep. The familiar click-clack of rolling railway wheels, the compartment with its fine woodwork, the switches, and the sense of easy, fast travel, all reminded me of America. I was told that when the late Wendell Willkie found the Green Express, after his hard, dusty journey across the Northwest, he felt so at home that he didn't want to leave it. I could well understand why.

The train pulled into the station at Sian at ten in the evening. I went to the China Travel Service Hostel, a spacious modern building built in the years before the war when Sian grew in importance and there was a movement afoot for making it the "secondary capital" of China.

Lying in bed at the hostel, I felt excited about the things I had to see. Sian was the capital of China's three greatest, longest, and most illustrious dynasties, the Western Chou, the Han, and the Tang, known to students of history and poetry as Changan. The name called up pictures of fabulous luxury, romantic poets, cultured courtesans, righteous scholars, turbulent generals, and tragic queens. It was the dream of all scholars to come to Changan and see its wine shops, its gay women, its decorated carriages, and its imperial trains. Because the dynasties of Han and Tang lasted so long, Chinese stories always tell of "Changan" as if it were equivalent to the "capital." Li Po lay drunk here in one of the wine shops, declining the call of the Emperor. Tu Fu and Wang Wei had their homes near by. Scholars coming to pass their examinations would come by the mountain paths of the Chungnan Hills, and Tu Fu and Han Yu sending their friends off to the South would go to the bridge on the Pa River. The place names of this region were not just place names; they were part of well-known popular phrases expressing human longings and joys and sorrows. To follow the "quick route of Chungnan," for instance, was to pass the state examinations. To "have one's name inscribed on the Stork Pagoda" was to become a *chinsze*. The capital of Tsin Shih-huang was there, too, a few miles to the west, but the "Ancient Ferry at Hsienyang" was not just a ferry but an established poetic phrase, not a syllable of which must be changed. (It was somewhat bizarre to find later a steel railway bridge running at the "Ancient Ferry of Hsienyang," instead of cormorant fishermen covered by palm-tissue waterproof.) Here, too, was the Forest of Stone Inscriptions, where the originals of famous Chinese rubbings could be seen, written by scholars of the fifth to the eleventh centuries. And here, lying about studding the landscape, were the gigantic mounds in the shape of mud buns with the flesh of emperors and queens for their stuffings—the famous tombs. Here the Nestorian Tablet was found. Here the Buddhist Hsüan Chuang made his translations, and here Japanese students came to study Buddhism in the eighth century.

I could not sleep, and got up at midnight. I wanted, above all, to see "the streets of Changan," and this I could do immediately. The hotel was quiet and deserted; everybody had gone to bed. Silently I stole out. I wished I could meet the men and women of Changan as they were dressed and went about in the days of old, but this could not be. I walked down the cement pavement and past the steel railings of the modern hostel and stood looking about. Here was a modern, macadamized road, not one paved with large stone slabs. In the distance I saw a small night restaurant, with its dim lights burning, and went toward it. The kitchen was at the front, and there were bare, crude tables and benches. Li Po must have slept in such an inn. The chopsticks were crude; the bowl and china spoons were simple. There were only two or three customers at that time of the night. I ordered a bowl of beef stew. The broth was inferior, but the beef was cut in large, generous squares, such as eaters at wine shops love. For once I regretted that I could not drink. But it was almost what I wanted it to be. Thus I established my communion with the Changan of the past.

I was moved the next day through the courtesy of Governor Hsiung Pin, a scholarly and very kind old gentleman, to the Guest House of the provincial government, where I had greater privacy and comfort. It was in fact a luxurious house, formerly the private residence of General Yang Hucheng, with a charming garden in front and a spacious orchard behind, where some lucky peasant families, presumably the gardeners, were living in seclusion. That evening I went out of the rear gate. This was near the northern wall of the city, and there were country houses and stretches of clear vacant ground and ponds and yards for threshing wheat, all presenting a mass of white barrenness. It might have been Peiping itself. Like many such open spaces near the city walls of Peiping, the earth was of a pure grayish-white, solid and dry, and the roads were anywhere you could walk through the vacant patches. The men were dressed as in Peiping and chow dogs curled their tails, and there was an atmosphere of peace and serenity at twilight.

I strolled toward the city wall, and discovered that a row of houses built against the wall was a radio station. The city wall proved most useful during the war as a place for air shelters. I found a footway leading to the top of the wall, where I got a full view of the city and its historic environs. The city was three by four miles, and its gate towers with curved roofs were still visible in the haze of the darkening distance. The wall was over twenty feet wide, and one could walk comfortably on its pavement, made of very large-sized bricks. In the eastern center of the city was the former Manchu quarter, and to the north outside the city lay the ruins of the Tang Palaces. The city wall and general aspects suggested something of the vanished splendor of Sian.

While I was sitting in a corner of the wall, two country women came up, one middle-aged and another younger, her married daughter or daughter-in-law. They were apparently residents in the neighborhood and had come up to enjoy a moment of peace and beauty after the day's work was done. The older one had bound feet, and was being attended by the younger. But the last thing I would attribute to the peasant women of China was frailty. This one might be a Grandmother of the Guerrillas, and so might many others. Again and again I was struck by the vitality, the self-assurance, and the natural leadership of China's women. Going about in pajamas, as Chinese peasant women do, may have something to do with it. A few days later I was to watch a singular scene. I was in the upper story of a decorative tower in the Central Park of Sian. As I went around the veranda, I saw a young peasant woman shadowboxing alone in the late afternoon. The place where she stood was partly covered on one side by a low mound, but still it was a part of the public park. Her trouser-ends were tied around her ankles, and she wore a waistband outside her jacket in true boxer fashion. Alone and believing she was unobserved, she was doing the boxing of Primeval Unity, or *taichi ch'üan,* a form of boxing that consisted entirely of uniformly slow, circular movements of crouching and stretching and bending and winding and writhing. It is primarily for exercise, rather than for attack or defense, but the principal idea is that it takes more muscular control and grace to lift an arm or a leg slowly and keep it in position than to snap it up or down. It is a system to develop muscular and breath control. Why did that country woman do that? I could not quite make out. But this was the North, and our histories and legends are full of women leaders of pirates and guerrillas. I was beginning to understand the North. She was as distant from the concubines of Kiangsu, with their rouged cheeks and willowy waists and sighing whispers, as heaven is from the earth.

7

ANCIENT SIAN

I WAS fortunate in having Mr. Kung Hsien-ming as my companion in my explorations of the neighborhood of Sian, not only because he knew better than others the history and archeology of this region, but because he was such a good, upright man. He is still young and has a clean, honest face and talks in a low split voice. Mr. Kung was a professor, teaching at an academy, and leave was granted him to accompany me on my trips. Once he was a more important man. He was on a committee for developing Sian into the second capital of China. For Sian had fallen into decay in the past decades of war and famine and turmoil. He had a profound love for the local history of Sian, had made several discoveries, and had theories about certain historic spots; he had laid out plans for the motor roads, and knew every bypath of the region. The chairman of the committee had complete trust in him, and he went on enthusiastically with his plans. Then the chairman's wife appeared on the scene. This marked Kung's downfall. All Chinese would understand this. For she was a feminist. This term, I always thought, was a misnomer. The Western "feminists" should have been called "masculinists" in view of such male virtues of theirs as smashing windows, and the word "feminist" should have been reserved for the effeminate men who cultivate the virtues of the opposite sex, like giggling and having a slick pomade on one's hair.

Now dissociated from this already moribund committee, Mr. Kung retained a quality of imagination and a sigh of enthusiasm that is so appropriate in archeologists. Many of the visits to the environs of Sian we made alone, and I learned that he had the habit of looking at the good side of things and was reluctant to talk about his personal hardships. Some of the stories I had to pull out of him, but then they seemed to him just like stories that happened so many years ago that he could laugh over them. He was getting about $2,000 a month, which was a starvation ration, but he had the strong spirit of inner content, of taking reverses philosophically. He wore a Chungshan uniform, made of native wool, which his wife kept spotlessly clean. His socks were well mended and his shirts were clean. I knew he had a happy home. That was what kept the flame of his uprightness burning through these hard years. Suppose this man had been married to a virago, or a feminist. She would be disappointed in his outward failures and try to prod him on to a successful political career, so that she could shine socially, until the man would hate himself and would not know whether life was worth living or not. I have seen quite a few such cases among my friends. Why doesn't someone write the inner history of those doleful husbands? It is such a sad theme.

I wish I could describe in detail and in the more leisurely manner of a travel sketch my visits to the historic sites of Sian, which exist in vast profusion both inside and outside the city to a distance of some ten or fifteen miles. For Sian is a city where one can take an outing of an afternoon in the suburb and kick up tiles from the palaces of Han or stumble upon Tang tablets or rare pieces of ancient sculpture now half sunk in the ground, if one has luck. It would be an excellent place for amateur archeologists and idle scholars with a sense of history to roam about. I wish I could describe the details of a trip to Lintung, where I saw the tomb of Tsin Shih-huang, and bathed in a modern white-tiled sunken pool where Queen Yang Kweifei took her perfumed bath. I saw the bullet holes in the walls and windowpanes where Chiang Kai-shek fled from his sleep one early morning in December, 1936, and I followed his route of escape to the hill behind, where many inscriptions now appear on the rocks commemorating the incident. I might describe another exciting day roaming through the ruins of the Tang Palaces and on to the old capital of Han. I went to the famous Nightless Palace *(Weiyangkung)* and verified the marks of a fire on the east city gate in the year A.D. 16, where the clay was burned into masses of variegated colors. Yet another day I visited the tombs of ancient emperors, particularly the Mouling, that of the great Han Wuti whose empire extended to Turkistan and beyond. There I saw big foxes scampering away across the open country on our approach and noble horses grazing and galloping freely over the wheat fields. The sight of these white horses standing in the wide spaces, etched against the tombs of emperors dotting the horizon, is difficult to forget. I was told that horses stamping and running over the wheat fields do the young wheat sprouts no harm, and it must have been true, for they were farmers' horses.

I wish I could express my feelings when digging in the ruins of the tower where Queen Yang Kweifei lived, or when I saw cottages standing over the ruins of the Chienchang Palace of Han, and farmers making their homes in caves under the Horse Race Terrace of Tang. I would like to linger over my visit at the Forest of Inscriptions, the *Peilin,* containing the very characters that I used to copy as models of calligraphy in my childhood; the ancient Mohammedan Temple; the Confucian Temple, where other equally valuable and historically famous inscriptions stood; the Hsiasheng Dramatic School for Children, now nationally famous; the excellent orphanage of Sian, where the orphans looked well-fed and healthy; and the Tungyomiao, where peasant women sat on the ground of the spacious courtyard in the sun, making quilted bedding for Chinese soldiers.

At every spot, sacred with ancient memory, I saw the new, humble beginnings of the modern age. I saw a war orphanage established by Buddhists at the temple, the Hsingshansze, where Japanese students came to study in China in the eighth century, and air shelters dug out under the cliffs of the Shaoling Plateau sacred to the memory of Tu Fu, and student dormitories cut into the loess hilltop at the Hsingkuo Middle School, built on the site of an ancient flourishing center of a Buddhist sect. I saw women weaving on hand looms in a loess gulley below the Tang ruins, and a steel bridge spanning the Wei where the "Ancient Ferry of Hsienyang" stood, and a big cotton mill at the capital of the Tsin dictator. I should have liked to write such a booklet of travel sketches on my visits to Sian alone. But this I must forego here.

In Sian, the sense of history forever hovers over the sensitive tourist, even if not over the peasant tilling his field by the side of the Tang emperor's Cockfight Terrace or the women washing laundry and gossiping by a pool which was formerly the Lotus Lake of Queen Yang Kweifei. One day, five or six miles southwest of the city, I passed the capital of Emperor Wu of Chou, the city of Kao, established in 1121 b.c. It was older than Confucius. Confucius looked back upon it as we look back upon King John or Copernicus. It belonged to the remote origins of the Chou dynasty, embedded in songs and sacrificial hymns. Yet the city is there, now no more than a small walled village. I stopped at the gate, and caught a glimpse of the streets, houses, and yards inside. Outside the tower there was a stretch of green wheat fields, and beside a field a peasant woman sat on the ground nursing her child at her breast. Confucius trying to do some historic research on the early religious ceremonies despaired and regretted that they had vanished. Then Confucius passed on and became old, too. Yet that woman was there, clad in cotton, her eyes jet-black, her cheeks solid and firm and tanned a deep brick red by the wind and the sun, nursing her son. It was as if she had been sitting there patiently all through the centuries, all through the Hans, the Tangs, the Sungs, and the Mings, and nothing had changed. She had seen the oppression of tyrants and the toppling of empires, the coming of barbarians from the north, the invention of porcelain and paper and printing, and the change of man's costumes, but her philosophy and her way of living had not changed. She seemed a symbol of China, rooted to the soil, sitting by the wheat and enjoying a momentary peace with her baby after a day of toil.

Briefly, the ruins of the Tang Palaces lay on the north of the city, while those of the Han city were on its northwest, facing the Tsin capital just across the Wei River farther west. The old Chou capitals of Feng and Kao stood eight to ten miles to the southwest. Southeast of Sian, across the Pa River, rose Lishan Mountain, associated with a "capricious" queen, who was not capricious at all. (It was like the story of the boy and the wolf. The queen loved quiet and didn't want to laugh. The wicked Chou king made a false alarm by setting bonfires on top of the Lishan. When the barons arrived, the queen laughed. Next time there was real trouble, and the barons did not arrive. The king lost his empire, and history blames it all on the woman. History is wrong. Some Chinese woman should undertake to write Chinese history all over again.)

The region south of the city leading to the foot of the Chungnan Hills is of particular interest to lovers of Tu Fu. The Tang capital was about eight times the size of the present city, and the ancient city wall, now a stretch of broken and worn-down mud elevations, stands a mile or so outside the present south city. Here is the site of the former Chüchiang Park, celebrated in Tu Fu's verse, where the holiday makers of his time jostled and drank wine and made merry. Farther south stood the Wei town, or Weichü, home of the powerful Empress Wei of Han, and still farther south, the Tu town, or Tuchü, where China's "sage poet" once made his home. Mr. Kung, my companion, told me that in spring the country hereabout was covered with gorgeous peach flowers.

While we were waiting in a teahouse on the roadside for the mule cart to take us to Hsüan Chuang's temple, Mr. Kung suggested that we should follow the good road in our car to take a look at the river. We came to the river, and the car slid smoothly along a stretch of a hundred yards of cement bridge and road. I got a momentary sensation of fast and safe and comfortable driving, and told Mr. Kung that was what driving on American highways was like. Standing on the low cement bridge, we looked over the rain-soaked countryside and down into the little river chattering across its pebble bed. It was clean mountain water, and a delightful stream for the village children to swim in in summer. Even Tu Fu, who I am sure could not swim, must have been tempted to sit on the pebble beach and dip his feet in the cool water. He must have spent many pleasant hours lingering on the waterside, until he came home leaning on a cane, pleasantly tired. The Chungnan Hills, on the south close by, were hidden in layers of mist. The broad valley was enclosed by the Plateau of Divine Grain on the west and Shaoling on the east. The country hereabout had that colorful mixture of slopes, valleys, rivers, and hills that is often characteristic of the foot of a mountain. On clear, sunny days the Chungnan Hills were softly delicate and not austere, but they had just enough rock to give them weight and solidity. South of the city lay the Ts'an River, the Fan River, the Chüchiang Park and other places celebrated in Tu Fu's poetry. Many things of Tu Fu's day have vanished. The city park at Chüchiang frequented by pleasure seekers of Tang is now only desolate countryside. A Sung writer, two or three centuries after Tu Fu, trying to find General Ho's Forest mentioned by the poet, already could not find it. But the general type of scenery was still there.

> Coming back from office I daily pawned the spring dress,
> And every day I came home from a drink on the bank.
> Loans for drinks are common experiences enough,
> But rare is the mortal who reaches three-score-and-ten.

93

I discern butterflies threading in and out among the branches,
And slow-flitting dragonflies skimming the brook.
Tell my friend that the river of time is flowing on.
Let's enjoy this day and not let it pass by.

Tu Fu also lived the life of a war refugee, like so many today:

Since Tungkwan fell last year,
Long have I been separated from wife and sons.
This summer when the vegetation was deep,
I escaped alone to the west.

. . . .

Then I heard that many were butchered,
The slaughter extended to chickens and dogs.
In the leaky mountain hut,
Who would be leaning against the doorpost?

. . . .

Since I sent a letter home,
Ten months have already passed.
Instead I am afraid to hear news from home—
Heart, O heart, be still!

Farther south, reached by a country path branching off from the good motor road leading to the Chungnan Hills, was the Hsingchiaosze, situated on top of a gentle slope. The temple buildings had been newly rebuilt and therefore did not interest me. Only the remains of Hsüan Chuang were buried there under a tall stone pagoda. Hsüan Chuang was one of the few ancient Chinese who traveled to India, where he remained to study Buddhism, being absent from China for eighteen years, A.D. 627-644. His fantastic journey gave rise to many legends, now incorporated in the novel *Hsiyuchi*. He brought back with him six hundred fifty-seven Sanskrit classics, and devoted his life to translating them. When he died, he had translated seventy-five sutras in more than thirteen hundred volumes. The effect of his travels on the China of his time was similar to that of Marco Polo on the Europeans of the Renaissance.

It was because of the scholarly translation by these Buddhist monks that Buddhism enjoyed such a high regard by Chinese scholars, which is not the position of Christianity today. Someone ought to put the Christian Bible into good Chinese, if Christianity is to earn the respect of Chinese scholars. There is no reason why it should not be translated into good Chinese prose. The trouble with present translations is that

94

some Western missionary who understands Hebrew and Greek undertakes the good work with a Chinese pundit. The pundit is paid by the missionary. Whenever a point comes up about the translation of a particular term or passage, the missionary who thinks he knows Chinese insists on what he thinks is a satisfactory translation with respect to fidelity to the original. The pundit is not only ignorant of the original but is also paid by the missionary; he is therefore mentally and financially dependent, and with Chinese wisdom is willing to let a horrible idiom stand, knowing that it is all wrong to Chinese ears, but deciding that nothing can be done under the circumstances. Some of the hymns and litanies were so funny that I could have screamed when I first came upon them in my college days. Now whether a translation carries the sense effectively to Chinese readers, pleasing the ears, the mind, and the soul, requires subtle judgment. To achieve this would require the sure hand of a master, with an ear for the rhythm of the language and an eye for its suggestive imagery. So far there are no modern Chinese who command the necessary Chinese pen, and the knowledge of Greek and Hebrew. Such a man will appear when the time comes. It is not sufficient that he write idiomatic Chinese prose; he must have real literary talent to hit upon the right word for the foreign idiom. He must be a student of Chinese philosophy, and know how to clothe the great, simple old words in a new garb and give them a new meaning. If he had that literary talent, and a flair for Bible English, he would not even need to know Hebrew or Greek, for there is ample reference material on the Bible in English. But he should have a catholic taste and appreciate the sound qualities of good prose, the gentle simplicity of St. Matthew, the mysticism of St. John, the passionate and sometimes impetuous eloquence of St. Paul; he should have a sense of the tragic in *Job,* of the lyric in the *Song of Solomon,* of religious passion and parallel rhythm in the *Psalms,* of history in the *Chronicles* and of the legend and saga and the epic in *Exodus,* of the prophetic fire and perhaps also a bit of prophetic venom in *Ezekiel* and *Jeremiah,* and of the practical, worldly wisdom of *Ecclesiastes* and *Proverbs.* And he would have to reproduce all this by a pen with a wide range of power, and almost *create* his own language. Lastly, he must be a profound believer in Christianity, for only by such inner belief and affection can such a work be created. The Bible can be read as literature and should be translated as a *literary* masterpiece.*

* My friend, Dr. John C. H. Wu, a Chinese scholar and a Catholic, has been commissioned by President Chiang to make a new translation of parts of the Bible. The *Psalms* he translated struck me as delightfully Chinese, but I have not seen other parts of the translation still in progress.

North of the Wei River the flat country is marked with gigantic mounds, the tombs of Chou and Han emperors, some requiring a whole day's trip for a visit. The mounds are a hundred fifty feet to two hundred feet high, and the tomb of the great Han emperor, Han Wuti, rises about three hundred feet, of the size and shape of the Egyptian pyramids.

There ought to be a systematic excavation of some of these tombs. They are not just mounds any more than the pyramids are just a pile of cut stone, but have passages, rooms, altars inside. A popular misconception about "robbing the tombs" seems to stand in the way of such excavation; in the first place, the people would regard it as a sacrilege, and in the second place, experts know that several of the tombs have already been looted of their priceless treasures. That is not the point at all: we would not be after the pearls and the gold and quicksilver. The inner structure, the vaults, the sarcophagi and bronze coffins and gates, the unremovable stone sculpture, the stone altars and benches and remnants of ancient offerings of carts, model houses and sacrificial vessels, bronze and otherwise, would still be there. I have seen a stone bench dug out by accident at the top of the Nightless Palace of Han, now covered by mud, removed to a school at the site of the Tienloko, and also sections of an ancient drain pipe found in the neighborhood, which should never have been removed at all. History records that by the side of the Tienloko there was a *Shihchüko* (or Stone Drainage Tower), both of them being Imperial libraries, and the drain pipe must certainly have been a part of the "stone drainage" and should be left where it was found. There ought to be a better plan of excavation and preservation, which is the very antithesis of sacrilege and plunder. The correct thing would be to declare such areas the property of the state and transform them into national parks, with a state commission entrusted with the duty of excavating, developing, and preserving the historical remains. But no doubt this will have to wait until China can manufacture tanks and guns!

The tomb of the First Emperor of Tsin, who built the Great Wall, stands at Lintung, with a circumference of about two miles, a hill by itself at the foot of the Lishan Mountain. That the First Emperor was the cruelest of tyrants, the conscription of men to build the Great Wall is ample testimony. The Emperor was a bastard, and was described as high-nosed, hawk-eyed, and having the rasping voice of a wolf. The historian Szema Chien, writing within a hundred years after the First Emperor, tells us that "the First Emperor began to excavate the Lishan. When he had subjugated the whole of China, he ordered seven hundred thousand men to dig underground and pour bronze to make casings for the coffin and palaces and towers and ministers [*i.e.,* human figures], and filled it with rare objects of art. He made craftsmen build automatic bows and arrows, to shoot any one who should approach it. He made canals and lakes of quicksilver, which flowed into each other. Above, it [the vault] pictured the heavenly constellations, and below, it pictured the topography of the earth. He made candles of the fat of the *wawa* fish, so planned that they should be able to burn for a long time. . . . When his body was laid down, someone said [to the Prince] that the craftsmen who built the mechanisms knew all about the treasures, and these treasures would become known to the world. When the ceremony of burial was over and the middle gate was already shut, an order was given to close the outer gate so that none of the workmen escaped. Trees were planted on top to make it resemble a hill." Toward the end of his days, this tyrant, in fear of assassins, slept in any of the two hundred and seventy underground palace chambers, keeping his whereabouts a complete secret. He had one of the gates to his palace filled with natural magnets, so that anyone carrying concealed weapons would be detected. Being unable to overcome death, he built himself an underground fortress for his remains, in fear of revenge by some of the hundreds of princes whose kingdoms he had demolished, and whose wives and concubines he had taken for himself. That his tomb was looted shortly after his death and the collapse of his empire is a known fact. It was said that Hsiang Yü's army plundered the tomb for twenty-eight days, carrying away the mountains of treasures gathered from all the palaces of China. But for the serious scientist the vaults and passages and general grand plan must still be there. The plunder was never thorough; many cartwheels and harnesses and spearheads and costumes were of no value to the looters, but would be of inestimable value to the modern historian.

The ancient Chinese kings' tombs consisted of a "tomb garden," *ling yuan,* with an enclosure and trees and temples of worship besides the mound itself planted with trees; the temples and surface structures are gone, and only those mounds remain in a bald, denuded countryside. Still there are things to discover. Only the year before last, a king's vault was discovered and opened up just a mile outside the West Gate of Chengtu. It was no more than a mound about forty feet high. Legend had incorrectly, though poetically, associated it with two ancient lovers of the Han dynasty. When digging for an air shelter, the workmen struck the brick wall at the back of the vault. Systematic excavation by scientists enabled us to see the thirty-foot-high vault, the triple bronze-plated doors, the terrace on which the coffin was placed, and the details of the sculpture. When I visited the place, artists were busy copying the figures under electric lights. It is strange that with all the enormous wealth of the tombs of Chinese kings, this is the only interior that has been preserved.

Many tombs have never been looted. The famous Mouling, tomb of the great Han Wuti, is not known to have been robbed. It is a pyramid, and it took me seven or eight minutes to get to the top of it. It is natural to assume that the great emperor's coffin was not placed a short distance from the front of the mound, but in the very center, and that there would be passageways and halls and stone sculptures and models of houses and stone benches and altars and lamps. There are tombs of his queen and of his two generals near by, with shapes which suggest a definite architectural design. At the tomb of one of his famous generals, Ho Chüping, nine extraordinary pieces of Han sculpture have been found. These are in the shape of various animals. There are a life-size buffalo, and several life-size horses, one standing with his hoofs dug into the chest of a defeated bearded Turk, in celebration of the general's many Turkish campaigns. There is a gigantic bear, and a dragon said to be clutching a "frog." This is, however, not a frog, for it has what seem to be the hoofs of a lamb. The style is massive, strong, and "impressionistic," and unlike any other Chinese sculpture that we have seen. These were scattered halfway up the mound in tumbledown fashion, but Mr. Kung and his group had them moved down and placed upright in pavilions built below. I noticed several stones now lying sunk in the ground, which bear definite marks of the sculptor's chisel. The upturned flat bottoms and the peculiar shape and size of these stones, similar to those already discovered, convinced us that these were part of the series. But even as those discovered had lain unheeded, so do these now lie on the ground. It would only take one day's labor of twenty or thirty men to turn them over and perhaps disclose some of the rarest pieces of Chinese ancient sculpture.

The fact that such sculptures were made for the general's tomb makes it certain that similar sculptures must have been placed in the tomb of his lord and emperor. The tomb of the other general, Wei Ching, who shared the honors with Ho for the Turkish campaigns, is worth looking into, for it has a zigzag pattern suggesting basic structures of some design.

The country round this region was so studded with such mounds that I could not count them. There was a particular tomb of the father of the megalomaniac Empress Wu of Tang, the Shunling, which was so out of the way that few people in Sian knew of it. In four directions half a mile from the center of the tomb stood pairs of lions, horses, and other animals that for size and workmanship are without rival in China. I lay down under the belly of one of the horses and could barely touch the insides of its front and hind legs. Yet it was all carved out of one piece, and on many parts of it a thin shining coating of some kind of metal the color of copper still remained.

One day west of the city we passed a village which, according to legend, was the home of Hsu Fo. This Hsu Fo apparently played a trick on the First Emperor, and incidentally may have been responsible for colonizing Japan. Hsu Fo was a magician, and the Emperor had for years been searching for the pill of immortality. Hsu Fo, who was a native of Shantung, told him that there were three fairy isles in the Eastern Sea where immortals lived. Seamen had seen the mirage of three islands, but when they reached the place, the islands had vanished. He proposed to send an expedition of boys and girls to those islands. Why it was necessary to send boys and girls to these fairy isles was not explained, but it was probably connected with the idea of virginity, as "impure" bodies would not be fit to see immortals. "Thousands" of them were put on ships and sailed for the islands and never returned. This was in the year 219 B.C. I dread to imagine that some of the descendants of these Chinese boys and girls, who succeeded in escaping the first dictator, took part in the sneak attack on Pearl Harbor. The colonization, if it took place at all, must have been very imperfect.

There was a sequel to this story. Helpless in the hand of the magicians, and unable to obtain the pills of immortality after waiting many years, this prototype of Hitler was driven mad with fury. The bastard tyrant loved no one, and no one loved him. Although he had taken all the queens and princesses of the kingdoms he had defeated and put them in over three hundred palace buildings, there is no record of his attachment to any one woman. The story of his quest for power is not relieved by one episode of love or romance, or humor. Once on the Siang River in Hunan he met a storm. He inquired what goddess was in charge of the Siang River, and his followers informed him she was the daughter of Emperor Yao and queen to Emperor Shun. He was furious at her impertinence and ordered the burning of the mountain dedicated to the goddess. His successive expeditions to obtain the magic potion had failed. He had spent great sums of money,

99

and after waiting for years, was both disappointed and worried. His magicians had pleaded for time long enough and were afraid. They explained that there were wicked monsters in the Eastern Sea who always raised storms and drowned his ships. On his next visit to the coast of Shantung he dreamed that he struggled with a spirit of the seas, in the form of a human being. His interpreter of dreams told him, "Your Majesty has been unable to see the spirit of the water because of the monster fish and dragons who surround him. Your Majesty has dutifully worshiped at his shrine, and yet there are such spirit monsters. You must kill the monster spirits before the good spirits will appear." Therefore he ordered fishermen to go out on the sea with apparatus for catching big fish, while he himself waited with a powerful bow to shoot the monster fish when it appeared. From Langyeh to Yungchengshan he could not find any, but at Chefoo he saw such monster fish and shot and killed one of them. Thereupon he took fright and became fatally ill, and died a thousand miles away from his capital.

Fearing rebellion and plotting for the succession of the throne by another than the Crown Prince, his ministers kept his death a secret and put his body in a cool, covered carriage. But it was a journey of months and the corpse began to stink. The minister then ordered a ton of abalone to go with it, so that the smell of the imperial corpse would not be discovered. *Sic transit gloria mundi!* Certainly if the abalones had been alive, they would have protested against His Imperial Majesty's company. What started out to be tragic drama had to end up as a comic opera, with the spirits of the abalones chanting:

"Oh, how the Emperor stinks!"

The whole story of this prototype of Hitler would make a fine drama, if handled with Eugene O'Neill's brooding sense of mystic terror and of the tragic.

I stood on the Ofangkung Palace of the wicked emperor. It was fifty feet high, five hundred feet deep, and five hundred yards wide, a terrace of smooth earth now, which would make an excellent, ready-made runway for airplanes. The Ofangkung was celebrated in history; it consisted of a series of several hundred palaces and underground chambers (the name meaning "Palace of Near Chambers") connected by walled and paved broad walks, leading from Hsienyang across the river to the top of the Chungnan Hills on the south and Lintung on the east ten or twelve miles away. It was yet not quite finished when the Emperor died and was completed by his son, and the burning of the palaces by Hsiang Yü six or seven years later was said to have lasted three months. The Ofangkung, or rather the series of such palaces, was not confined to one spot, and where I stood was but the "Front Palace." The dimensions given by historians seem to be correct, and history says it could accommodate ten thousand persons on top, and below were planted banners fifty feet high. The terrace sloped gently toward the south, while on the west the perpendicular wall stood fully fifty feet high above the ground.

This was the first dictatorship in China, an attempt to rule the people of China by force, based on the fascist philosophy of Shang Yang. But the people revolted "with bamboo poles," and it was the shortest dynasty in China. The Great Wall was but a monument to human slavery. It is curious to note that the Sui emperor who built the Grand Canal around 600 A.D. founded a dynasty that was equally short-lived. This was the kind of thing that the people of China would not stand for long. Dictatorships founded upon human slavery always left some architectural wonders, but had always to pay the price. While Emperor Yang of Sui was sitting in his pleasure boat in the newly built Grand Canal, towed by groups of maidens dressed in silks of different colors, he was already planting the seed for the destruction of his short-lived empire. Invariably the long-lived dynasties began with rulers who were kind. The first swashbuckler who rose to the Dragon Throne had to be followed by a son who was kind and wise and civilized, like Emperor Wen of Han, Emperor Taitsung of Tang, and Emperor Kanghsi of the Manchu dynasty. One of the wisest Confucianist scholars advised the First Emperor of Han, who was really a village bully and ne'er-do-well, "Your Majesty has conquered the world on horseback, but don't expect to rule the world on horseback also." But the dictator of Tsin had no chance for a civilized successor to follow; his tyranny was too unbearable, and revolt spread all over China a year after his death. It was a revolt of the people, joined in by the revolt of the police force.

The Ofangkung was in a sense a disappointment. It was a mud terrace, leveled and bare, with only one stone statue standing and another sunk in the ground. It had nothing of the permanence and inspiring quality of the Roman Forum. Where had all the bricks and stones gone? Carved stone was rare in this country, and no doubt successive dynasties had despoiled the structures of anything valuable. There were at least twelve bronze giants, fifty feet high and with feet measuring six feet. While ten of these were later melted to make coins, two had survived. Centuries later, when a king tried to move them to Loyang, the plan had to be abandoned because of their weight, and they were left on the bank of the Pa. It would be easy enough to discover them with a magnetic detector. The stone inscriptions of the following dynasties, containing calligraphy of priceless value, had been collected and carefully preserved in the Forest of Tablets *(Peilin)* inside the city. These are truly national treasures, and the more valuable ones were covered with mud half a foot thick to prevent damage from flying shrapnel.

Some extraordinary tablets showing inscribed sketches of Tang beauties with very peculiar costumes were stored away at Chingliang Temple, three or four miles outside the city. Two artists were living there in ascetic simplicity. They had just come back from a trip to Tunhwang, and had given an exhibit of their copies of the Tunhwang frescoes. After a lunch that might satisfy monks, I was shown the exhibits. The ten beauties were not there, but I saw copies of them, made from rubbings on the stone. They were so extraordinary that I could not believe my eyes. These were feminine figures sketched in outline, and the artist had colored them with his own imagination. The faces were Chinese, but the costumes were modern European. I never knew Chinese ladies to have worn hats, but their cute headgear tied to the hair and tipped a little to one side was almost Parisian. The dresses had low-cut collars, which was not surprising in ancient costumes of women, but there were also what might be considered modern overcoats, coming below the knees, and trousers with upturned cuffs. The shoes were buckled and quite different from the usual Chinese women's shoes, even those for unbound feet. I cannot be sure that these tablets were Tang or that they were the common costumes of Tang women. I felt inclined to think they were sketches of foreign costumes. There was a residence for Persians in Sian, in the Tang dynasty, but these costumes were not Persian either. Mr. Kung told me that these pieces of stone had been used as pavement for a courtyard in some building, in a little village outside the city, and were recently discovered by someone interested in preserving ancient inscriptions.

The Tunhwang cave paintings represent a period of medieval Chinese art that was rich and important. There are over two hundred caves in the cliffs of Tunhwang with Buddhas in them, on the border of the desert of Chinese Turkistan, and every corner of the caves is filled with paintings of celestial musicians and Buddhist legends, and stories of wars and hunts. The artist Lei told me that some of the sketches resemble Matisse, but I rather think that Matisse resembles the Oriental painters. They were so ancient and yet so modern. Since a few years ago, these wall paintings of Tunhwang have become known and have become quite a fad. A number of artists have flocked to that desert town, spending months copying them, each choosing what struck him most amid the thousands of paintings in what must be an artists' paradise. The Tunhwang paintings may have an important influence on contemporary Chinese art.

There is a current discussion of which city is to be the postwar capital of China, and the Chungking papers from time to time publish articles on the question. One theory is that Sian should be the capital, on account of the future importance of China's Northwest, and on account of its rugged northern atmosphere, its healthy climate, and its history. I think, however, that the capital will go back to Peking (Peiping), for the simple reason that none of the government leaders will vote against it when the question is brought up. Arguments in favor of Peking are almost unnecessary. The Northeast will be equally important, and China cannot afford to retire behind the coast. If it is the policy of the government to get back to the strength and simplicity of the North and avoid the pitfalls of Kiangsu luxury and its somewhat effeminate culture, there should be no other choice but Peking. By that time Peiping will become Peking again (because "king" means capital) and Nanking may have to be changed to Nanping. The two cities will thus have to exchange their end syllables.

The theory is based on the influence of geography on morale and men's thinking. Some contemporary historians have stoutly maintained that the strong and illustrious eras of China were always based on a capital in the North, and although I am a southerner, I must agree. By the same token, the foggy climate of Chungking should have an influence in befogging the thinking of its residents and foreign reporters. No one dares to suggest Chungking as the future capital. Chungking must remain in the nation's memory as the symbol of China's years of trials and stout-hearted resistance. She must wear that simple mantle of glory, just that and nothing more.

8

THE "CIVIL WAR"

SIAN is also an important political and military center. Here are the Chankantuan (War Area Service Staff Training Corps), the great Military Academy of General Hu Tsungnan, the Training School for Guerrilla Fighters, and most interesting of all, the Laotungying, or Concentration Camp containing Communist followers.

Little is heard abroad of the Central guerrilla fighters, a supplementary force of the National Army, operating in Kiangsu, Shantung, Hopei, Hupeh, Anhwei, and Honan. Little also is heard of the Kuomintang underground operating in all occupied areas, doing intelligence and espionage, building up a core of resistance, evading the Japanese, the puppets, and the Communists, fighting a grim battle of silence with constant danger of arrests and assassinations. Young men and women, after receiving their training in guerrilla organization, in War Area Service staff work or in political service, are sent out to various parts of occupied China to do their dangerous work. The Kuomintang party has a secret underground system for sending messages to any part of occupied China, including Manchuria. Meanwhile, thousands of people have returned to Free China from the occupied areas and passed through Sian.

The route from occupied China to Free China ran to the border at Chiehshou, a small town in Honan, thence north to Loyang, westward through Sian, and south to Chungking. Students escaped from Peiping or Shanghai, crossed the border after a dangerous journey, and arrived at Chiehshou penniless, waiting to be sent to government colleges. Young man freely left Shanghai and went up through Nanking and Hsüchow, disguised as merchants. Strangely enough, the Japanese did not bother them. At the border they all said they were just going to the next town to visit relatives.

Some were sent to Loyang and were held up there for lack of funds, while others better provided for trickled westward to Sian, and to Chungking and even Kweilin and Kunming. This strategic position of Sian as the only connection between Chungking and Central China must be borne in mind when we discuss the question of the "blockade" of Communists by China's troops stationed in this area.

Therefore at Sian one gets a fair picture of the condition of the occupied areas, which is on the whole one of confusion, starvation, and unbelievable hardships in the countryside. In some *hsien* there are three magistrates: a puppet magistrate, a Chungking-appointed magistrate occupying one part of the *hsien,* and a Communist magistrate occupying another.

I had the good fortune to run into Professor S———, an old friend and colleague of mine. I cannot reveal his name or identity because his family is still in the occupied area. He is not a party man, but having escaped to Free China, he took up work in connection with the occupied areas. His heart is very much with those working behind the enemy rear and with the relief of college students who have escaped inland. Once when he was speaking at Tungkwan to the soldiers, he mentioned the fact that the people of Peiping felt like subjugated people who had "lost their country," and he stopped and his throat choked for half a minute before he was able to go on. Then he expressed his gratitude to the soldiers, and said, "It is owing to your heroic defense of the country that we are still free." He told me how pitiful the condition of the students at Chiehshou was. Having lived under enemy rule, the young men glamorized the war of resistance, dreaming of living in freedom. Many, though not all, of them had risked many dangers and hardships before they finally reached the border, and they felt a sense of liberation and elation. But many were poor and without means of support. The Ministry of Education provided scholarships for students from the occupied territory, but there were thousands of them, facilities were limited, and the colleges were spread out over the entire inland. Moreover, they could not bring their school certificates along while traveling through enemy territory, and means of identifying them and certifying their school credits were required. All this meant red tape, and communications took time, especially at Chiehshou. Even at Sian one read Chungking newspapers half a month late. Some government agency at Chiehshou or at Loyang gave the students food and shelter and floors to sleep on. Some didn't have enough clothing when the weather changed. So from their sense of elation they sank into disillusionment and despair. Professor S——— did what he could for some of them by helping to certify them and place them. A great number of these young men and women joined the War Area Service Staff Training Corps in order to go back to work in the enemy rear.

Through Professor S——— I arranged to see some of those young men. The conditions they told me of in Hopei, particularly Peiping, were horrible. The Central guerrillas, the Communist guerrillas, and the puppet troops subsisted on this land. In areas controlled by the Communists, the latter would disappear and hide away whenever the Japanese came in, and the enemy would sack and burn the villages, after which the Communist troops would dribble back. So a great number of the villagers found it impossible to live on the land and flocked to the Japanese-ruled cities to pull rickshaws. But rice was not only expensive in Peiping, it was unobtainable, and hundreds of the poor died on the roadside every day. The enemy sold a kind of "mixed flour," also called "fifty-four-assortment flour," brackish, of a deep brown color, made up of fifty-four kinds of husks of different grains and barks and roots and dirt, and sold to the public. It tasted like mud and was likely to produce diarrhea. A Chinese would like of course to glamorize any part of the war, including the guerrillas, but I came to the conclusion that the enemy has been able to get all the manpower and resources from these occupied areas that he wants. I only pray that the people of China be spared the fate of the farmers in these areas.

The students said that tens of thousands of the country population have been sent to Manchuria, by a system of conscription by family and land unit, and by burning the villages and generally making it impossible for them to make a living on the land. One told me that at Peiping the sale of gramophone records of Stephen Foster melodies was forbidden. I suppose the Dixie Land melodies, being American, had a corrupting effect. White men had to wear armbands of different colors corresponding to their nationalities, the American color being red. In the papers and slogans, the words for England and America were written with the "dog" radical. (The "dog" radical or classifying component is generally added to words denoting wild beasts and savage tribes.) I was also informed that the English and American teachers of some universities in Peiping were now living in a concentration camp at Weihsien in Shantung.

The students told me also their personal stories of escape. Some of them came through safely and uneventfully by the eastern section of the Lunghai railway. All of them had to leave the railway at Shangchiu and travel a stretch of several days by hand-cart to the border. Others, who came by way of Shansi, went through gruesome experiences and untold hardships. One student by the name of Yen, who had just graduated from the department of chemical engineering of a missionary university in Peiping, told me of his trip from Peiping to the Free China border which lasted from July 26 to October 12, 1943. He and his companions went through a jigsaw-puzzle combination of

Communist-held, National-held, puppet-held, and Japanese-held territories. They tried to cross the Yellow River at several points and were turned back by Japanese machine-gun fire, until one night they succeeded with a hundred other refugees in crossing the river in spite of the fire of two machine-gun nests. When I saw Yen, he seemed none the worse for his experience.

One evening in Chungking I talked with some gaily dressed modern Shanghai girls who had recently crossed the border on hand-carts. Nobody would think these stylish girls could have made such a journey. The hand-cart is a primitive contraption, made of a broad wooden plank fixed to two wheels and pulled by a man in front like the rickshaw. The travelers lie on the plank, head first, exposed to the wind and sun and rain. There were no inn facilities, and they stopped at whatever village house they could find. One night the girls traveled late into the night and after finding a farmhouse for lodging, were taken to an attic and slept on a bedboard with their feet against a coffin. After passing Loyang, they got on a railway train which had to dash through enemy gunfire from across the Yellow River for a stretch of about a hundred miles to Tungkwan with all lights blacked out. Every night the train went over this stretch, and although sometimes it was hit, it always got through. This was called *ch'uang kwan,* or dashing through the pass. At places where the railway ran close to the river and was exposed, mud walls were thrown up for protection, and at other places detours were built.

I had the chance to talk with another group of eight party workers in the War Area Service, now back in Sian. They were able to picture the confusion and sabotage, and both open and underground work, in occupied areas. There were two from Hopei, two from Kiangsu, and one each from Liaoning (Manchuria), Hupeh, Shantung, and northern Shensi. All of them were graduates of colleges or normal schools, and one was a graduate of the Meiji University, Tokyo. The pictures they gave were horrible, intimate pictures of the incessant undeclared civil war which has gone on since 1939 in Hopei, Shantung, Anhwei, and Shansi, in a grim struggle for supremacy. They enabled me to understand not only the deep misery of the peasants in these areas, but also why the guerrillas were less effective than they should be, and why the Japanese were able to hold the towns so securely these three or four years, and why fighting has practically come to a standstill there since 1940.

One man told an amusing but sad story of how they set a trap and made the Communists "fight the Japanese by mistake." The Chinese term for guerrillas is *yuchi,* which means "float about and fight." "The Communists float about, but don't fight," this man said. "When the Japanese come, they float away, and when Central troops are there, they fight." The Japanese were stationed at a fortress at Huang-chiatun, controlling the highway from Fengjun to Chunhwa in northeastern Hopei, near the Great Wall, and the Communists were at Tukutun. They had minor complaints against each other, but were otherwise living at peace. On August 18, 1941, Colonel Wu of the Japanese-controlled puppet First Regiment received orders to protect a convoy of eighteen trucks loaded with ammunition coming down the highway from the Great Wall. A Kuomintang party director, Fu Chehlin, set up a plan, which was technically called "adjusting spark plugs," to draw the Communists and the Japs into a fight. He mined the highway near the point controlled by the Communists. The mines destroyed seven trucks and held up the rest. Meanwhile he had disguised some of his men in Communist uniform to throw hand grenades at the Japanese fortress, and he spread the rumor through the puppet troops that the Communists had blown up the convoy. At the same time, he disguised some of his men as Japanese soldiers to attack the Communist garrison, luring them back to a deep gully at Tuku-chuang. Soon the Japs and the Communists found themselves fighting each other, the Japs from above the gulley and the Communists below, both sides suffering severe casualties. This trick of setting "spark plugs" was repeated several times successfully that year, until the Communists found it out and captured the Kuomintang man Fu and buried him alive (to save ammunition).

My informant told me that at Fengjun where he was working with Fu, the Communists buried over four hundred people alive in 1941. He had a hair-raising story of his own escape. He was strangely rescued by an unknown railway workman who handed him an open telegram directing his escape. He had roamed all the way from Peitaiho to Tientsin, protected by the invisible hand of the Kuomintang underground. He didn't know who helped him at any point, and the story seemed to him like an incredible miracle. These people all seemed to have gone through dramatic experiences, like all secret agents. They assured me that their comrades had faced death, arrest, and torture, but were carrying on undaunted. Hundreds of patriotic youths had died unsung and unknown. This was a side of the war of resistance that I had been totally unaware of. It will constitute a sad and moving chapter in the history of the war. I was told that some of the peasants so hated the Communists, through personal happenings to their families, that they joined the puppet troops in order to fight the Communists.

I questioned my informant closely on the stories about burying people alive. Another man's eyes flashed. He had been stationed at Lingshou in central Hopei, and he asserted that at Chengting more than a thousand people had been buried alive. The terror had been especially severe in 1940 when the Communists had just arrived and had had to do this to consolidate their control of the area. All who refused to co-operate or take their orders were given the label of "traitor" (since they refused to co-operate with the anti-Japanese Communist army) and were killed, sometimes by big knives, also to save ammunition. I find it hard to believe these stories, but they were first-hand and the testimony was unanimous. It will be a simple matter to investigate these charges on the spot at Fengjun and Chengting after the war.

One of the men in the group of party workers at Sian was from Shantung. He told me the story of the wiping out of Chin Chiyung's forces, which I later found was known to everybody in Chungking. General Yü Hsüehchung's twenty thousand troops were being transferred, and a force under another commander was being sent to replace them. Before the new troops had arrived, one of the Communist leaders, Li Fo-cheh, led his troops to attack the Central troops from the south, while the Japanese attacked them from the north. Being hopelessly outnumbered and surrounded, Chin committed suicide rather than surrender, on August 7, 1943.

The man from Liaoning, a province of Manchuria, informed me that all able-bodied men from twenty-one to thirty were under draft for one year's service out of five, and that a severe system of census and *paochia* (collective responsibility) was enforced there. Children under six and people over sixty were not given rations, but their families had to share food with them. All spoke of the Communist idea of "individualism" encouraging the breakaway from the family system. This seemed the most unpopular feature of the Communist rule among the common people. Family loyalty is such a deep tradition among Chinese people of all classes that while they submit to the Communist rule, they all inwardly disapprove and resent it. It affected the parents chiefly, since the Communists work through the young people, calling them away from their "feudalistic" ties to their families. But Chinese, young and old, are inherently loyal to the family first. I suspect that the subconscious conflict must always be there, except for a few very "enlightened" comrades who know that they are being very modern by breaking all "feudalistic" family ties. But even the young people suffer. They avow that their women can divorce them under the protection of the Women's Union and the National Salvation Association, and they have no choice but to submit. They must write a legal acceptance of the divorce, else something may just happen to them. They will be found to have become puppets, traitors, or even Trotskyites; even if they do not know what the word means, they know they will not live long. This is part of the "emancipation of women." Once a wife becomes a member of the Women's Union, she has the whole party machine behind her and is more powerful than her husband, unless he, too, occupies an important party job. The chairman of the National Salvation Association officiates at the new wedding, and the *tiwei,* short for *tifang weiyuan,* or "local commissar," is the official go-between. The *tiwei,* or local commissar, is the real authority from whom the elected magistrate takes his orders, at the risk of becoming a Trotskyite himself, to be replaced by another "elected" magistrate in his place.

One cannot escape the conclusion that in this grim struggle for supremacy and control of occupied areas, the party interests were regarded as paramount and overruled the patriotic interests of national unity and struggle with the enemy. In the first two years of the war, the Communist guerrillas attracted a great number of young patriots who were more interested in fighting Japan than in party politics. Once among the Communists, however, it seems to have become impossible to be interested *only* in fighting Japan, for one who is not with them is regarded as against them and stands in danger of "liquidation."

There was the case of Hsiung Tacheng, formerly tutor of physics at Tsinghwa University. When the Marco Polo Bridge incident took place, he was teaching at Tientsin, and he left his teaching post to join the guerrilla army of Lü Chengchao in central Hopei near Chengting. Lü himself was a major under General Wan Fulin and was not a Communist. Hsiung helped in bringing four or five hundred teachers and students from Peiping and Tientsin to join the ranks, organizing and expanding the guerrilla forces until Lü's army had fifty thousand men controlling central Hopei. As a physicist, Hsiung was the chief of the supply service and brought in technicians from Peiping and Tientsin to organize the production of ammunition. There was no doubt that Hsiung was interested only in the war of resistance. Major Lü also took the same line and employed men regardless of party connections.

Seeing the growing force of Lü, the Communists filtered in and bored from within, until Lü one day found that even his cook and his orderlies were Communist partisans. He knew that he was completely surrounded and that his life might be in danger. When he had a chance of seeing General Sun Liangcheng, he entrusted his horse to the latter's care as his parting gift. In March, 1939, the physicist Hsiung was arrested and detained under orders of the Communist command. Lü himself was sent up to Yenan to receive "training." Over one hundred eighty students and teachers who had refused to become Communists were also involved. Thus a successful "purge" was effected and the Communists gained complete control of the central Hopei guerrillas. This is typical of their method of extending their control. Among those who were detained and put in "traitors' camps" (ch'uchienpu) were Li Meng, a student of Yenching; Liu Wei, a student of the School of Engineering of National Peking University; Li Kwanghsin, a student of Tsinghwa; Chang Fang, a student of Chilu University and postgraduate student of Yenching; Miss Liu Weichen, student of Chilu and friend of Chang Fang; Chang Chen, assistant tutor of Fujen (Catholic) University; and Huang Chung, a well-known Christian leader of Peiping. These were students and teachers who had joined the guerrillas through Hsiung's influence. Pai Lu, a Catholic theological student of Poyeh, Hopei, was arrested because he went to Peiping to buy some medicine Hsiung needed. That friends of Trotskyites are Trotskyites seems a well-established logic according to Marxian dialectics.

So the patriots are thrown into "traitors' camps" in Communist-held areas, and Communists are thrown into "concentration camps" in National areas.

All this is hardly pleasant reading, and it is not pleasant writing for a Chinese. But the truth has to be told to understand the nature of the conflict. There is undoubtedly another side of the story, but this other side has already been so ably, constantly, and effectively propagandized that the reader probably would like to hear the untold side. In order to get a balanced picture, I refer the reader to Edgar Snow's *The Battle for Asia*, pages 353 to 356, where the Communist side of the story may be heard. The pro-Communist charges against Chungking have been rather fulsomely repeated in America, and the other side has refused to tell its story at all, regarding it as a domestic issue. The result is only confusion. The government has strictly censored anti-Communist news both at home and abroad. Rightly, it does not wish to present a picture of disunity and hesitates to tell the story of Communist sabotage of the war of resistance. But one must either ignore the Communist question, or stand above both parties and hear both sides.

In summer, 1943, when the National Army was surrounded and outnumbered by the Japanese on three sides and surrounded by the Communists on the fourth side in the Taihang Mountains, the result was the capture of two generals. The Communists united with the Japanese in destroying the Twenty-seventh Army of the National forces and ambushed and wiped them out at three places, Pingshun, Kaoping, and Kuhsien, on July 8, 1943, according to the official telegram of General Chiang Ting-wen. After several such clashes had taken place, a government official told the facts to a foreign correspondent, but *the story was then banned by the Kuomintang censors themselves*. I was in New York then, and I could not understand the capture of these two famous generals, until I went to Chungking and heard the full story.

The question of the undeclared civil war should either be ignored by the outside public as something too complicated for outsiders to understand, or it should be treated with the thoroughness and sincerity which it deserves. In view of the importance of the subject, it is my opinion that the American people are fully entitled to hear the facts about the history and origin of the conflicts. The Chinese government does not wish to tell the story for the sake of face and appearance, and the Chinese Communists do not want to tell the story because it makes ghastly reading of their record in this war. Thus a complete black-out on the six-year-old civil war is established. But obviously, without knowing the character and the extent and magnitude of this civil war, there can be no intelligent discussion of its solution, peaceful or otherwise, and no understanding of the grim struggle that looms ahead for the future of China.

The history of this fratricidal conflict constitutes the most inglorious chapter of the China war, and I have no desire to let the Japanese gloat over it. Unfortunately, the Japanese already know the full story and have been known to "celebrate" frictions between Central and Communist troops. It is doing nobody any good to minimize this civil war and call it occasional "clashes" when battles lasted as long as fifteen days, troops involved at one time numbered 40,000 men, when systematic and organized campaigns were carried on for years from one province to another, with the intent of annihilating the opponent accomplished by determined pursuit and wiping out of remnant forces, and when they involved successive attacks on three provincial government offices, the hounding out of the provinces of two governors and the capture of a third. Nobody's interests are served by glamorizing the Chinese Communists or by underestimating them as a harmless, innocuous party of political innocents. For it is my conviction that, following their aggressive tactics of expansion, against which the Central troops are powerless unless Chiang orders an open war, the Chinese Communists will have control of half of China if the Japanese succeed in cutting China in two and if another year lapses before they are driven out.

The facts themselves are sufficiently clear. The Chinese Communists have now established themselves, though incompletely, in five or six provinces of the occupied areas. As these areas were in the enemy rear, the Central control was incomplete and they were ideal ground for freebooters. But from the very beginning, there were Chungking-appointed civil administrations and military commanders of war areas, with guerrillas and regular troops, responsible for carrying on operations in Hopei, Shantung, Kiangsu and Anhwei. Governor Lu Chunglin was in charge of Hopei, with General Sun Liangcheng as commander-in-chief of guerrilla forces in four columns, and General Chu Huaiping as commander of the regular Ninety-Seventh Army. Governor Han Tehchin was in charge of Kiangsu, with General Ku Chutung commanding the regular troops. Governor Shen Hunglieh was in Shantung, with General Yü Hsüehchung's troops and others. General Li Tsungjen was in charge of the Anhwei area. Governor Yen Hsishan was in Shansi, in control of his army. Besides, there were many People's Armies (*minchün*) of different sizes, and Peace Preservation Corps (*paoantui*) organized by the villagers for self-defense. There were Chungking-appointed magistrates in every *hsien,* Sanmin Chuyi Youth Corps, War Area Service Corps, and Kuomintang agencies doing underground work. These were all organized under designated "war areas" by the Military Affairs Commission with National units in charge. The operational area assigned to the Communist troops, first known as the Eighth Route Army and later as the Eighteenth Army Corps, was in northern Shensi, eastern Suiyuan, Chahar and northern Hopei, which includes the Peiping and Tientsin area. The other Communist army, the New Fourth, was assigned an area on both sides of the Yangtse river, between Nanking and Wuhu, covering sections of Anhwei and Kiangsu. If this disposition of troops laid down by the national unified command had been obeyed, there would have been no friction at all.

Naturally, in their plan to seize control of these areas not designated to them, the Communists found it necessary to eliminate both the Central troops and the People's Armies, and to attack Kuomintang agencies and Kuomintang-appointed county magistrates and governments. Granted that the Communists thought it their patriotic duty to take over the entire occupied areas, they could have done nothing else. In this war of penetration, they had every advantage. The Central troops, not being ready for open war, could not plan concerted large-scale campaigns against the Communists, while the latter could and did do so. Time and again, they were overwhelmed by surprise attacks with converging powerful forces. Arresting county magistrates and surrounding small-sized local self-defense units were easy for the well-organized Communist Army. The main advantage of the Communist Army is that of a determined aggressor against a defender who has not made up his mind for defense. A further important incentive was the fact that it was much easier to capture rifles and ammunition from their Chinese brothers than from the enemy. After every victory, the Communists became stronger by so many rifles. Everywhere they went, their first job was to capture rifles and ammunition from the *minchün* and the *paoantui* and collect grains and cash. The Central troops further had the disadvantage of being far separated from their bases. Time and again, they fought until their ammunition was exhausted.

The plain fact then is that the Central troops have not gone into Communist areas to attack them, but the Communists have come out to attack other Chinese units in occupied areas in the name of fighting the Japanese. The Communists openly admit now they have run all over Shantung, Hopei, Kiangsu, Anhwei, and even Hupeh, and are a little proud of their victories and their growing strength. But they have not captured these territories from the Japanese but from other Chinese by bloody battles. From the very beginning, the process of penetration and expansion was characterized by armed and underground conflicts with other Chinese soldiers, and by extremely subtle and able tactics of boring from within. In no instance have the Communists been able to capture territories which the Japanese intended to hold. As they have not yet been able to establish perfect control over the occupied areas, where Central military and civil organizations are still operating today, the result is a continued futile and disheartening fratricide, while the Japanese have been able to get all they want in manpower and resources.

The history of this six-year-old civil war will fill a whole volume.

I must be content with an outline sketch, with sufficient details to give a picture of the character of the campaigns. I base my material on Chen Chung's book, *Four Years of the Chinese Communist Party,* published in April, 1941, which contains the facts of the civil war ending with the clash with the New Fourth Army. If the book were translated, with its material on sabotage and political machinations, I believe no political party in the world with such a record of internal disloyalty during a foreign war could retain the respect of decent-thinking men, I shall, however, confine myself to the military aspects, with sufficient data to give some idea of the war's character and magnitude.

Briefly, this is the story of Communist expansion, beginning from central and southern Hopei, from below Chengting, starting as far back as 1938, aggravated in 1939, and completed with a large-scale three-month campaign in the beginning of 1940. Growing strong with this victory, the Communists penetrated into Shantung with large-scale overall operations in 1940, although preparatory disarming of local self-defense units began in 1939. Encouraged by this success, the Yenan headquarters planned to squeeze out the Central forces in Kiangsu by converging attacks by the New Fourth Army from the south and columns coming down from Shantung in the north, a campaign which aborted on account of trouble in Anhwei. By the fall of 1940, the Chungking command ordered the cessation of hostilities in northern Kiangsu, and in order to avoid future clashes, the New Fourth Army was ordered north. The time limit for the execution of these military orders was repeatedly changed and ignored. Rampages in Anhwei north of the Yangtse were going on in the winter of 1940, with attacks on county governments, massacres and disarming of people's self-defense troops. One part of the New Fourth Army was south of the river a little above Wuhu, ordered by the National command to cross the river north at this point. As a delaying tactic, it refused to move unless its demand for half a million dollars in cash and a half million in ammunition was granted first. Meanwhile it had turned south instead of crossing the river. General Ku Chutung's Fortieth Division was returning from south Kiangsu for transfer and had arrived at Sanchi, south of Wuhu, on January 1, 1941. The Communists had come down as far as Moulin, within eighteen kilometers of Ku's troops. According to the Kuomintang story, Ku's troops were ambushed and attacked on the night of January 4. Ku turned and attacked and by the 12th, the New Fourth Army was defeated and disarmed and the Communist general, Yeh Ting, was captured. The Yenan command demanded the release of Yeh Ting and an apology from Chungking in the terms of an equal and hostile army. Chungking ordered the disbandment of the New Fourth, and Yenan countered by appointing a new commander.

The campaign opened in central Hopei and pushed down south. Skipping over the clashes in 1938, the conflict with the Central guerrillas under Chao Yunhsiang at Hsinho in January, the disarming of the Seventh Regiment of the Second Army at Poyeh in December, the capture of the ammunition of the People's Army at Shunchung in December, and the attacks on the Fifteenth and Fourteenth Regiments of the People's Army under Wang Tseyao in April of the following year, we find that large-scale systematic operations began in June, 1939 and lasted till the end of March, 1940.

General Chang Yinwu was commander-in-chief of the Hopei People's Armies and at the same time Commissioner of the Interior of the province. His troops occupied a circular area east of Chengting on the Peiping-Hankow railway (covering Sulu, Chihsien, Hengshui, Hsinho, Shenhsien, Tsinhsien and Kaocheng). It was a flat country; nevertheless the People's Armies had fought seven successful guerrilla encounters with the Japanese in this area. The Communists could and should have been useful allies. On the night of June 21, 1939, the headquarters of the People's Armies was suddenly surrounded by two Communist regiments under Ho Lung. The battle lasted two days and two nights until Chang's ammunition was exhausted and his troops were completely disarmed. He was also head of the Hopei Sanmin Chuyi Youth Corps, and the Corps was executed wholesale. Then the battle spread over 120 kilometers and over forty thousand Communist troops were employed, under Ho Lung, Liu Pocheng and Lü Chengchao. Chang's troops escaped toward west of the Peiping-Hankow Railway, but the 129th Division of Liu Pocheng, the 120th Division of Ho Lung and the Youth Guards of Lü Chengchao followed in hot pursuit until they completed the annihiliation or disbandment of the People's Army. The troops of the People's Army thus disarmed and liquidated consisted of three divisions, one special brigade, one independent regiment, a signal corps and a supply corps. A great amount of ammunition went to strengthen the Communist Army.

The Communists pushed farther. Toward August, a concerted movement was formed from the east and north, and another column of Youth Guards came up from the south at Hsingtai, threatening the 11th Brigade of the People's Army under Wang Chih-ho, stationed at

Tsanhuang, 50 kilometers below Chengting. On August 1, the encirclement was ready and the attacks began. Finding itself completely surrounded, the brigade surrendered with over 100,000 rounds of ammunition, over 1,000 rifles and 500 soldiers taken prisoner. The Chinese Communists had thus completed their control of both sides of the Peiping-Hankow railway immediately below Chengting, and again gained much ammunition.

This was followed by the attack, on December 2, on the "Hopei Chahar guerrillas," organized out of the people's self-defense units, under the charge of Sun Chungwen. Again, Sun was caught by a surprise attack by more than 2,000 Communist troops under Hsing Jenfu. His corpse was subjected to unmentionable inhumanities.

The stage was set for squeezing the Central troops out of southern Hopei entirely. The Central guerrillas commissioned by the Chungking government were under the command of Sun Liangcheng, with four columns straddling the Peiping-Hankow railway farther south. On January 12, 1940, Communist troops set upon the 2nd column under Hsia Weili at Hsingtai, the 4th column under Hou Juyung at Yuanshih, and the People's Army units under Chiao Mingli, which were on their way for inspection. Over 1,000 Chinese were killed and the official guerrilla inspectors sent by the Military Affairs Commission were murdered.

On February 8, the Communists started attack on the headquarters of Sun Liangcheng himself and on the 3rd guerrilla column under Chao Yunhsiang, which were stationed far south in the very tip of Hopei province (at Neihuang, Chingfeng, Poyang). The attack was launched in strength and after a six-day pitched battle the Central troops escaped into Shantung and Honan, hotly pursued by the Communist troops as far as Yungyang in Honan. The Japanese could not have done a more thorough job. This campaign lasted fifteen days in all.

The Communist control of central and southern Hopei was now complete, with the exception of the 97th Regular Army under General Chu Huaiping, which by the way had an established record in fighting guerrilla warfare with the Japanese. This last campaign took on the character of an army battle, with the Communist troops numbering more than 40,000 (ten regiments of the 129th Division, part of the 115th Division, and Youth Guards and Youth Vanguards). The battle lasted seven days beginning March 4. Again Central troops found themselves surrounded by previous encirclements and their line of escape in the mountainous region was blocked by ambushes at many places. This was probably the bloodiest battle and the slaughter of troops was terrible.

Now Governor Lu Chunglin was shorn of his wings, and after the attack on his provincial government headquarters, the white-haired old man, who had braved dangers to fight in the enemy rear, escaped almost alone back to Chungking to tell his story. According to Governor Lu's own story, the Communists were able to prevent the farmers from selling grain to his troops by calling them puppets and by a system of fines. When Central troops passed through certain areas in secrecy, the Communists staged loud cheering processions of welcome to advertise their whereabouts to the enemy. They were obeying the Chungking government by acknowledging Lu's authority and tolerated him as long as they found it convenient to do so.

All this happened while a foreign war was supposed to be going on and the nation was supposed to be united in struggle with an external enemy. But I rather think it happened because a foreign war was going on.

Under peace circumstances, the Central troops would not have allowed this state of things to drag on. But if Chungking had accepted the challenge, there would have been open civil war, and this had to be avoided at all costs. The situation was therefore ideal for the Chinese Communists. What they could accomplish in Hopei, they could accomplish elsewhere as well. The different campaigns form a well-thought-out sequence following a steady southward direction. Victorious over their Chinese brothers and growing strong on Chinese defeats, the Communists pushed on from Hopei to Shantung. One need not go into all the campaigns in Shantung, Shansi, Anhwei and Kiangsu. The tactics of penetration, of preparatory disarming of small *paoantui* units and people's army units, obtaining control of outlying *hsien* towns, accumulating supplies and arms, followed by strong, powerful sudden thrusts in overpowering numbers and encircling movements, were of the same general pattern, directed and carried out with determination, cunning and superb courage. One must admit that General Chu Teh is one of China's best military strategists, and Mao Tsetung one of the best tacticians in political propaganda.

In Shantung, many local people's self-defense units had already been disarmed in 1939. With the triumphant conquest of central and southern Hopei, the Communists pushed on into Shantung in 1940 with renewed energy and increased strength from their captured ammunition. Chen Chung's book mentions twenty-seven such armed conflicts in Shantung in that year alone. I need mention only a few cases. Over

Japanese women prisoners (in cotton uniform) who have joined a wool spinning group of the Chinese Industrial Co-operatives in the Northwest, together with Chinese girl workers (in overalls).

A Hunan peasant woman shortly after she had been raped by a Japanese soldier.

A repaired section of an ancient military footway (third century) at the Stone Gate Pass. On the opposite bank is the modern motor highway between Shensi and Szechuen.

The author in his traveling outfit.

Part of machinery for a paper mill made by the Shen Hsin Textile Mill at Paochi.

A view of the electrically lighted underground tunnels of the Shen Hsin Textile Mill, the biggest underground factory in China, dug into a mountain.

Chinese women making bed quilts for the soldiers at Sian, under the Chinese Industrial Co-operatives.

Chinese soldiers in Hunan at mealtime.

Girls of the Sian Orphanage in their dance costume.

Children of the Sian Orphanage learn switchboard work and radio repairs, and make their own violins.

Miss Chin Yuhua, the author's adopted daughter.

An aqueduct over the Chingyi River, part of the many water conservancy projects in Szechuen.

View of 2,000-year-old flood control and irrigation system at Kwanhsien, Szechuen. In the distance may be seen the bamboo-rope bridge.

Salt boats of Szechuen.

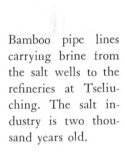

Bamboo pipe lines carrying brine from the salt wells to the refineries at Tseliuching. The salt industry is two thousand years old.

General Hu Tsungnan, one of China's ablest commanders, in a picture taken with the author at Sian. His troops were responsible for stemming the Japanese advance across the Salween in 1942.

General Hsueh Yueh, the "Little Tiger," who thrice defeated the Japanese at Changsha.

Major General Ou Chen, one of the heroes of the battle of Changteh.

35,000 troops of the Communist forces joined in an attack on the government commissioner's headquarters in the Seventh District. Over 5,000 Communist troops under Peng Mingchih attacked the Seventh Brigade of the *paoantui* near Shuhsien and Szeyang. While the Japanese were attacking Chihsia, the 5th column (*chihtui*) of the Eighteenth Army Corps took the opportunity to attack the Central 27th Brigade and the county government at Chaoyuan. This is but a sample of what happened on a larger scale later in the overpowering attack on Chin Chiyung, mentioned before. They had as much interest in wiping out the Central Chinese troops as the Japanese. When the Japanese retreated, the area would be theirs. The same pattern in Shansi. The same pattern in Hopei, Honan, Anhwei, Kiangsu. For the motive behind such a pattern alone can account for the large-scale civil war. The Communists, however, to date have not obtained complete control of these provinces, but have made enough trouble for the Central guerrillas not to be able to concentrate their energy on Japan. Neither the Communist guerrillas nor the Central guerrillas are fighting there for more than mere survival.

Perhaps what happened in Shansi may be more illustrative of Communist plans and fratricide tactics. Chen Chung's book, on which this account is based, quotes many minutes of Yenan party meetings, decisions of the Yenan military command, and orders issued to fighting units. The verbal accuracy of these quotations may be called in question, but in view of the many Communists who have come over to the Chungking side, and the many captured documents, the knowledge of such orders and instructions occasions no surprise. According to Chen, the Eighteenth Army Corps held a conference on May 16, 1940, arriving at the following main principles, besides more specific instructions for military and political workers:

1. Give the troops in Shansi and Suiyuan the label of pacifists, and gradually eliminate them.
2. Bore the Central guerrillas from within and then plan to destroy them one after another.
3. Avoid direct frontal clashes with Central regular troops, for the the present. Split them politically and watch for an opportunity to destroy them at a stroke.

In March, 1940, an emergency military conference was called in Shansi, at which Chu Teh, Liu Pocheng, Peng Teh-huai and Ho Changli were present. After General Chu Teh had given his report of the international situation, they arrived at the following resolutions:

1. The troops of the Eighteenth Army Corps are not to wear caps bearing the Kuomintang emblem of a white sun against a blue sky, in order to improve their morale.
2. Strengthen our base in southeast Shansi and win back the lost political power there.
3. Destroy the troops of Shih Yushan and Lu Chunglin.
4. Clean up southeast Shansi by first destroying the Independent 8th Brigade and the entire (Central) guerrilla forces of the Second War Area.
5. Accumulate food supplies to the limit.

Following this conference, the Eighteenth Army Corps mustered 50,-000 troops from eastern Shansi and Chahar and stationed them at Pingshun, Lingchuan and Hukuan. With the help of the 688th, 689th and 369th regiments of the 115th Division and another brigade of over 2,000 men, the "cleaning up" campaign in southeast Shansi began. It will be recalled that this followed immediately the defeat of the Central forces in southern Hopei, when many of these troops came over the border.

When the Japanese attacked Wutai Mountain, the Communist base in Shansi, in 1940, the Communists, following their tactics of fighting only when having preponderant numbers, abandoned the base. But when the Central troops under the Second War Area command decided that Wutai was to be the base for the New 2nd Division, General Chu Teh flew back with his Communist forces to wrest control of the area. When the New 2nd Division was on its way to Wutai, it was subjected to hit-and-run attacks at Taliushu, at Shouyang *hsien,* and at Tsaochiachun on the Chengtai highway, where a battle was fought for two days, and was again ambushed at Shunan by a force of over 800. After staging such harassing attacks on the way, from which the Communists greatly profited in terms of scores of mules and much valuable ammunition, they finally made the main attack on the New 2nd Division at Yushuhsien. By that time, the New 2nd Division had already exhausted its supplies, and was doomed. Naturally many Chinese officers and soldiers were killed. The 130,000 dollars that its commander Chin Hsienchang was carrying for his troops were taken as part of the Communist "booty." Two companies escorting the mules were massacred, and only one cook and one muleteer escaped. It is hard to understand how such destruction of Chinese manpower was to help in the war against Japan, by the weirdest stretch of materialistic dialectic. Multiply these cases by the thousands, and we can understand why there is no unity but only mad confusion in the guerrilla warfare against Japan.

After the comparative success in southern Shantung, the next slice of territory to be pocketed was northern Kiangsu. According to captured documents, of which many were found after the defeat of the New Fourth Army, the plan for the attack on northern Kiangsu was formulated at Peihsien early in 1940. The minutes of the conference of political and military workers contained the following:

1. A report was made that our (Communist) Party is determined to exert its best to capture political power in northern Kiangsu. This is to be divided into three stages, carried out in three periods. In three months, we shall be able to gain control of northern Kiangsu and the coastal region. The first period ends at Mid-Autumn Festival. The second period ends on October 10. The third period ends on New Year's Day, 1941.
2. The first stage consists in creating unrest in the region and uniting the small local bands into larger units. Through local unrest, we can go forward with our regional work, start opposition to the Government, and store up grain and accumulate cash by taxation.
3. The second stage is that of sudden attacks. In this period, we are to concentrate strong forces, selecting the lightly-defended areas of the Central troops as our targets. We shall also disarm independent units and secure the ammunition of political agencies.
4. The third period is the period of encirclement and *coup d'état*. We shall occupy the whole of northern Kiangsu with all forces at our command.

Without going into details revealed by this and many other documents, it may be briefly stated the plan was for the New Fourth Army to cross the river north and the Communist troops in Shantung to press south, forming a pincer attack on Governor Han Tehchin's troops in northern Kiangsu. In July, 1940, the New Fourth Army attacked the Central base near Jukao and established its control over a small area. In October, two more regiments were sent north, making a total of ten regiments, which started to attack the Independent 6th Brigade and the 33rd Division. Simultaneously, Communist troops under Peng Mingchih, numbering over 5,000, descended from the Shantung border and captured Founing. From October till the beginning of December, battles were going on in the area between Tungtai in the south and Founing in the north. An especially severe battle lasted for a week beginning from November 29, without definite results. Then trouble blew up in southern Anhwei, and the Communists had to split up the campaign. The Military Affairs Commission at Chungking issued repeated commands to the Communists to move back to their original areas, in order to avoid further conflicts, but the orders were ignored and clashes therefore continued until the great open conflict flared up in April of the following year.

These are the preliminaries of the final clash with the New Fourth Army. When General Ku Chutung decided to strike back, the result was the clash with the New Fourth Army, which was disarmed. The Communists told the world that this was civil war. It looked indeed very much like it.

Even from such a brief survey, it appears certain that the campaigns were planned in long range, that there was a general purpose and line of direction and that these were not accidental conflicts. There can be no question as to who was the determined aggressor. It is not to be supposed that Chiang Kai-shek could not plan concerted attacks and encircling movements as well as Chu Teh. If Chiang had wanted civil war, Hu Tsungnan's troops could easily have gone into Yenan and crushed the Communists and didn't have to be satisfied with a "blockade." Naturally, the conflicts continued and flared up again and again with greater severity, as in 1943. It is because of the planned and premeditated character of this aggression against Central forces that I believe the Communists will, by following the same tactics, soon obtain control of Honan, Hupeh, Hunan and Kwangsi, that is, wherever the Japanese come. I do not believe that, while this situation continues, there is any way of stopping them short of a declared civil war. But I think that the Chinese government will continue to appease them by letting them advance steadily from province to province rather than risk a civil war in the midst of the war against Japan.

The past record of the Chinese Communists exhibits sufficient astuteness in propaganda and unscrupulousness of method to warrant the assumption that, after the war, they will adopt whatever tactics and put on whatever front they may deem necessary to achieve political power in China and accomplish their final, unchangeable objective. Their unscrupulousness in creating ruthless internecine warfare even when the enemy is still on Chinese soil is matched only by their slickness in championing China's national unity abroad. And while they do not even pretend there is freedom of the press or of thought or individual rights in Yenan and have established the most rigorous party dictatorship, they have succeeded in making themselves out as steady champions of freedom of the press and constitutional democracy in Chungking. We may therefore expect that, in the postwar period, they will not only put on a democratic front, but even a procapitalist front, as the American Communists are doing, in order to achieve political power. And because I have great respect for Mao Tsetung's political genius, I believe he will soon abandon violence and seek a legal position by "constitutional" means, planning to end up as China's Reichs-Chancellor. The greatest harm the Americans can do themselves is to underestimate the Chinese Communists. A whole nation can stupidly misread history being enacted before their eyes, unable to understand the forces at work, until they are one day rudely shaken by events. I suggest that the forces at work today in China have something to do with China's international alignment in the next world war.

In the light of these facts, the pronouncements of Mao Tsetung may be read with interest. They seem to point to the origin of the whole civil war. In Chapter One of his book on *Reconstruction of the Party* (*Tang ti Chiensheh*), he says, "In the present stage of the Chinese revolution, the most fundamental objectives are: expansion and strengthening of the Communist Party, guaranteeing the complete independence of the Communist Party in its political structure, guaranteeing the iron-like union between Communist elements and the Bolsheviki . . . as a preparation for revolution aiming at a socialist society."

In *On the New Stage*, he says, "In order to overcome difficulties and win over the enemy, the Communist Party must expand its organization."

In the inaugural number of *The Communist* (*Kungchantang Jen*), p. 19, he preaches "armed struggle," *wuchuang toutseng*, which in Chinese cannot mean struggle with an external enemy. "The experience of the eighteen years teaches us that the United Front and armed struggle are the two weapons for victory . . . And the Party should control these two weapons of the United Front and armed struggle." Again, in the same essay, he says, "In the last eighteen years, we have learned and clung to armed struggle. We understand very well that in China, apart from this line, apart from armed struggle, the Communist Party would not be able to hold its position. In the past eighteen years, the strengthening, expansion and bolshevization (*pu-erh-she-vi-ke-hua*) of our Party have proceeded in the midst of revolutionary wars and cannot be separated from guerrilla warfare. Without armed struggle, there would not be the Communist Party of today. I hope our comrades will not forget this lesson, a lesson of experience bought with blood." As this was written several years after the war started, the meaning of "armed struggle" and "expansion of party" is sufficiently clear in the light of the above facts.

Again, Mao Tsetung said in his speech to partisan students going out into the war areas, in November, 1940:

1. The international situation is not favorable to us. Therefore for the present we should do our best to expand our power, avoid sacrifices and conserve our resources.
2. Our Party should for the moment be content with an outwardly inferior position. But we should absolutely avoid appeasing the Central Government. We should take this opportunity to expand our army in preparation for what may come afterward.
3. Taking Shansi as our main base, we should extend our organization to Hopei, Chahar, Shantung, Honan and Suiyuan. Then we should gradually turn our attention to the plains and concentrate on our expansion in Central China.
4. The attitude of our troops towards the Central troops should depend on the strength of the Japanese forces. Where the Japanese forces are strong, we may give ground to the Central troops; in the opposite case, we should exert pressure on the Central troops, in order to increase our own strength.
5. We should strive our best to expand our Party, and gradually clean out all Central forces north of the Yellow River.

Evidently, some Communists among those who have escaped from Yenan are the source for the material in Chen Chung's book. There is a continuous stream of disillusioned Communists and non-communists who have come over. Of the 129th Communist Division alone, six to seven hundred officers and men have escaped from Yenan. Mao Tsetung would undoubtedly deny these reports as either fabricated or grossly distorted, although he could not deny the writings under his own signature. But there are a great many other captured documents which have to be explained away. Their authenticity, like that of the Tanaka Memorial, may be open to question. But like the Tanaka Memorial, they are already outdated by subsequent events. We have come to the stage where the actions of the parties concerned are better comments than anything they may have said in public or private.

The total impression of this review of the facts of the civil war is somewhat dismal, all the more so because such internecine war could and should have been avoided. The civil war has now lasted six years and covered seven provinces, developing to the size of the Taiping Rebellion. The Communist expansion they are now boasting about has not been a peaceful expansion, but one achieved by "armed struggle" and "bloodshed" in the exact words of Mao Tsetung. The Communist statistics must be read afresh. For every Japanese they claim to have killed, they have killed at least five Chinese. For every town they have captured from the Japanese, they have captured fifty towns from other Chinese. Of the hundreds of "clashes" per year they claim to their credit, a fair percentage must include those with the Chinese "enemy." While I take pride in the fact that they have captured ammunition from the Japanese, I am aware that half of their weapons have been robbed from other Chinese guerrillas and regular units. Against their claim to have held down 350,000 Japanese troops and 200,000 puppet troops in the occupied areas, must be counted the fact that they have held down half a million Chinese soldiers holding down the same Japanese and their puppets in the same areas. Alongside their vociferous criticisms of the absence of free press in Chungking and their energetic demand for national unity, the Chinese Communists and their American fellow travelers shrink from giving us some idea of the free press in Yenan and the facts of this civil war as they see it. They have preferred to present the "blockade" as an unaccountable mystery. Incidentally, neither Edgar Snow nor Mme. Sun Yat-sen nor the most rabid pro-Communists deny that there is no freedom of thought or freedom of the press in Yenan, that it is a totalitarian régime with the smoothest regimentation of ideas, comparable to that of Soviet Russia. The facts must first of all be correctly stated; whether one likes them or not is a matter of personal opinion.

One wishes that all this were untrue, but things that have been happening for five or six years cannot be wished away. Among my friends or people I trust, three cases have come to my own knowledge. First, Bishop Paul Yu Pin told me how his brother told him with tears in his eyes how, when he was with troops in Shantung, fighting the Japanese, they were attacked by the Communists from the rear. Second, Mrs. Chao, the "Grandmother of the Guerrillas," told me how her son was shot by the Communists from the riverbank, when he was in a boat with troops fleeing the Japs. Third, a friend of mine, an engineer now living in New York, told me how he lost four or five brothers in the war. One was working with the Kuomintang office in guerrilla area in Wusih, near Shanghai. He was shot in the back while walking in the streets by Communist partisans working for control of the same area. These three cases cover widely separated regions from the neighborhood of Shanghai to Shantung and north of the Yellow River, and range in time from 1938 to 1943.

It seems to me that expansion into areas for the patriotic purpose of fighting a common enemy could, and should, have stopped short of armed clashes with other Chinese units, if patriotism was the sole motive, and when it was seen that such conflicts were inevitable. The Communists could at least have fought as allies, which they did not do. They could have moved into areas where there were no Central troops—northern Hopei, for example—in which case there would have been no conflicts; and if they wished only to reinforce the Central troops, some working relationship could have been worked out with the local commanders even though they did not recognize the National command of Chungking. Since the Red troops had other objectives in mind, there was no point in their coming to an agreement on fighting the Japanese as allies with the Central troops. Whatever their motive, they failed to do so. Naturally, the result is, Chinese have killed Chinese. If this is not fratricide, what is it?

The paramount question for China is national unity. Who sins against unity in time of war sins against the nation as a whole. The problem of China's unity means exclusively the problem of the Chinese Communist party. Without the problem of the Chinese Communists, there is no problem of unity at all, since even the most backward provinces are not under suspicion of planning an open or secret revolt against the government. I may specifically mention the Kwangsi generals, Li and Pai, the Shansi general Yen Hsishan, and the "Christian general" Feng Yuhsiang, all of whom have fought repeated campaigns against Chiang Kai-shek, but all of whom have had the sense to forget old quarrels in time of war and national invasion. The Kwangsi generals threw in their entire resources and Kwangsi soldiery into the forefront of the battle in Shanghai without a thought of building up their own armed power for future control of portions of China. General Li Tsungjen has been serving on the Hupeh front now, and on every other front in the beginning of the war, for these last seven years, though one seldom sees his name in the papers. General Hsu Yungchang of the Shansi army, who steadily fought against Chiang in past campaigns, has been quietly directing campaign strategy at the Chungking Supreme Command all these years, and enjoying the complete trust of the Generalissimo. The Szechuen "warlords" have been fighting in Hunan, or directing the administration and development of Sikang. No possible disunity can arise from the generals or "warlords," and no one suggests it. No one suggests or even dreams of revolts from Yünnan, Szechuen, or Sinkiang. This fact alone, the unselfish devotion of all generals and all factions to the cause of the nation above the cause of private expansion, has made it possible for China to fight against Japan.

I wonder what would have happened to China if the so-called "medieval" and "feudalistic" warlords had acted in the same manner as the Chinese Red Army, and each unit had taken the matter in its own hands, fought Japan in its own way, and started fighting other units. No amount of guerrilla fighting would have availed if the whole national front collapsed and Free China disappeared from the map. The conditions of the entire Chinese Republic would then approximate the conditions obtaining in the famed guerrilla areas in Shansi, Hopei, and Shantung. These conditions, I repeat, are a national disgrace. I am sure that if the generals who fought against Chiang had refused to co-operate by surrendering their individual armies to a unified control, or had freely expanded into other areas against orders, they could have advanced the same reasons for distrust of Chiang, and the Allies would greatly regret it, but would also come to the conclusion that they had no good reasons in view of the past bitterness. But to a Chinese, this would have sounded a death knell of defeat and slavery for our people. In time of war, unity comes first, and I would prefer the most benighted feudalistic warlord who supported the United Front to the most enlightened materialistic dialectician who broke it.

The issue of the civil conflict has been curiously confused with the question of the constitutional development of China. There should be a distinction between the cause and the solution for the conflict. Obviously, the only alternative to a solution of the problem by means of violence is to grant the Chinese Communist party political rights and set in motion the methods for reducing party problems by peaceful, legal, and democratic means. The cause of the conflict, however, had factually nothing to do with the absence of a constitutional government. The cause was a military one, that the Chinese Communist Army broke its pledge of September, 1937, to take orders from the Chinese High Command and proceeded with the organization, disposition, and movements of its troops in defiance of the Chinese War Department. The Chinese Communist party should either have refused to sign the pledge to place its army under the direction of the High Command, giving as its reason the fact that there was yet no constitutional government in China; or it should have made the pledge and kept it. It should not have made the pledge, knowing the facts, and then suddenly discovered seven years later that there was no constitutional government in China and that therefore it was justified in keeping a separate army to back up its party claims. If that were a legitimate cause for revolt, all China's generals would be entitled to the same right, and China might as well not have started the war against Japan at all. The delay in constitutional development is historically unconnected with the Communist revolt. The cause of the Communist revolt was the opportunity the Chinese Communists saw in the war against Japan to expand their territory.

I have in all my previous writings taken a sympathetic view of the Chinese Communist Army, though not of the Communist writers' ideology; but I cannot condemn too strongly their fratricide even before the war is finished. It seems to me that, at the worst, they should have set up an independent kingdom administratively, but fought as allies in military operations. Such are the normal reactions of a common citizen when his country is at war, and such should be the paramount standard of judgment. This they have not done. In the first years of the war the Chinese Communists fought side by side with the Chinese Army, up to 1939, when they precipitated clashes by infiltrating into southern Hopei, and up to 1940-41, when the great clash of the New Fourth Army was precipitated—and up to that time, I had admired them for their patriotism as I had admired them for championing the release of Chiang at Sian. But things have changed since then, greatly. My first feeling of alarm came in the spring of 1940, when in a parlor group at Hong Kong consisting of Communist sympathizers I heard them *sneer* at the Chinese victory at Nanning, as one sneers at enemy claims. "They," said the Chinese young man with a snicker, meaning Chinese soldiers and not the Japanese, "lost a hundred thousand soldiers." I had a feeling of positive revulsion that I could not get over. It seems to me armed clashes with the national army, in time of war, would be called treason in any modern country, and such leaders would be relieved of their posts in short order and court-martialed. I do not think the people of Soviet Russia would stand for a cocky, benighted general who preferred in infinite love of his fatherland to clash constantly with the Red Army, defy Moscow's orders, and call the Ukraine his own, even though he might be fighting the Germans. And I do not think Americans, in time of war, would stand for an army, of whatever color or creed, which moved freely from Wyoming to California and started clashing with other American Army units stationed there as soon as it arrived, and then proceeded to attack, arrest, and torture Federal officers and employees and ended up by collecting its own taxes and printing its own currency. On such military matters, I think General Eisenhower or General MacArthur is a better judge. As far as the people of China are concerned, their feeling is not very much different from what American and Russian people would feel in similar circumstances.

The question of civil war is on every American's mind whenever the question of China is brought up. Therefore I have to write about it here. Moreover, it is essential to an understanding of the whole China situation. So far the public abroad has had a decidedly one-sided picture. American commentators talk as if, first, the Chinese government were deliberately discriminating against the Red Army and were seeking a civil war for the pleasure of it; second, as if the Chinese government were not fully determined to avoid a civil war and solve the Communist question by political means; third, as if the government ought now to give the Red Army supplies with which to fight its own National Army; and fourth, as if help given to Chungking would be used in fighting the Communists rather than Japan. These are untrue and uncharitable assumptions unworthy of a great ally.

If I were an American hearing only the Communist side of the story, my sympathies would be entirely on the side of the Chinese Communists. I would be hearing that the Chinese Communists were the only people fighting Japan, and that for no reason whatsoever the Chinese government started "blockading" these heroic fighters, that these Communist troops were not paid by the government, that certain parties in Chungking were "fascist, pacifist, and pro-Japan," etc. But I would remember one fact: that, in the entire seven years of war, the Chinese government publicity has not let out one unkind word about the Chinese Communists, and that there cannot be found in the entire American press a Chinese government story of the six-year-old conflict. When the question of the Chinese Communists comes up, the Chinese government shuts up like a clam.

It is possible for a Chinese to take an objective view of the situation and see it from the Communist side. The Communists did not hesitate to sabotage American supplies for Chungking by telling the world that if supplies were given Chungking, they would not be used for fighting Japan but for fighting them. Who else could have invented such a baseless rumor? But in their position, Chungking's strength is their weakness, and Chungking's weakness is their strength. Brooks Atkinson pictured the situation correctly when he reported that, in the negotiations between the government and the Communists, the Communist position had become stronger because the Central troops had suffered recent reverses in Honan and Hunan. This explains why they did not derail a single train when they saw for a month Japanese troops pouring down the Peiping-Hankow railway to destroy the Central troops in Honan through at least four hundred miles of their famed guerrilla territory. The truth is bitter, but the Americans must hear it. Naturally the Communists would fear nothing more than five hundred airplanes and three tank divisions for the Chungking forces. By the logic of their circumstances, they must combat it. Whether in this they are acting as patriots, however, is another question. The Communists have merely drifted into a position where they must discredit Chungking and, in discrediting Chungking, discredit China as a whole.

For after having fought the Chinese government and captured, imprisoned, and tortured government personnel, they are now afraid of the consequences of their own acts. They are sincerely worried over a reckoning of accounts. Few people see the connection between the dissolution of the Comintern in May, 1943, and the sudden flood of anti-Chungking propaganda after the event. Because of America's looming importance and coming help to China, and because of the dissolution of the Comintern, they come to America in the cloak of injured innocence and try to scare away help to Chungking by saying that such help will be used against them only, and by talking of a civil war, which apparently the government desires and they do not, and of which they would be innocent victims. American writers who certainly know that this struggle has been going on for years have concealed one side of the conflict from the American public because they are campaigning for the Red régime in China. At least, they should have the sense of humor not to complain of the Chinese government for failure to pay regularly an actively hostile army fighting itself. General Lee did not complain to France about not being paid by General Grant. Incidentally, there is a humorous touch to the picture. Chinese (Chungking) currency is contraband in Communist areas, confiscable by Yenan law, proclaimed as far back as January 30, 1941. Article II of the "Regulations" says, "Any transaction within the region not made in terms of *pien pi* [border currency] shall be considered as an act of undermining the currency, and the offender or offenders shall be punished accordingly and the money and goods involved shall be confiscated." Yet Chinese fellow travelers in Chungking had the artlessness to complain to Americans that the Communist Army had not been paid in this contraband.

From the Chinese Communist viewpoint, next in importance to sabotaging war supplies for Chungking is the creating of the impression that the Chinese government, instead of being interested in the war against Japan, is more interested in fighting them. Rumors of impending civil war cropped up among the foreign correspondents in Chungking again and again, contrary to the truth. In February, 1944, when I was in Chungking, such rumor was at its peak. Two press dispatches about an imminent civil war were sent by foreign correspondents and held up by the authorities. General Ho Yingchin however, was able to satisfy the correspondents, including Brooks Atkinson, that the rumor was unfounded. Curiously, no such rumor was heard of at this time among the Chinese, either the man in the street or those well informed. I do not believe that the foreign correspondents invented the rumors. They must have been engineered specifically for foreign consumption from quarters interested in discrediting the government and preventing help from coming to Chungking.

Third in importance is to paint Chungking as shot through with pro-Japan elements, and single out certain anti-Communist leaders of Chungking for attack. Like the other rumors engineered specifically for foreign consumption is the accusation that General Ho Yingchin, War Minister, and Chen Lifu, Education Minister, are pacifist and pro-Japan. The Chinese Communists would not dare to make such a ridiculous charge before the Chinese community; consequently, the Chinese people have not even heard of it. General Ho signed the Ho-Umetsu Tangku Agreement before the war under the direction of Chiang Kai-shek, which is the only basis for this persistent charge. If the Chinese Communists attacked Chiang as "pro-Japan," the charge would sound too ridiculous. Their tactics are to uphold Chiang and paint him at the same time as an all-powerful dictator and also as an utterly powerless figure, surrounded by pro-Japanese intriguing underlings. Even though both cannot be true at the same time, it is a carefully thought-out propaganda policy, at which the Chinese Communists display extraordinary intelligence. And while I do not share Chen Lifu's party views, I would be less than an idiot to believe such a rumor of him.

All these charges are directed toward the outside public solely for their consumption. They are distinct from other criticisms of government failures, like internal corruption and incompetence, inflation and absence of a free press, etc. These three charges—first, that American supplies would be used for fighting the Communists and not fighting

Japan; second, that the Chinese government is trying to start a civil war instead of trying to avoid it with the greatest patience; and third, that Ho and Chen are pro-Japan—are so ridiculous that the Chinese public never hears of them, except as cabled back from American papers. When the Chinese hear these charges, they smile. As a Chinese, reading both English and Chinese papers, and talking with the Chinese people, I can remember my astonishment when I first came across this charge of being pro-Japanese against General Ho in the writings of an American fellow traveler.

But the Chinese government, for the present at least, will not talk about domestic troubles. This has created a curious situation. The government is placed at every step in the utterly false position of having to deny things that exist. I met Mr. Richard Watts after he had come away from a press conference. I asked him if it wasn't a dull conference, and he said, "No, on the contrary, it was a very lively meeting." Some correspondents had forced a discussion of the perennial report of a "blockade" of the Communists. The Chinese spokesman could have outlined a full and honest picture of the strategic position of Sian, saying that it guarded the historic route to Szechuen; that defense of this vulnerable area was of basic importance; that the Allies would be very sorry if Hu Tsungnan's troops were not there; that Japan could threaten Chungking once she got to Sian; that good and effective defense was always "idle" even as the Russian garrison on the Manchurian border was "idle"; that, moreover, "the blockade" had the double function of preventing both the enemy and the Communists from running rampant over the rich wheat fields of southern Shensi; that the Communists would certainly forsake the barren plains of northern Shensi and come down to the rich southern plains if they could do so, as they have repeatedly done elsewhere; that in such an event, communications of the National Army with Honan and the whole North China would be cut off; etc., etc. Instead, the Chinese spokesmen were compelled to quibble and ask, "What do you mean by blockade?" Then the correspondents went to Chou Enlai's office, and the Communists in Chungking like Tung Pi-wu asked, "Why don't you go and see the blockhouses on the border?"

Again, some time ago, the correspondents asked if it was true that the Red Army hadn't been paid. It would have been easy to explain why the military headquarters could not be expected to pay very promptly a hostile army that was daily engaged in fighting its own troops and attacking government offices—acts tantamount to rebellion. Instead, the spokesman denied the charge. The correspondents then asked, "When did the headquarters pay the Red Army last, and how much per month?" The answer was vague. The government kept up the fiction that the Red Army was still a part of the National Army, and therefore entitled to receive pay, and the Red Army kept up the fiction of obeying the Central government and fighting on a United Front.

I reserve my criticism of government failures and mistakes for the final chapter. Here I am dealing strictly with a question of historical fact, and with the question of China's unity in time of war, in which I am all for the government. The government has launched an anti-Communist program as a basic part of its state policy for the last seventeen years. It fought a civil war with the Communists for about nine years up to the Sian Incident. It is fully engaged in exterminating Communist thought among the youth of China now. The then Nanking government dealt with the same problem with the same methods: it shut up over a thousand political prisoners in Nanking; it had a secret service and a strict censorship. Their programs for national development were the same; their policies and methods the same; the men were the same. No one can deny that it was the Nanking government before the war that was giving China a new spirit and a new strength, with all these anti-Communist measures going on. The Communists have been calling the Kuomintang government fascists, dictators, comprador-landlords, imperialists' running dogs, butchers, and gangsters for the last seventeen years, and are now merely reviving the old charges. Yet without being willing to admit the existence of this policy now and the reasons for it, on account of the war, the government is compelled to resort to press censorship, and is at a loss whenever the Communist question is brought up. But while the government is determined to settle its domestic dispute internally, the Communists have no such scruples about taking their case abroad. The Chinese government still prefers to keep its mouth shut, like a witness on the dock trying to protect someone he loves. That may be an admirable trait; but if the government fully realized how this question of "civil war" had been played up abroad and was seriously worrying the friends of China, it would take the outside public into its confidence.

I have been compelled to tell the full story of this Communist trouble, because it is affecting American supplies to China and the international position of China after the war. I wish I could say that there were no "Chinese Communists," that they had co-operated splendidly and unselfishly in the war, and that the whole problem was unimportant, as some Chinese propagandists try to suggest. I am afraid that refusal to face the truth of the conflict may yet cause endless troubles in the years to come.

In the final chapter, I shall give an analysis of the character of the Chinese Communist party and of the prospects and principles of a peaceful solution, as the majority of the common people of China see them.

9

YOUNG CHINA AND THE WAR

IT WAS during these days, some of the most memorable in my life, that a new person came into my life. This is Chin Yuhua, now my daughter. I had come back from an exciting day's trip, had sat on the ruins of the Hanyuan Hall of the Tang Palace, communing with the past and looking northward to Queen Yang Kweifei's Tower, had then gone on to the Han city and mounted the Nightless Palace, and had returned in the afternoon from a visit to the Ofangkung and the ancient capital of Chou, where Mr. Kung had spent an hour with me trying to verify the ancient site of the Kunming Lake by studying the strata of earth formations of the region.

That night there was a concert given by the Sian Orphanage for war orphans. The night before, there had been a play in song and dance, having as its theme what happened to a Chinese village when the Japanese came. There was a dance of nurses, clad in white, and a dance of farmers. The whole show was not only creditable: it was excellent. A Korean had written the music play, and there were four violins in the orchestra. Among the twenty to thirty girl dancers, there was a child in front, who was both graceful and good. You can tell whether a girl is good or not even on the stage. She was not the most beautiful, but she struck my fancy.

I had had always in mind the adopting of a war orphan and was more or less on the lookout for one. I had not learned her name the first night. The second night she appeared twice, once singing a war song, and once at the piano, playing Weber's *Invitation to the Waltz* in duet with a boy. She was sweet and gentle, her arms were graceful, and she always stood erect. I looked for her name on the program. It was a good name, meaning Jade-Flower.

I said to myself I wanted that child. I whispered to Mrs. Ku, the director, asking if it was possible for me to adopt her. She told me that it was impossible, that it was against the rules. Many people had approached her and she had had to refuse. Moreover, the children did not want to leave. This orphanage was unusually well managed, better than any I had seen, and the children had rosy cheeks and were apparently as happy as they could be. However, after some whisperings with the other teachers, she told me that it might be all right, if Mme. Chiang approved. It would be quite an exception since I intended to bring the child to America with me to live with my family, and take care of her really as my own child.

Yuhua was twelve years old, and her mother was still living. I asked Mrs. Ku to approach the child and her mother and see if they would consent. Very luckily, they did, and they came the next day to see me. I had taken a chance on Yuhua's two appearances on the stage, but I was not disappointed. I liked her more and more, and I was proud and very happy. It was a new and exciting human relationship. Perhaps the older we grow, the fonder we become of the young, since we have seen so much of futile maturity. That is so in my case at least. Grace and charm dwell in all children before they grow up and resemble us. Yuhua had, as good children have, a natural dignity, and she was happy with me. I bought her some little things, such as gloves and mufflers, and told her to prepare to leave with me for America, if Mme. Chiang should consent.

But when I saw Mme. Chiang about it, on my return to Chungking a month later, she said she was sorry she could not break the rules. She told me even Mme. Kung's adopted children had to be returned to the orphanage for fear of setting a precedent. Mme. Kung had taken two sick ones to her home and nursed them back to health after nine months and returned them to the orphanage. Mme. Chiang was afraid that when the children were adopted in homes, some people might treat them as slaves working without pay, and she would not be in a position to check up. Moreover, the children might be deprived of a regular school education. The rule was a sensible one, and when she mentioned her own sister's case, I felt I had nothing to say. But I didn't tell her how much I loved the child and how disappointed I was and Yuhua would be. Mme. Chiang has been extremely kind to me in many things, but she could not grant me this favor. She said I could still adopt Yuhua, but not take her out of the orphanage. I could support her in a private school when she was ready and could moreover take her to my home after the war. That is what I am going to do.

I tell this story, which is strictly personal, because it is so much a part of my trip to Sian, a part of my inner experience and a permanent gain, which will last longer than all my excitement over the historic ruins. It was to me personally perhaps the most important event of the whole trip to China. When my wife and daughters learned about it, they were amused and said I had not adopted a boy because I wanted to be the only man in the house. There may be truth in this, but really I have no hankerings for sons (how strange!). I am so used to daughters in the house that I feel the presence of a boy would be strange and incongruous. Yuhua was twelve that year, and she would be a good companion for my youngest daughter, and I just cannot conceive that a boy would be. But now that I have adopted Yuhua, I imagine there is another reason why I have done it. I am perhaps frightened by the thought of my children growing up, and I must always have children in the house. My children are already beginning to be more sober and don't scream with laughter quite as much as they did and don't demand to drag mattresses down from the bed and sleep on the floor for a change, or do those foolish and brave and exciting young things any more.

I struck up a friendship with General Hu Tsungnan. He had easy, simple, and rather warm manners, and easily broke into loud laughter. He is the commander of the fine troops that the Communists say are not fighting Japan, and is known as one of China's ablest commanders. It isn't true that he was given the best-trained Central troops to command, for the flower of the Central troops was sacrificed in the battle of Shanghai. He simply had the gift of creating a fine army out of raw recruits and whipping them into fine shape. He had an immense pride in his troops, like all good generals, and he had the right to have it when one saw his creation. His short stature, his massive forehead, full face, very full chest, and square shoulders strongly reminded me of Napoleon. His hands, too, were unusually warm and soft, almost feminine, like Napoleon's. His, however, was essentially a military, and not a political, mind. He was strikingly young in appearance and yet unmarried, and he seemed to be too happy to be a brooding Napoleon. The impression was rather that of a man with a strong self-discipline, who was doing his job well and knew it, and could afford to be friendly and familiar with his staff.

At Sian I had to see the Concentration Camp and the Military Academy. Here, as in all the military academies which I visited in the North, I found a high standard of neatness and discipline, partly due to General Hu Tsungnan, and partly, I am sure, due to the tradition started by President Chiang Kai-shek.

At the Military Academy far out from the city I watched General Hu's troops, including cavalry and tanks, during one of their field exercises. The young soldiers were tall, healthy, and strong. For the first time in my life I heard the terrific rattle of machine guns going off ten feet over my head as I crouched in a hole under a mud ledge. The field practice had for its object the storming of an enemy barbed-wire line covering a distance of fifteen hundred yards in open country. Flares were fired from guns as signals, mines exploded, and the soldiers crawled toward the barbed wires with bullets whizzing low over their heads. The sounds and sights of battle were far more realistic than any actual battle on the screen. The sound effects, reverberating across the valley, were quite different, and I believe cannot be reproduced in a closed theater.

I demanded a visit to the Concentration Camp, or Labor Camp (*Laotungying*), because I had heard so much about such camps, and wished to see one for myself. This was one of the biggest, and contained over a thousand "students," as those sent up to the camp for "training" were called.

I had pictured barbed wire and decrepit huts, but what I found was a complete surprise. In general appearance it resembled a military academy, of which I saw many in China. It was in a very large enclosed compound, probably containing three hundred acres, with drill grounds, courtyards, extremely good buildings, better than some school buildings I had seen, and gardens and vegetable fields. It contained mostly young men and some forty young women, of college age or over, who had escaped from Communist areas or who had been found involved in, or perhaps only suspected of, Communist activities in Free China.

When I arrived at eight in the morning, they were drilling on the parade ground. They wore cotton-padded gray uniforms such as I saw at all the colleges, training centers, and schools I had visited. At first when I had seen a troop marching in the streets, wearing that belted uniform and cloth shoes, I had naturally taken them for soldiers. On inquiry I had found that they were college students marching to a celebration. The college dormitories have adopted the military way of making their beds, with bedding folded into severe squares. Usually at assembly the students stand in rows like soldiers in an auditorium without chairs. This is one of the changes in college and school life brought about since the war.

The Concentration or Labor Camp was the cleanest place, truly, that I had seen in China, and perhaps cleaner and neater than many American college grounds. I felt sure they had cleaned up the place particularly for my benefit. But granted that, I still say it was the cleanest place in China that I had seen. The hard mud yards and roads were swept, and there was a spic-and-span quality and a trimness about everything which would satisfy the most exacting colonel on inspection day. Not a disorderly corner was to be found. Not a stone was out of place. The flowers stood neatly in orderly rows along the mud paths or in raised beds. In every yard there was a rockery, each one different, made of broken porcelain with burnt clay pagodas and houses to resemble a miniature landscape. Some had pebbled designs or lettering on the ground. These were the work of the students, and I imagine there was a kind of competition. I walked from courtyard to courtyard and wished all Chinese schools could be kept as clean and all students could live in such compounds. It would be ironical to call this the "bright spot" in China, but there was no question that the place was unusually well managed. I wish the New Life Movement would forget its moral exhortations for the moment and just concentrate on teaching the people of all towns to enforce a high standard of municipal cleanliness. That would be a distinct contribution. The New Life Movement during its tenth anniversary last February did start such a competition at Chungking, and its agents went in search of dirt in all government and school compounds. I think the Executive Yuan and the Central Training Institute won by a draw.

I was amazed at the display of artistic talent in this colony. There are many artists among the Communist students of China. In every separate house unit, there was a social and reading room, called Chungshan Hall (named after Dr. Sun Yat-sen), and these social rooms were the individual creations of each house unit. In each there was an earthen mantelpiece which was the main point for artistic showmanship. Some were simple and severe, with Greco-Roman columns, and others were more ornate, and there was always a pleasing, bold touch of color. The chairs and armchairs were modeled out of loess and there were mud settees, generally of a modernistic design, though a little hard to sit on. On the tables were magazines and compositions by the students, and on the walls were portraits in charcoal and water color. In one of the social rooms I saw remarkable portraits of Roosevelt, Churchill, Stalin, and Chiang, painted by some student, and in the main building there were water colors and ink paintings in the classical style by a student who seemed to me an exceptional artist.

The students evidently had been encouraged to do these things in their hours of leisure

A "concentration camp" is certainly nothing to rejoice over, but granting the political necessity of such evils, one is nevertheless happy and relieved to find that there is no unnecessary cruelty or inhumanity connected with it. The trainees were of course given classes in Sanmin Chuyi for ideological indoctrination, in which the comparative merits of Kuomintang and Communist principles and ideals were discussed and China's plans for civic reforms and national development were taught. They were also required to grow their own vegetables and tend the gardens.

As I stood before the students assembled on the drill ground, I felt I knew them well. In no way were they different from other young men and women students of China. I knew their minds, their thoughts, and the authors they had read. Since they were radicals, they must have read and thought harder than average students. All of them must have taken part in political or patriotic movements. They seemed to know me chiefly through my magazines, particularly the magazine of humor, *Lunyü,* and were therefore in a laughing mood, that morning at least.

They were supposed to be in all stages of conversion and semi-conversion to Kuomintang ideas. Many of those who had escaped from Communist areas may have needed no conversion, but since Communist agents were filtering into the country, the government could not be quite sure of their sincerity and had put them here, when they came over. I was told by Mr. Ku, the director, of a significant change in the last years. In the first years of the war, the general movement of young students was toward Yenan; in the last years, the direction was reversed.

There must be others who remained unconvinced, and preferred not to court trouble by expressing their Communist faith. The test of sincerity was necessarily difficult to make, since they would express only agreement with the Kuomintang ideology, in order to be released. I told them that they all knew more about Marxist doctrines than I did, but I knew more about the intellectual background of mid-nineteenth-century European thought from which Karl Marx's thoughts and doctrines took their color. I said no Marxist could be a Confucianist, because the humanistic and materialistic viewpoints were so far apart. They were a warm and apparently receptive audience and laughed readily.

After my lecture, I asked for a conference with some of the students.

I felt that every one of them had had an exciting and bitter story of personal adventures of the mind and body to tell. Probably some regretted that they ever left home. One of them had been the chief of staff of Ho Lung, the Communist general, and told me of their fights with National troops. Another was a graduate of the Normal School at Hanchung, Szechuen, and told me that he had escaped from a "traitors' camp" at Yenan, where he had met one of his friends who had joined the K'angta (Resistance University) in the first years of the war, but had refused to join the Communist party.

All of them of course talked of their hatred of the Communist rule, but the officers being present, I could not be sure that they meant what they said. All this I had to discount, no matter how sincere they appeared. Apart from the physical appearance of the place and the students, I had no way of telling what was really going on inside their minds. But certainly they did not look ill or undernourished. What I could not quite make out was what the officers told me, that many of them could go out to the city on week ends, and that I could see them walking in the streets of the west city on Sundays in their uniform. I was, on the whole, so impressed that I told President Chiang later that foreigners should be urged to visit the place and see it for themselves.

This camp, I understand, is being cited as a "fascist" feature of the Kuomintang rule; but I wonder what American critics would do if they were in the position of the Chinese government and found secret agents of a hostile "Bund" masquerading as patriots in their own country. It is admittedly a difficult question. This was the only concentration camp I saw and I could not be sure the others were maintained with the same high standard.

I was able to persuade Professor S——— to go with me to Tungkwan and Huashan. We used to be associated with each other in Sinological research, and our talks often went back to our colleagues of the Peking National University, the old friends and acquaintances of those early Peking days, and the present conditions of the residents of Peiping. He had passed through Tungkwan, but had not seen its military establishments, and he had never gone up the famed Huashan Mountain, celebrated for its hard climbing. I was particularly fortunate to get the right companions when going on a mountain trip, because on that alone the conversations at night in mountain temples would depend. There were five of us. Professor S———, Mr. Kung, whom I had specially requested to come along, myself, and besides, two excellent young men (although I could not call them "young men" in China, their age being over thirty), both of whom had studied abroad, one in France and one in Japan. They were Chang Tatung and Chao Tsaipiao, from the staff of General Hu Tsungnan, accompanying us on this trip. Both Mr. Chang and Mr. Chao were good in Chinese and mature in outlook. Mr. Chao, in foreign dress, showed his scholarly traits in his slender fingers, his fine features, and the low voice of his comments. Mr. Chang, plumper and a better talker with a sense of humor, had a way of talking in a soft, low gurgle. All five of us were inclined to be "literary" and had more or less the same outlook. Mr. Chang had a warm corner in his soul and it was not till we slept in a temple on top of Huashan that I found out the secret in it, and was sorry for him.

This was to be one of my discoveries on this trip; many college graduates were working with the Army. Wherever I went, I found such men as Mr. Chang and Mr. Chao; for instance, those working with the staff of Hsueh Yueh in Changsha. In Kweilin, Kweiyang, and Kunming, I ran across people in soldiers' uniform who might be taken for Hopei or Hunan peasants from their ruddy faces and creased, padded uniforms, and yet in conversation turned out to be graduates of Peita or Yenching or Johns Hopkins. If one did not go to the Army, one would not see them, and if one did not talk with them, one would not recognize them as college graduates.

It was a short journey of a few hours by train. The train stopped a little beyond Huayin, for it was a little dangerous to go by train farther, and there we were met by General Wang and Division Commander Kao, who took us in a jeep to Tungkwan. But not all of us could be accommodated in a single jeep, and some of the party went by railway handcar. We drove for a quarter of an hour through what was called a "communications trench." This was a broad motor road, cut into the loess hills fifteen to twenty feet deep, so that army transports could not be observed by the enemy across the river.

Tungkwan is a well-shelled and well-sheltered town, on the bend of the Yellow River, which comes down from the north and then abruptly turns here into an east-west course. Standing at the junction where the great Tsinling Range sweeps toward the Yellow River, the city occupies a narrow strip of land of the highest importance, holding the only access to Shensi and western China by land from central China. Its name "kwan" signifies a pass, and the plains of Shensi west of it are known in history as *Kwanchung,* or "Inside the Pass," and the region on its east is known as *Kwanwai,* or "Beyond the Pass." There are in fact several passes along the land strip running along the south bank of the Yellow River where many historic campaigns were fought. In many past dynasties, China's capital ruled from "Inside the Pass," as it was invulnerable with a good army, and he who controlled this area controlled China. At Tungkwan city the mountain lies directly on its back, so that part of the city wall runs up along its slopes. There have been shellings back and forth across the river, but the hillside here is so studded with gun emplacements and machine-gun nests that the enemy has not seriously attempted to take it.

We entered the city gate, where the tower had been shelled so frequently that only a skeleton remained. The streets were practically bare of civilian population, and what shops there were were half closed, looking more like homes than shops. We went straight to an army headquarters at the foot of the city wall which ran along the bank some fifty yards from the water's edge. At the headquarters I met and talked with a group of nineteen girls working in the War Area Service Corps.

The purpose of our visit was to see the trenches and fortifications. As these are military secrets, I cannot go into descriptive details. Suffice it to say that we walked along a long tunnel and an intricate system of underground trenches, in parts dark and completely protected, and in parts camouflaged at the top, with gun emplacements where through a field glass one could see the enemy on the high cliffs across the bank. Near the gun emplacements were always underground sleeping quarters for the gun crews. The underground trenches connected with various dugouts, with tables and benches, where the soldiers could rest. In one of these rest rooms, two girls of the Service Corps were attending the soldiers, playing chess with them.

Once I came within fifteen feet of the water's edge in a specially protected corner. The Yellow River was here only about two hundred yards wide, though the distance from the enemy fortifications on top of the high cliffs was very great. There were soldiers on the watch at different points, and at the sight of anything moving on the opposite shore, the machine guns would crackle. The same was true when the enemy detected any movement on our side. It happened that while our party was going through the tunnels, Japanese bullets began to whistle and puncture the earth above us. Whether they had caught glimpses of our moving figures or not, it gave me a welcome sense of nearness to China's war front.

We went to the soldiers' canteen for lunch. In Chinese it was called *chiupao* or wine bar, but there was no evidence of wine. This was a kind of club run by the group of nineteen girls. While waiting for lunch and resting, our party spent a hilarious hour there, chatting with the girls. Most of them were college students, a few graduates of colleges in Peiping who had been sent here in the last few months. There was a girl from Manchuria who knew some words of Japanese, and she was persuaded to sing a song in Japanese for us. They had read my daughters' books in Chinese and we felt as if we had known each other for a long time. I learned that they slept in separate quarters and seemed to be quite happy about the work they were doing. When lunch came, I found that the girls were actually serving as waitresses, standing by to refill our rice bowls, and I felt ashamed of myself.

The military establishments were scattered for miles around. We visited an artillery corps, with guns and a complete array of the most modern survey instruments, all bought from Germany in the first years of the war. Here in a field demonstration, about three hundred soldiers were engaged in capturing a fortified position near a village. A tank corps was attacking a position in practice. These were baby tanks, and there were precious few of them, but as far as a layman could see, the marksmanship was very good, for the bullets from the advancing tanks hit the target very closely every time. And there were antitank guns firing tracer bullets.

No one could have seen these soldiers of Hu Tsungnan's without being greatly impressed, and I was thankful that this gateway to western China and to Chungking was in the hands of a man in whom one could have such confidence.

I must discuss here the real nature of the "blockade" of the Communists by Hu Tsungnan's troops stationed near Sian. The Chinese Communists are broadcasting to the world that they are "blockaded" by these troops. The fact is that the Communist guerrillas have never been able to hold towns, but subsist on the countryside only. If they had been able to come down south, it would mean handing over Sian and the Lunghai railway to the Japanese, constituting an immediate menace to Chungking, since the vulnerable side of Chungking is from the north. The defense of the Tungkwan-Sian area not only covered the vulnerable angle of Chungking, and not only stopped the enemy from crossing the Yellow River to Shensi. Strategically, it prevented Chungking from being cut off entirely from the whole of North China, including the Northwest and the Northeast and the whole of Central and East China north of the Yangtse. If Sian were lost, Chungking would be cut off from Sinkiang, Tsinghai, Shensi, Shansi, Shantung, Hopei, Anhwei, Kiangsu, Honan, and northern Hupeh. That is exactly what Japan and the Chinese Communists want.

The danger is this: Should the enemy gain control of Sian and the Lunghai railway, the Communists would co-operate as little as they did—whether through inability or unwillingness—when ordered in May, 1944, to cut the Peiping-Hankow railway. Then Japanese troop trains were pouring down from Manchuria to destroy the Central troops in Honan through at least four hundred miles of the famed Communist-controlled guerrilla area. The government spokesman, Liang Han-chao, has stated that the Communist troops had been ordered by Chiang Kai-shek to mobilize against the Japanese supply line passing through their territory, but they not only did not act, but even ignored the order. This was the first time the Chinese government was willing even to hint at Communist non-co-operation in the war against Japan, perhaps because the situation had become too outrageous. These are facts of past history that intelligent outsiders should ponder carefully, alongside the great military significance of Tungkwan Pass in Chungking's grand strategy of defense against Japan.

Even if Tungkwan had no strategic importance, it is highly regrettable that good troops had to be stationed against other Chinese troops. The Communists have not fought as allies of Chungking or agreed upon respective operational areas for different units, as the American and British Armies are doing. Wherever they could do so, they have broken loose into areas designated for other Chinese units and fought them both openly and underhandedly. Where they could not do so, as in the case of the Tungkwan area, they call it a "blockade." If the Central troops had wanted civil war and had acted as the Communists did elsewhere, Hu Tsungnan's troops would not "blockade" them, but could go into the Yenan area and drive them out with comparative ease. Since Yenan has regarded even Chinese currency as contraband ever since January, 1941, I hardly think it is fair to talk of the "blockade" as a one-sided affair.

Furthermore, it was Hu Tsungnan's troops under Sung Hsilien that stopped the Japanese at the Salween in 1942. Hu's troops, accused of being "idle," passed in a steady stream through Luchow, Szechuen, on the way to Yünnan, and if the foreign observers had not been asleep, they should have known the fact. The gross ignorance and distortion of the facts show that partisan propaganda has been active and that there has been some very low-grade reporting from the China front.

In view of the facts of the situation, would any sane American commentator suggest that these troops of Hu Tsungnan be moved out of southern Shensi and let the Communists and therefore the Japanese

144

occupy the area as in Shansi? Would an American chief of staff, entrusted with the defense of Chungking, do so? And does any one doubt that the Chinese Communists, in view of their records elsewhere, would move into the rich southern Shensi if they could, instead of staying up in the barren North? The Japanese would then descend upon the plains of Szechuen as easily as I did a week later. The Allies should be thankful that Chungking still stands and is under no immediate menace from the north, because of the presence of Hu Tsungnan's troops. Yet the effective defense of Tungkwan has become now probably the most outstanding and best-known criticism against Chungking. China stations also some of her best troops under one of her best commanders, Chen Cheng, to guard another possible approach to Chungking south of the Yangtse, toward Ensze. These troops, too, are "idle," as the Russian garrisons on Manchurian frontiers have been "idle" for the past seven years; but because there the line of defense does not inconvenience the Chinese Communists, Americans do not charge it against Chungking. Certainly somebody has not been playing fair with the American public, or with the commentators themselves.

10

HUASHAN

THERE is a Chinese saying that every man must visit Huashan once in his lifetime.

Standing at Hukungtzu, a modern building at the very foot of Huashan, and looking up at the rocky peaks, I well understood why it was famous. The rocks of Huashan seemed like a protest against the law of gravitation. The rocks on the other mountains more or less formed the general pattern of triangles tapering toward the top. Not so these rocks of Huashan. They stood at the most tumbledown, illogical, senseless angles, and some of the peaks, not satisfied with being sharp precipitous cliffs, leaned forward at the top. They were "awesome" and romantic, not classical. They should never have been scaled at all!

The weather was cold and uncertain. But I had had a gown made for this journey, with the long, fine Kansuh sheep's fur on the inside and the popular deep blue cotton cloth on the outside. It was both practical and warm, and it was the only one I wore until I got back to

Chungking. I also had bought a Siberian beaver hat which made me look like a regular northern merchant.

The Huashan peaks are part of the great Tsinling mountain range that is just layers and layers of dog-tooth jagged rocks south of the Sian plains, any one of which would be as difficult to scale. But long ago the Taoists were determined to capture and occupy the place, as one of the strategic points in the cosmogony of the universe. Huashan was the Western Sacred Mountain, one of the five in ancient China (East, West, North, South, and Center) corresponding to the Five Elements in the scheme of things. Moreover, Taoist saints had lived and died here, or rather were reported to have gone up to heaven when their days on earth were numbered. So no Buddhist priest need think of invading this sacred territory.

I had a feeling that I might find Laotse himself still living here, transformed into a sheep or a donkey, cogitating the universe. Anyway, Laotse passed through Tungkwan on buffalo-back and disappeared from mankind. Legend said he told someone to meet him in the shape of a black lamb in Szechuen, and someone did meet him in Chengtu, at the point where the Black Lamb Temple now stands. But the legend might be incorrect, or he might be simultaneously in two places, appearing as a black lamb in Chengtu, while his spirit was really roving among the peaks of Huashan.

It was getting dark and I smelled the keen mountain wind and felt the approach of a snowstorm. Mr. Chang and his companions had been delayed in the city on a private mission, whose purpose I was to discover two days later. I was hungry, and when at last they came, the hot meal was welcome, as any traveler who has spent a cold day at the foot of mountains knows. A basin of charcoal was put in each room, and after supper we sat around the charcoal fire, the five of us, relaxed and comfortable. Then we began those chats that are among the unforgettable experiences of this trip.

There was provided here, as is usual at such places, a set of volumes on local history, containing the history, geography, and legends of the place, together with the lives of distinguished people born here, and poems of scholars celebrating their visits. Professor S—— chose several volumes and retired to his room, and I chose one volume and lay in bed reading until I was tired and went to sleep, with a faint excitement about the Green-haired Maiden and the many fairies that had inhabited this mountain retreat.

The next morning we were told it would be fairly cold at the top of Huashan. One could not be certain of the weather at this time of the year. The others had army overcoats, but I had to go up in my Chinese fur gown, which was inconvenient for mountain climbing. We also had blankets, as we planned to stay up overnight, and I later discovered that we had even brought some chicken sauté. How thoughtful this was, and how incredibly ill-disciplined and unfit for immortality our sensuous tastes were, I was soon to find out. We were unfit to live in that rarefied atmosphere on top, where we should only drink dew and feed on pine seeds and *huangtsing* roots, which the Taoists did as a concession to this mortal body!

The land began to rise gently as soon as we left the inn, and after a while we "entered the mountain" through a winding road along a half-dry mountain gully. For about three miles we could go in sedan chairs, but when we came to the steep ascent, we had to abandon them. I had looked at a map of the mountains and had thought the temples and roads spread out in all directions over a wide area. On the contrary, they were piled close one above another, to be scaled over impossibly steep stone steps with the help of iron chains.

The Taoists had wanted to escape from the world; some certainly had wanted to escape from political tyranny in times of chaos. They had therefore come up to this forbidding fortress, perched on top of sloping granite, which was ample evidence that they had left the world and wanted no harm to anybody and wished only to be left alone. But history and legend grew up, and the world would not leave them alone. Women pilgrims scale those treacherous rocks that scare away many less pious men who are scholars merely in search of fun. From the Tsingkoping to the top, the climb consisted of a series of obstacles of a wide variety, like an obstacle race. Now we were sunk in a perpendicular shaft between giant rocks, now we were trudging along a giant ridge that sloped several hundred feet downward on both sides like the roof of a Chinese house. Now there was a footway of shaking wooden planks jutting out from the face of a precipice over a deep chasm four hundred feet below. This was the Bridge of Faith, and only the devout who had complete trust in God could have gone over safely. This obstacle race was enjoyed for its own sake, for its challenge to the spirit of man, and thus the Huashan became famous. Unlike the other famous mountains of China, the attraction of Huashan was not in its grandeur or beauty, or waterfalls or snow. It was simply in its danger.

Before we came to the sharp climb, the guides pointed out various points on the side of the cliff along the road that had been inhabited by hermits. A hut would perch dangerously on a narrow ledge forty or fifty feet above the gully, accessible only by tortuous climbing. As we climbed a slope, we saw on the opposite cliff a cave which was supposed to be the resting place of the famous Taoist Chen Chuan (*alias* Hsiyi). As far as I could make out, there was now no way of reaching the cave except by the most hazardous climb up the crevices of the cliff. Hsiyi lived a hundred and eighteen years, from the end of Tang to the beginning of Sung, passing through the chaotic "Five Dynasties" (tenth century). When he came here from his retreat in the Wutang Mountain, he was already past seventy years old. He had stopped eating grain of any kind, and he used to sleep more than a month at a stretch. A woodcutter happened to see a heap of skeleton covered with dust, and recognized him only on close approach. After a while he woke up and said, "I was enjoying a sound sleep. Why wake me up?" Later he was supposed to have died with his left arm propping up his head, and a multicolored cloud guarded the entrance for a month. There used to be an iron chain hanging down from the cave, and a priest had gone up it and found Hsiyi's bones, pinkish color and "emitting an extraordinary fragrance." Later someone went up and stole one of his toes. The Taoists were enraged when they discovered this and took down the chain. Since that time, no one has been able to go up and visit the cave.

On the opposite slope were the cave and temple of the Green-haired Maiden. She was a rich lady, by the name of Yüchiang, who lived in the time of the Tsin dictator. Toward the end of the dynasty, she brought a stringed instrument and came up to live here as a nun. She ate only pine seeds and *huangtsing* roots. In time green hair grew all over her body, which had become "so light that she could fly," the legend says. The place was inaccessible except by going through thick underbrush, and it was easy to understand how a monk living in such a retreat had to live on fruit and berries and walnuts. But the fairy was still a living spirit, I was told by a Taoist priest. As late as 1935, a woman over seventy years old had come here with her grandson to offer a new robe to the fairy. It got dark before they reached the place, and the child begged his grandmother to go home. The grandmother told him to go down and wait for her at the Jade Fountain Temple at the entrance to the mountain. She was determined to carry out her offering to the Fairy and went up alone. Her pious heart touched the Fairy. A tiger appeared, and the old woman fainted with fright. When she came to, she found herself safe at the temple. The only possible explanation was that the tiger had been sent by the Fairy to carry her up, because of her touching devotion. The Taoist priest who told this story could give her name and birthplace, as proof that he was not lying. Once here, one felt disinclined to dispute the honesty of the kindly old priests. The country was infested with snakes, and the priests were not afraid of them. Finding one near their bed, they would take it up gently with a pair of tongs and drop it outside the house, saying, "Please go away." All priests living in such mountains had to learn to be unafraid of two kinds of callers: snakes and tigers.

We began now to go up through the series of "obstacles," where apparently the road was closed in on all sides by cliffs. The first two were the "hundred-step" and the "thousand-step" climbs, almost perpendicular through shafts between rocks. There were convenient notches cut into the rocks on the roadside for the climber to grasp, and on one side, a strong iron chain suspended on iron bars driven into the rocks provided further support. Leaping up those steps in a Chinese long gown was not exactly easy. But when one heard that thousands of women pilgrims, including grandmothers with bound feet, came up and down this place annually in spring, any man would be ashamed to turn back. The steps were narrow, but on busy days the men and women had to pass in opposite directions. Really the descent was more frightening than the ascent. Somewhere along the route there was a "Heart-turning Rock," which was supposed to turn the traveler's heart cold, discouraging some from further strenuous adventures of this kind.

After going up those shafts and emerging on top, we came to a short stretch of level ground, with several tea houses on it. On top of the exit, there was a trap door. When this was closed, it was impossible for anyone to come up to the upper level. It was a place where one man armed with a good sharp sword could defy a whole army. As each head popped up from the narrow tunnel, it would be easy to chop it off.

Following the level stretch, we found that the road came to a dead stop after a short distance. Here was the "Ladder for Scaling Heaven." It was not hard climbing, for the ladder, a series of stone steps cut into an absolutely perpendicular rock, was only sixteen or eighteen feet high and was provided with iron chains on both sides. After this, one stopped at a picturesque temple, where one could look back to the gully and beyond to the Yellow River, visible on clear days. We did not see the river, for a cloud had covered the valley behind us and was threatening to rise farther and block out the mild winter sun. The Northern Peak, the nearest, towered above us, seemingly close by. But before we reached it, we had to follow "Laotse's Plow." Although frightening when looked at from a distance, this was really quite easy to go through, being a path of steps cut diagonally across the granite. I do not know what the priests meant by hanging an iron plow at the Northern Peak, back of the temple, unless they meant that Laotse himself had plowed up that stone groove for the convenience of travelers.

When we reached the Northern Peak, we were ready for lunch. The temple was built at the point of a rocky promontory, reached by a narrow ridge. Why should anyone choose to live in such a place? Other mountains provided just as beautiful views without such a treacherous approach. There was not even a plateau here. The Five Peaks of Huashan (named after the directions, plus the center) are a group not more than a mile or two apart, but separated by treacherous descents and ascents. Together they form the "Western Sacred Mountain," which again is one of five, the Eastern being the Taishan in Shantung and the Southern being the Hengshan in Hunan. But they were nothing but rocky peaks that under ordinary circumstances would not be scaled or inhabited. If the tops of other mountain cliffs were similarly developed with a system of steps cut into the rock surface, they could be equally "dangerous."

The priests were very hospitable, and we were entertained with tea and walnut and various seeds. The air was intensely cold. We relaxed on a broad couch in a room which used to be the guest room of the China Travel Service. The temple was built over the promontory, and there was a trap door in the floor, through which a priest descended to a room on the lower level where food was stored. The *huangtsing,* which I tasted for the first time in my life, was produced on this mountain. According to the dictionary, the Latin name for it is *Polygonatum falcatum,* and the popular English name is "deer bamboo." It belongs to the family of leeks, onions, and wild lilies. It tasted almost like salted turnips and should "prolong life" only in the sense that salted turnip would, when there was nothing better to eat. The Taoists evidently made a virtue of necessity by calling it the "yellow essence of life." We had brought our chicken, and while the vegetarian monks objected to the smell of meat, they were used to us carnivorous animals and were gracious enough about it and lent us their bowls. We used them in the knowledge that the bowls would have to be rinsed carefully afterward. There were, however, potatoes offered by the priests, and Mr. Kung Hsien-ming, who had studied in France, went to the kitchen and taught them to prepare the most delectable French fried potatoes.

Many travelers stopped here and did not venture farther, but we had planned to stop overnight at the Western Peak. The Northern Peak was connected with the rest by a narrow ridge. It was this place that was a trial of one's courage. Actually the danger was more imaginary than real, provided one kept steady nerves. The path was cut out of a rocky ridge, which sloped down at a sharp angle on both sides, in a stretch of a hundred fifty feet. Walking on it was like walking on the ridge of a roof, except that the ridge itself sloped up. The path was fully three feet wide, and was provided with steps, with chains on both sides. It was this place that had trapped two famous scholars of the past. It was generally known as the "Place Where Han Yu Wept Out Loud and Sent Down a Message for Help." (Han Yu was the great prose writer of the Tang dynasty.) More recently, in the eighteenth century, a Confucian scholar and governor of Shensi, Pi Yuan, was able to go up but unable to come down. His followers had no choice but to get him dead drunk and carry him down wrapped in a blanket. My courage was superior to that of these Confucian scholars, but inferior to that of the bound-footed women pilgrims.

By the time we reached the Western Peak it was growing dark. The Western Peak Temple was a new solid stone building, built over a stone foundation of thirty or forty feet, situated on a wider ledge than the Northern Peak. It was a favorite stopover for pilgrims and had ample accommodations. The priest was an impressive old man in Taoist and Ming robes, tall and wearing a beard, and he spoke in a thick, lusty voice, in spite of his great age. That night we had a delightful conversation. The weather had turned bitterly cold, but our room was heated.

The next morning when we woke, we found that it had been snowing, and there was a thin sprinkle of white on the ground. We discovered that Mr. Chang had brought up some incense and candles to pray for his beloved wife's spirit at the temple. He did not like to talk about it, but told us to go ahead and visit the Southern Peak and he would be coming along later. I learned from his companion, Mr. Chao, that his wife had died three or four years ago after a short, but very happy marriage. He was so in love with her still that he would not marry again. To offer up prayers for her at the top of Huashan was one of the purposes of his trip. I think it was near the anniversary of his wife's death. It was because he had to buy incense that he had kept us waiting on the night of our arrival. I see nothing wrong about such prayers when the sentiment is so sincere. It is better to express remembrance of one's dead ancestors and relatives through a pious ceremony than not to remember them at all. Thus are social and religious customs rooted in human sentiments. A friend of mine, who was educated in the United States and whose mind is entirely modern, sets up an altar on New Year's Eve to worship his deceased parents as a matter of sincere principle.

The Southern Peak, where there is a spacious temple, and behind it a pavilion, is the highest point of the mountain. Here we had a full view of the Tsinling Range, stretching out into the clouds in sharp, grayish-black, jagged cliffs in ranges and ranges as far as the eye could see.

A smooth-faced precipice rose up from the valley four hundred feet below the pavilion and there was a road leading to a cave a little below our level on the face of the cliff, ending in a narrow footway of planks two feet wide, suspended against the side of the rock. How anyone should choose such a cave to meditate and die in was beyond my comprehension. It looked more like the abode of a man suffering from a persecution complex or at least one who hated to see his fellow men. I decided that old Taoism was a very sad religion. This, it was pointed out to me, was the Bridge of Faith. Anyone who had sufficient faith in the Taoist Jade Emperor of Heaven could pass over successfully. I scrutinized the bridge. The ropes were old and the planks not too well laid. My faith in God was not great enough, and I decided sensibly there was no point in risking my life for sheer bravado. Yet I was told women pilgrims had passed over successfully. Religious fanaticism is something difficult to understand, but apparently the theory was that the greater the hardships and self-tortures on the pilgrimage, the greater was the merit in heaven. No one need tell me now that Chinese peasant women have no courage or cannot go wherever they please with their bound feet. In Soochow I was carried once in a sedan chair by peasant women, feeling, of course, tremendously ashamed, but these had natural feet, and when the men were too lazy, as Soochow men are usually, their wives had to come out and carry chairs for a living. There was nothing to be said about it. But the Shensi women seemed even to beat them.

Then there was pointed out to me another path that led out from the further side of the cave. This path had a series of stone steps cut into the perpendicular side descending some twenty feet before it led to another spot where some other hermit preferred to perfect the art of prolonged suicide. It really would seem much easier and simpler for the hermit to have pretended he had slipped and just fallen down and died and called it a day, since he seemed to hate his fellow men so. The other way was too laborious and complicated. I did not care where the path ended or whose cave it was. I was no longer interested in such foolhardy adventures and could not be tempted by another choice bit of trapeze excitement.

We got a good glimpse of the Eastern and Central Peaks, and saw a knoll below the Eastern Peak, where the Taoist Chen Chuan used to play chess. As it was inaccessible from below, it could be reached only by an overhanging cliff, so that those who wanted to play chess there had to crawl upside down from the projecting top, in Blarney Stone fashion. This place was called "A Kite Turning Tail." I decided that it was far too romantic for a man of my disposition.

We turned back on our way down the mountain. Three of my companions went to the other two peaks which were quite close by, but Professor S——— and I went back straight to the Northern Peak. A thermometer at the temple showed that it was twenty degrees below zero, and we did not want to risk being in the open too long. Professor S——— had only a thin black spring overcoat on, and I, when away from my wife, always remembered to take care of my health.

We could have taken the train to Sian that evening, but we were a little tired and thought a quiet night in that mountain retreat would be good for us. Besides, the company was congenial and the previous evening chats had been very delightful and we were reluctant to break up. So we decided to stay another night and have the whole next morning free.

We told stories and exchanged news of old friends separated for years. In time of war, the question was always who remained true to the cause of resistance and who had turned puppet, and if one had turned puppet, what were his motives, and had there been extenuating circumstances? The war cut a deep line of cleavage, and I regret that at least one whom the Chinese intellectual world had respected had forfeited our friendship. He had a Japanese wife, which was no excuse because it should have been easier for him to leave his family behind. He was Lusin's brother. Professor S——— and I both knew him well, but after he went over to the enemy, Professor S——— had stopped seeing him. Professor S——— said the least he could do was to resign his post as president of Peking University until the enemy had stopped torturing our men in the university. The prison was in the front building, and the classrooms were behind, and teachers on their way to classrooms had to hear the cries and screams of our young men. Professor S——— spoke with great emotion. He thought there was no excuse for the man and that the only reason for his turning puppet was his addiction to animal comforts. Professor S——— told me that if he had chosen to resign, the Japanese could have done nothing to him, for many scholars lived in Peiping in seclusion without having to join the puppets. Another man we knew had accepted the presidency of the Peking Women's Normal College. He was fool enough to presume that he could run the college in his own way, and when the enemy told him to take one of their men on the faculty, he was fool enough to ignore it. He chose rather to resign, and he did. Something might be said for such a person; not so with the other one. His funeral notice should have been written already, and no one among the thousands of his former admirers and friends would shed a tear over him. He had sold himself, body and soul.

Chou Tsojen is dead, and there is no "Alas!" It is said that we cannot judge our contemporaries, but I doubt it. I doubt that the dispassionate judgment of posterity is correct, and I further doubt that posterity should judge the beauty of a man's prose without reference to his moral character. How much, we contemporaries have the right to ask, is all his culture worth, if he is wrong in the elemental things, if in a time of war, with such a stout national leadership, he remains unmoved? I knew him well, and always thought that beneath the genial charm of his prose, he had a cold heart. The difference between him and his brother was that he was essentially a cynic and Lusin essentially a hot-blooded rebel. What a world of difference that makes! Lusin had a deep cynical quality underneath, too, a withering cynicism about all of China's culture; but that common quality in the Chou brothers had vastly different results because of differences in their psychological make-up.

A true analysis of Lusin would be resented in China. But at least this may be said: Lusin has a profound insight into the dark corners of men's souls, their stupidity and hypocrisy, in which he admitted he was influenced by the Russian writers. His profound cynicism enabled him to write so understandingly of that stupid, moronic, and ridiculous "Ah Q." What Ah Q represents is an unsettled question. Before Lusin joined the Communists, *The Story of Ah Q* was bitterly denounced by them as the product of a decadent and reactionary bourgeois writer, writing blasphemy of the illiterate masses. Lusin was unable to stand all alone against the crowd, or else he was convinced by them. He fought them for one year and then went over. After that, *The Story of Ah Q* became suddenly for the Communists a masterpiece of proletarian literature. Such vagaries show that sound literary criticism is not possible when it must follow the party line. We don't have to try to understand these things.

We also talked of lighter topics, and spoke of ghosts and fairies and Taoist priests. Professor S—— introduced a game, a literary one. He would quote a line of poetry, leaving out a crucial verb or adjective, and the others were to supply the best or most effective word. This excellent practice in writing amounted to matching our talents against the established poets. I remember that one line described a waterfall coming down from the mountain crests. The verb left out might be "flow," "overflow," "splash," "spray," or "fly." We found that the original word was *hsieh,* meaning "pour," but really nearer to the English word "flush," and we happily agreed that the poet knew his job.

Another game was to scramble the order of words in a line of verse and to give out the words one by one, and each man was to supply a word of opposite meaning and tone (like "earth" for "heaven" and "pace" for "flow," etc.). When all the words were given, the original line was revealed and the competition was to see who had made the best couplet with the original line. Sometimes extraordinarily good lines were produced in this manner without one's intention or knowledge, so that it suggested poems dictated by ghosts at *fuchi,* or the Chinese planchette. Professor S—— also cut out a piece of paper, folded it several times, and cut it with a pair of scissors. The resulting pieces spelled out a broken swastika (standing for Germany), a broken cross (standing for Italy), and English letters forming the word "HELL" for Japan, which was perfect. The amazing thing, which gave it a touch of prophetic mystery, was that the same pieces spelling out "hell" in English could form the word "empty" in Chinese and furthermore the word "finished" in Japanese. This, he said, was a very popular game with the schoolchildren in Peiping.

There were a number of places near by that were full of legend, and I regretted I did not visit the Yuntaikwan and did not meet the fairy that Tu Tsechun met there. It is an interesting story characteristic of Taoist tales, and typical of many associated with the mountain, so I might as well tell it here. Also it illustrates a human truth. What that human truth is, I shall leave to the guess of the reader. It is a long story, told with considerable charm, but I will condense it.

155

Tu Tsechun was a rich man's son in the time of the Five Dynasties. He had squandered his fortune in drink and women and, spurned by all his friends and relatives, had become a beggar wandering in the streets of Changan (modern Sian). He was an unusual man, however, and when begging in the streets, an old man leaning on a cane came up and asked him why he looked so dejected. He was angry at all his friends and relatives who had deserted him.

"How much cash do you need?" the old man asked.

"Oh, I suppose thirty or fifty thousand cash would be enough for my purposes."

"That is ridiculous. Ask for more," said the old man.

"A hundred thousand then."

"That won't do."

"A million, then."

"Still too little."

Finally Tu was persuaded to ask for three million cash and next day the gift was duly presented to him at the appointed place. A thousand cash make a dollar, but still it was a lot of money.

In a year he had squandered that, too, and he met the old man by chance again. The old man was surprised but this time gave him ten million. After three or four years, he had squandered that, too, on wine and women of Changan, and became a beggar again. The next time Tu saw the old man, he was too ashamed to meet him and turned away. But the old man caught hold of him and would not let him go.

"What do you want of me?" asked Tu.

"You have learned some lessons," replied the old man. "Now I want you to do some good works."

Tu swore he would reform and accepted thirty million this time.

"When you have done what you want to do, meet me at the Huashan," said the old man as he departed.

Tu really reformed this time. He went back to Yangchow, and built fine mansions and collected all the orphans and widows and the poor in the neighborhood and gave them rich land as their own.

When he had done this, he went to find the old man at Huashan, at the appointed place. After going into the mountains for a dozen miles, he saw a beautiful mansion with storks circling above it. There was the old man in a Taoist dress, surrounded by beautiful girls, sitting around a hot oven, trying to transmute metal into gold. The old man needed a man who had done philanthropy to help him succeed in his magic.

It was the last night, the crucial night for the experiment. Everything depended upon Tu's behavior, and whether he was sufficiently cultivated. Giving him three pills and a cup of wine to swallow, the old man gave his instructions:

"Be absolutely silent and remain calm whatever you see. You have to go through certain ordeals. You will see devils and vampires and wild beasts and monsters. You will even see Hell, and your own relatives tortured before your eyes. Whatever you see, do not utter a sound, but remember that they are unreal. Everything depends upon your co-operation. If you go through the ordeal bravely without uttering a sound, our medicine will have been made and we shall both be immortal."

The Taoist then left the room, and Tu was all alone. The mansion had vanished and he found himself in the wilds. First came robbers who threatened to kill him, but he was undisturbed in spirit, so they vanished. Second came wolves and lions and tigers and snakes. Tu met them with perfect calm and the beasts ran away. Then came a thunderstorm and earthquake and the earth yawned open beneath him, but he was unmoved. Finally came the ox-headed and horse-faced devils who dragged him to Hell and were going to throw him into a big caldron of boiling oil. Even then, Tu was unafraid and refused to utter a sound.

"This is a monster from Huashan," said the King of Devils. "We cannot destroy him by boiling him. Let's send him back to the earth, to be born as a woman."

So Tu became a woman, born in the house of Wang Chin in the county of Shanfu, district of Sungchow. This woman grew up to be beautiful, but still refused to utter a word, and therefore became known as a "dumb girl." A scholar in the same town was fascinated by her beauty, and said, "What's the harm if she is beautiful? I shall be the envy of all husbands of chattering wives." So he married her and after several years begot one boy and two girls, whom the mother loved exceedingly. Her husband petted her and embraced her and still she would not say a word. The husband then became furious and said to her, "The wife of Baron Chia refused to talk with him because she despised him. But when she saw him bringing down a pheasant at the hunt, she forgave his ugliness and talked and smiled. Now I am not as ugly as Baron Chia, and as a scholar, I can do better things than shooting pheasants. Yet you refuse to speak to me! When a man is thus despised by his wife, what is the use of having a son?"

Thereupon he took his young boy and hurled him down on the

stone of the courtyard. His skull broke and his blood splashed over the court. Thereupon the mother forgot herself and cried out, "Ai-yah!"

At this cry all vanished and Tu found himself sitting alone in front of the alchemist's oven. It was almost daybreak. The whole experiment had been spoiled. Fire had broken out and flames were lapping the roof. The Taoist priest came in and cried, "Ah, now you have spoiled all my plan of years!" He cut some of his hair and put it in the water jar standing in the yard and sprinkled the water and the fire was extinguished.

"How difficult it is to be a fairy," remarked the Taoist sadly. "You have overcome all mortal emotions except one. Because of that, you will remain a mortal. I can begin the experiment over again, but you will live within mortal coils. Now go away."

Tu Tsechun went back home. In later years he revisited the Yuntai Peak but found that all human traces had vanished, and he went home with a sigh in his heart.

Huashan is the world of wonder, where myths grew up like wild berries and the making of them is still possible today.

11

PAOCHI AND THE JAPANESE PRISONERS

COMING back from the world of magic, I was to journey back to Szechuen, following an ancient route into an ancient region. Yuhua came to meet me at the Sian station, and I stopped over at Sian for another day. We went together to the Chungnan Hills, where we stopped at a hostel overlooking a mountain lake and the views celebrated by Li Po and Tu Fu. The day was clear and mild, ideal for an outing.

The Guerrilla Training Center was closed for the time, a class having just graduated. But the beautiful red national flag waved proudly in the sun over a big evergreen tree as we approached. In the distance on another hill rose the peaks of the Five Buddhas. General Hu Tsung-nan was completely at ease with his officers and punctuated the conversation with his laughter. At lunch a little wine was served, according to custom. Being unable to drink, I coined a Chinese phrase on the inspiration of the moment. After one cup, I decided I would

158

not drink any more and turned the cup over on the table and called it
"*jengpei kwanyin.*" The phrase is hard to translate, but literally it
means "sealing the cup and enjoying the look of drinking guests." It
was my last day at Sian, and I was sorry to part with so many good
friends. I hummed a little verse under my breath:

For a half month, I busied myself here and there;
The clear days of early winter were yet warm.
I stumbled among the bricks of Tsin and the tiles of Han,
And lingered over the inscriptions of Tang and the rubbings of Sung.
The hill called Chungnan held a prophecy,
And the village name Huangfu also contains a pun.
But looking back, there is an endless thought yet unexpressed.
The hills and rivers of the old country are yet not regained.

The pun here comes from the coincidence that General Hu *Tsungnan* was stationed at the *Chungnan* hills and that the ancient village
of *Huangfu* here was now *Huangpu* (Whampoa).

On our way back to the city we visited the cave of Lady Precious
Stream at Wuchiapo. It was only three miles off the main road, but I
had been unable to reach it on a previous trip because of the muddy
roads. Now the mud was dry and hardened.

In Tang times all this region had been a busy city park. There were
terraces and towers and bridges and canals and ponds, but now the
Chüchiang Lake was all dry. We lost our way when we came to the
end of the road, where there was only a stretch of wheat fields and
country paths. A soldier in a camp near by was good enough to go
along with us. We had to leave our car and walk through a winding
dry river bed. The cave was a perfect loess shelter, two stories high,
reached by a dark and winding staircase, lighted by a candle. But on
the top floor there were many rooms, looking down on an enclosed
court. There were statues of Lady Precious Stream and her warrior
husband, but no relics. Here Lady Precious Stream lived eighteen years
waiting for the return of her husband, until her baby child had grown
up into a young man. It was essentially the story of Penelope waiting
for the return of Ulysses, while her son Telemachus grew up. How
could she have guessed that she would be celebrated a thousand years
afterwards in London, and that her joys and tears would still be shared
by us latecomers in this day?

That night my friends came to say good-by at the train. It was hard
to leave people who had been so kind. Yuhua and her brother were

going with me on the train as far as Paochi, and her mother came to say good-by also. Someone was thoughtful enough to give me a box of cigars made from tobacco grown in Honan, which I found had an aroma as rich and mild as the best Havanas.

There had been a conspiracy to force me to stop at Wukung for a day. Here was the biggest agricultural college in Shensi, with over a thousand acres of land, and such big modern buildings that the Japanese had bombed it repeatedly. There were over a thousand boy and girl students, and fairly decent teachers' residences. The students' faces were healthy and full of life; I thought it would be hard to be ill in such a healthy, sunny plain. When I spoke to them, I told them how little Confucius knew about agriculture and horticulture.

My real reward for this break in the journey was seeing the irrigation canals along the Wei River. Water conservancy is probably the most noteworthy aspect of the reconstruction projects in Shensi. The foundation for it was laid some fifteen years ago when T. V. Soong took an interest in it. The work was so successful and so appreciated by the farmers that the provincial government has gone ahead during the war, and has built five or six canal systems along the turbulent and unnavigable waters, with gates and dikes for regulating the irrigation of the fields. Practically all the important rivers of the province have been or are being harnessed for irrigation. All these dikes are named *hwei-chü,* or "benefit canals," preceded by the name of the river. Thus the Wei system of dikes is called *Wei-hwei-chü.* The peasants were so grateful that the French-educated Chinese engineer, Li, who built the first canals, and his wife, have become a god and goddess and are worshiped just as Li Ping, who built the famous Szechuen irrigation system two thousand years ago, was worshiped. At the time I was there, they were buildling a canal regulating the Ching (King) River farther north, and had mobilized half a million of the local population to do it. Strangely enough, no newspaper story has appeared about such gigantic, important, and interesting reconstruction projects going on during the war. One does not hear about them unless one goes about and takes the trouble to look for them. We hear, also, strikingly little of the extension of schools to all villages and the weeding out of illiteracy, going on at full speed, or the New County System and preparations for local elective government, or about the extension of railways in Kweichow, or even of the striking dock and canal systems only a day's journey from Chungking. When one sees these things being pushed through during the war, one has the right to hope that much quicker progress will be made when the war is over.

Paochi was formerly a small town, but since it became the communications center between Chungking and Sian, controlling the entrance to Szechuen, it has suddenly grown up in a few years.

The name means Precious Cock, but the legend regarding its origin is confused. An ancient Tsin emperor discovered a stone cock of beautiful liver color here and set up a temple to it. But this stone cock had some sort of control of the weather. "When the spirit came from the Southeast, it made a tremendous booming noise like thunder, and all the cocks of the universe would crow."

Early on the morning after my arrival I set out to visit the workshop of the Lunghai Railway. The maintenance of this railway during the seven years of war was a saga in itself. It was, like everything else in Free China, a tragic and brave struggle of human will against circumstance, worthy of a song to celebrate the men whose toil and brains and courage kept the road going, and so much more so because they took it all for granted as part of the war of resistance. A railway extension to Lanchow was planned, by building first an extension to Tienshui. The line ran through extremely difficult terrain, requiring dozens of bridges and tunnels, and the work was held up on account of the shortage of steel. I have already referred to their work in maintaining a nightly service "dashing the pass" through enemy artillery fire along the Yellow River, east of Tungkwan and as far as Loyang.

Even the maintenance of the locomotives without spare parts for seven years was a feat. Realizing how the engines would run down and get out of order, Director Lu had set a competition in locomotive repair, with rewards for extra speed. This had doubled the number of locomotives available for service. I saw how the workmen were salvaging parts of old locomotives and making them into new ones. Director Lu said the locomotives would be insufficient when the time came for a counteroffensive and soldiers had to be transported to the East Coast. He told me how sadly he needed certain things from the United States, which had been ordered for years but could not be flown in. I was asked to talk to the mechanics, but what could I say except that they were the pioneers of a new class of industrial workers, that China needs not hundreds, not thousands, but tens of thousands of men like them, that China was entering the period of industrialization and that they should be very proud of their profession? I said it was foolish to talk of training up a fine army, without having industry and trained mechanics, that this was the lesson of this war and China had learned it, bitterly.

We went by a railway handcar to the Shen Hsin (Sung Sing) Cotton Mill, about a mile away. This is one of the greatest marvels of the Chinese war, and I wonder that the journalists have never written about it. There are many underground factories in and around Chungking, but none on such a big scale as Shen Hsin. This factory has an oversize power plant which supplies the electricity for the city of Paochi, and the electric lights of Paochi are unusually bright. The factory and plant were removed from Hankow in the last days of the evacuation, together with its thousands of men and women workers. I had seen by this time many textile factories, including a huge one in the ancient city of Hsienyang, but had never seen so many carding machines and spindles going inside a mountain. There were twenty-six entrances and exits, and the electrically lighted tunnels added up to some three miles, running at right angles to each other like the streets of a city inside a mountain. Besides the cotton mill with 23,000 spindles and 400 looms, there were also a flour mill, with a daily output of 90,000 pounds of flour, and an iron works complete with foundry to make and repair the milling and textile machinery. Many of the machines and lathes were the product of the iron works, including complete paper-making machinery copied from an American model.

When the plant was moved to Paochi, the place was practically unknown. It had neither power nor material, and no skilled or unskilled labor, and the reorganization and setting up of the plant were the improvisation of genius. Now there are thirty-five hundred workers. Food and living quarters are provided free of charge for all employees, with separate quarters for married couples. Juvenile workers are required after an eight-hour day of work to attend classes for two hours in the evening. There are also a kindergarten and a primary school for the children of the employees. Other welfare facilities include a hospital, clubs with libraries and recreation grounds, a co-operative store, a restaurant, a savings department, and a system of life insurance. I saw equally efficient welfare arrangements at Arsenal Twenty-One (which has the largest swimming pool in Chungking) and at the Shasi Cotton Mill near Chungking. If any of the hundred little things being done under the Kuomintang rule had been found in the Communist areas— the schools, the orphanages, the co-operatives, the dikes, the relief projects, etc.—the American reporters would have fallen into a fit of ecstasy. The problems of capital and labor are the same the world over, and enlightened capitalism faces the problem in the same way in different countries. In order to make the workers produce, it has to make them happy. Men facing the problems in real life usually think out the same sensible answers without a theory to it. Among the managing staff at Shen Hsin, I met two Oxford-educated brothers, sons of the deceased owner. They spoke beautiful English, but I doubt that they ever studied business management.

I found myself not only taking more and more interest in China's industry during this trip, but also seeing a good deal of bankers and bank employees. Paochi had fourteen banks. Everywhere I went the bankers had a club. I sensed a significant change, new in the sense that the banks had absorbed a large number of young men, and that banking and public accountancy courses in colleges and evening schools always had large enrollments. These men going into business are keen, intelligent, and modern, and they take a wide interest in lectures and public activities. The Farmers' Bank at Chungking, for instance, is a colony by itself situated in the suburbs, with its library and clubs, and an extraordinary group of intelligent young men and women employees. This seems to indicate the rise of a new class in Chinese society, presaging China's entering into a business age. This class of young intelligent men in the rank and file of business corresponds to that class of modern-minded, middle-aged industrial leaders, whose rise I mentioned in a previous chapter. Businessmen used to be despised as a class; now business seems to be placed above literature and philosophy among the educated youth of China. This is an important phenomenon.

Now I come to the most interesting part of my experience at Paochi, the visit at the Japanese War Prisoners' Camps. I had arranged to go to Szechuen with the Northwest Tranportation Company, and on hearing that I was visiting the Japanese prisoners' camp, the vicepresident, whom they affectionately called Wei "Fuli," gave the whole staff a half-day holiday to visit the camp. So a group of two trucks and a car went out of the city one morning with a party of some fifty men and three girls, who were their librarians. Yuhua also was with us. The staff of the Northwest Transportation Company were dressed spic and span in their navy blue woolen Chungshan uniform. Most of them were high school graduates, and a few, I think, had been to college. They were well provided for, but they had only two days of holiday in the entire year, and were required to work hard. As I was to learn later on the highway journey, this was a most efficient and well-run business firm.

After driving for forty minutes through the countryside, we came to several shallow streams. The ground was broken into chasms where the streams ran into the river. The trucks forded two streams successfully, but when we came to a third, where the mud was treacherous, we forsook the trucks and started to walk on foot. The camp was still two miles away, hidden in a bend of the hills. Before we approached the village, there was another stream to cross by steppingstones. One of the girls had on high-heeled shoes. She should have picked her way over the small boulders slowly and surely, step by step, but she took fright and started to leap from one to another, and being unable to check herself, fell plump into the river. Luckily, it was very shallow, and only part of her dress was wet.

At the village where the camp was we were met by the commander, Mr. Ma, and Mr. N. Arno Bendtz, a Swedish representative of the War Prisoners' Aid, World Committee of the Y.M.C.A. We learned that there were several prison camps, widely separated, and Commander Ma wanted to send word to the prisoners of the other camps to assemble. I told him that we would rather see the camp near by just as it was. I didn't want the prisoners to line up: I just wanted to see how they were spending their time this morning, just like any other morning.

We were told that the prisoners were of two types, the converted and the unconverted, terms that at best describe general attitudes only. So we saw that day two camps only, one for infantry prisoners and the other for a small group of pilots.

The camp for infantry was small, holding probably a hundred and twenty men. The prisoners were dressed in deep blue quilted cotton, made, I thought, from better cloth than that worn by Chinese soldiers. Groups were lolling about in the sunny compound, and several were sitting on a narrow porch occupied in sewing or mending. They looked at us curiously, their attitude being neither very friendly nor very hostile. I went inside one of the houses. A dozen men were sitting with crossed legs on the big *kang* covered with mats, and some were playing cards. The sight was none too inspiring. I tried to talk with some of the men through an interpreter, but while they smiled, I felt they would rather be left alone. They knew they would be asked the usual questions, and something hurt in them. There was one who could talk Chinese fluently, and they found him in the yard outside. I sat down on a stone next to him and tried to be natural. He was friendly and talked Chinese intelligibly. He said he had owned a small shop at home. He had no complaint about his treatment here, and would often, on coming to a point, stop and laugh, seeming to suggest, "What is the use of talking?" He thought of his home, of course, but the war was an unpleasant topic that mystified him and that he could not think through. With him, as with the others, I felt a sense of hurt pride and a deep attachment to their own country which was natural.

I met a group of three or four women prisoners, who were either Japanese or Korean. I remarked that there was no important guard and no machine guns were at the entrance, and that the mud walls about six or seven feet high would be easy to climb. In fact, I saw some Japanese working at a back wall which had broken down. Commander Ma told me that there was no point in their trying to escape. A few had tried it and had been caught and sent back. Here they were a thousand miles inland. Those who escaped would after a day or two be driven to approach a village to ask for food. With their accent, their gait and the Chinese *paochia* village system, they would soon be detected and sent back to the camp.

Meeting the truculent air pilots was the most interesting part of this visit. Because they were extraordinarily frank in their opinions, I had a fascinating talk with them, and was able to learn a great deal. There were nine of them, all pilots who had been captured in the first year of the war, back in 1937-38. They were housed in a loess cave, looking out on a spacious yard. Commander Ma told me these were "unconverted," which made me want to talk with them the more. I found them seated on mats on a big *kang*. The *kang* was L-shaped and at the corner I saw some photographs and a Japanese wooden shrine to their Emperor which they evidently had made themselves. I sat on the edge of the earthen bed, and many of our party crowded into the tiny space inside the entrance and near the door to listen to the interview.

Commander Ma told them in Japanese that I had just come from America. He could speak Japanese very well, but with him was a Chinese interpreter who seemed to speak it perfectly. I myself could not understand a word of Japanese.

I didn't realize what I had let myself in for. I felt as if I were listening in at a meeting of the Black Dragon Society. The Japanese pilots were not only frank, but anxious to talk, sometimes several of them replying to my question simultaneously. From the Japanese point of view, their "morale" was still very high. Truculent, intelligent, fanatical, and unrepentant, they expounded their philosophy of war. They had not surrendered, but had been shot down and captured. The five or six years of imprisonment had not changed their ideas or their spirit. Most of them were young, the oldest seeming to be about thirty. Some had been trained from the age of fifteen or sixteen in

165

the ideas of the Japanese Army, the doctrines of war, the necessary struggle for power, and Japan's national destiny. All of them could talk and discuss their ideas like college-educated people. Some of the younger ones were a little too effervescent.

There was an older man who could discuss every point of Japanese nationalism from A to Z. He sat on his crossed legs with perfectly erect, square shoulders and needed only a sword to look like a picture of a *samurai*. But another thin man sitting next to the window, who talked curtly and sat stiffly, frightened me. There was a hardness in his look and a cunning in his mind that seemed to make Japanese militarism all at once intelligible to me. He seemed to be their master mind and would check or correct the others' answers, and had that peculiar guarded and set Japanese expression that seemed to say, "The world is my enemy." This was an exceptional chance for me to come into direct touch for the first time with the Japanese warlike mind.

Looking at the shrine on the wall, with Chinese words that I could read, I asked them what they thought of their Emperor. The question wasn't clear, and there was an exchange of Japanese among themselves. Then the thin man at the window, the master mind, replied, "In our unusual situation, we ought not to discuss the topic. If we think of the topic at all, we should commit *hara-kiri*." I whistled beneath my breath and knew what I had found.

"But do you believe he is a god?" I pressed. That was the question I wanted answered. I had heard about this, but I wanted someone to tell me to my face that he believed it was so.

The able talker replied, "He is both god and man. We believe he is a god and also a person. As a person, we think of him as our own beloved parent."

That put me out. I didn't want to challenge them on this sensitive point, although it was fantastic to hear a modern-educated man say it.

"Do you think that the Emperor is the state, and that the idea of the Japanese Empire cannot exist without the Emperor?"

There was a rush to answer.

"Definitely so," said one.

"Our Mikado is the symbol of Japan's national and world destiny," said another.

"We are representatives of the Emperor."

"He is the symbol of our nation. A nation cannot exist without a head. Your Confucius said so."

"Never mind about Confucius. After these years of contact with the

Chinese people, have you changed your ideas of us? I suppose—I know —you have been taught in your schools some nasty things about the Chinese."

Another man who had hitherto been silent spoke up. "No, that is not true." (I knew that it was true, that he merely intended to be polite, but did not dispute him.) "We were taught in our schools that America was our real enemy."

"You have heard about Pearl Harbor of course. And you know the course of the war is turning against you. I am sorry but you are doomed to defeat. It was very unwise of you to tackle America. Didn't you realize that America could outproduce you, and that you had taken up a task too big for you?" I said all this with a frank smile. It touched off some very emphatic remarks.

"We knew America was a strong country. We knew it. But she is our only enemy and rival in the Pacific. America must be defeated. To that end, we will move all our physical and spiritual resources for the conflict. The conflict is inevitable. It is a conflict of national destinies."

There was no tone of regret. I had not expected such a frank confession of opinion.

"So you were taught in your Army schools to think that war between Japan and America was inevitable."

"It isn't that we were taught to think so. It was inevitable. We knew it and planned for it. Strong, powerful nations must fight or die."

This was getting intensely interesting to me and they did not seem to be bored. They talked as if they wished to convert me. Possibly some of them had read my books which had been translated into Japanese.

I asked: "Don't you think that the Emperor was not to blame for the war policy, and that it was your militarists that led you into this war?" I used a Chinese phrase, "holding the Emperor to rule the dukes," meaning the militarists making the Emperor a tool to establish their own power and further their own ends. The interpreter made this plain and they understood.

"What do you mean by militarists?" flashed back the challenge. I was put on the defensive.

"By militarists, I mean a military caste ruling the nation and determining the policy of the state, instead of the civilians. The militarists," I explained, "are army men with army minds; they cannot think of foreign relations except in terms of war and conquest. When you have such military minds controlling the government policy of any

167

country, the result is war—as in Germany. Your country is so ruled, and your national policy is determined by a military ruling class. That is what I mean by your militarists."

I heard only clicks and hisses, which as translated meant: "They are not militarists. They are loyal servants of Japan."

I tried to do a bit of propaganda and, in a friendly spirit, I said, "The war will end in victory for the Allies and defeat for Japan. In the United States there are two schools of opinion. One thinks we ought to overthrow the Emperor, the other thinks we ought to keep him. But the people of the Allies are all agreed that the military caste in Germany and in Japan must be destroyed."

"We don't understand. There are no militarists in Japan."

There seemed to be a kind of deadlock. They were talking among themselves. *"Tsit-tsit . . . Nia-nia . . . harayama dyoshi . . . tsit-tsit arigato nogo hayashi"*—that was how it sounded to me.

"I mean people who are for war, who believe in war as an instrument of state policy. You all want the world to live in peace, don't you? How can there be peace if people believe in war?"

This produced a really zestful tirade from the laughing, effervescent young man, that made me realize the gulf was too great for any useful argument.

"World peace?" said one readily with a hearty, cocksure snigger. "You look at animals. Even insects and ants fight. There will always be war in the world so long as there are any human beings left on this earth. When all men are dead, yes, there will be world peace."

I was a little stunned. The interview was ended. I had learned a great deal.

Before leaving the village, I visited Mr. Bendtz's humble quarters. He said that in the beginning he had had to overcome a lot of suspicion of his motives, and that when he first had breakfast with the *samurai* captives, he was given an astounding reception. One Japanese pilot said that he and his fellow prisoners represented the heavenly Emperor of Japan and that only if Mr. Bendtz recognized that fact could they have any intercourse with him. According to Mr. Bendtz, there were twenty officers, twenty pilots, and thirty to forty university graduates whom I did not see. There were two factions, the officers and faithful representatives of the *samurai,* and the ordinary soldiers, and they seemed to have little to do with each other. Commander Ma was forced to make separate lodgings for the two classes. The university graduates were at first placed with the officers, but later requested to be transferred to the soldiers' camp, where they felt more at ease. Mr.

Bendtz had arrived a few months ago and had just got various educational and welfare committees started, headed by the prisoners themselves, with the co-operation of Commander Ma. He said that Ma had done an excellent piece of work and accomplished a labor of lasting value. He quoted Dr. McClure of the Friends Ambulance Unit, who had visited the camp, as saying, "This camp is wholly and fully up to the standards of the camps in Canada which I had the privilege of visiting a few months ago." I was proud and happy to find that China had lived up to the humanitarian traditions of the West in its treatment of prisoners.

Paochi was also the center of the Chinese Industrial Co-operatives, and I had a good chance to see their shops, their exhibits, and a most touching camp for orphans and Honan famine women refugees, and had tea with the children of their school for orphans. Rewi Alley was not there at the time, but Lu Kuangmien and Hu Shihju were very kind to me and showed me about. I shall not touch upon this because it is so well told by Mr. George Hogg in his book *I See a New China*.

Yuhua had been with me for the last four days, and we grew fond of each other. She had very good manners and yet was spontaneous and unconstrained. She asked me many things about America, and I asked her many things about her life in the orphanage where she was so happy. Here is a story told for her edification. It is an improved version of Æsop's *The Tortoise and the Hare*, with a reversed moral.

Once a Tortoise met a Hare on a meadow. The Tortoise boasted that he had great persistence, and ridiculed the Hare for his love of fun and running about all day. He told the Hare that if he didn't reform, he would come to a bad end in his old age.

"I shan't argue with you," said the Hare. "How about having a race? We shall ask Brother Fox to be the referee."

It was agreed, and the Tortoise crawled on. After crawling for a quarter of an hour, he had covered barely thirty feet. The Hare grew impatient and regretted joining in the race with him.

"The way you progress," said the bright Hare, "we shan't finish the race till evening, and my beautiful day will have been entirely wasted."

So the Hare forgot about the race. He went off where he liked and sported among the trees and the meadow and was very happy. But the Tortoise said to himself, "I have persistence. I will plod along, and eventually I shall reach the goal."

Toward early afternoon the Tortoise was nearly exhausted and sought shade, where he felt tempted to take a nap. But he had prejudice against an afternoon nap, and thought it immoral to be kind to himself, and plodded along. His shell was heavy and his head small, and as he lifted it to look about, he could not see five feet beyond him, and his eyes began to swim.

Now because the Hare was following his natural bent, he found the going a pleasure, and the more he ran the better he felt. He had gone half a mile when he came to the bank of a river, thought the scenery very pretty and took a nap. When he waked up, he felt thoroughly refreshed, and he had forgotten all about the race. As he was wondering what to do with the leisure, he saw a squirrel pass in front of him. This struck him as a very queer animal, and he decided to chase it to find out how big its tail was, so that he could go home and tell his mother about it.

So the Hare began to chase the Squirrel, and the Squirrel ran for a long distance until he saw a big tree and clambered up to the top.

As the Hare came to the foot of the tree and was staring up at the Squirrel, he heard a voice near by.

"Brother Hare, you have won!"

He looked round and saw it was the Fox, and the tree was the very goal of their race. The Tortoise was still panting and snorting half a mile away.

Moral: A tortoise should challenge another animal on anything except a race.

Children should enjoy their studies, or they will get nowhere at all.

I had bought a few things for Yuhua. The last few days had been wonderful. Now the time of parting had come. I committed her to the care of her brother, and we promised to write each other often. They saw my truck pull off about two o'clock in the afternoon, and I saw her little hand waving in the distance until our truck turned the corner.

12

THE NORTHWEST HIGHWAY

FOR the first half of my journey across the Tsinling Mountain, following the historic route into Szechuen, I had a seat next to the driver on a truck of the Northwest Transportation Company. This was a form of *de luxe* travel. On the ordinary passenger bus, about thirty passengers rode packed tightly on wooden seats, their hair, their faces, and their clothing powdered with dust like workers in a flour mill. There were also hazards and delays on the bus journey. A bus might break down halfway up the mountain road and passengers would have to pass a night as best they could. The Northwest Transportation Company, however, was famed for its fast and safe service. It carried chiefly cargo, but would take a few passengers who were willing to perch on top of the load, in the wind and the dust and the bitter cold. To be able to sit next to the driver was good luck indeed.

We went in a convoy of five or six trucks, necessary for mutual assistance in case of breakdowns. There were about a dozen passengers, among them several students of Yenching, who had escaped from Peiping and were going to Chungking. Two of them were girls, who were given seats beside the drivers. Each truck raised a trail of dust for half a mile behind, and the drivers tried to keep at a comfortable distance from each other.

It was a mild day, and the cold on top of Tsinling, which was only about two thousand feet here, was not as severe as one was told. The trucks went up the hairpin curves and reached the peak in an hour, and then took a whole afternoon to come down the gradual descent on the south side. As we had started late that afternoon, we stopped at Shuangshihpu that night. I put up at the office of the Northwest Transportation Company, where the man in charge was a Peita graduate. The mountain air was cold, but the room and bed were clean and warm.

The next morning I got up early to visit the Industrial Co-operatives and a Polytechnic School. The Polytechnic School, run by the government, fascinated me not only because I loved to see machine lathes going anywhere in China now, but also because it was typical of the things being done in those bare mountain surroundings. The dormitories and conditions of the students suggested pioneer days, yet the classes in physics and geometry and the power-driven machines apparently belong to the twentieth century. My greatest pleasure, however, was in seeing the Bailie School, situated a mile away across a small river. The forty or fifty students here were picked from the Industrial Co-operatives to receive elementary training in mechanics and co-operative management. I had the unexpected pleasure of finding Mr. George Hogg, the Englishman, in charge here. His personality gave the school a warm and cheerful atmosphere. He led the students in singing Indusco and patriotic songs with a lusty voice and an infectiously snappy rhythm, and the boys heartily enjoyed it with him.

They had keen, intelligent faces, and many of them, though war orphans, would be the equal of any, if they had a chance for college education. Mr. Hogg had a clean, really handsome face. In his speech in Chinese he even used some Chinese literary idioms. The students saw me off to the bank of the little stream, and I was really sorry to leave them.

I had to hurry back to start on the day's journey. Crossing mountainous territory, in two hours we came to Miaotaitse for lunch. Here was the place of retirement of the great strategist Chang Liang, now preserved as a temple to his honor. Situated on a picturesque slope, famous for its old cypresses, it had ample courtyards, winding corridors, pavilions, and an unbelievable number of tablets, which were tributes to this great and mystic character. After this man had helped the First Emperor of Han to establish a new dynasty (about 200 B.C.), he had the immense wisdom to retire and escape the fate of the other generals who had fought side by side with the Emperor. I could not help sympathizing with the other generals, one of whom quoted the proverb, "When the game fowl are killed off, the good bow may be laid aside; when the wild hare is exhausted, the hound may be boiled alive." Chang Liang, however, became a Taoist living in retirement, and died in happy old age. The First Emperor of Han rose to his position from that of a village subaltern, and one of his aides was a dog-butcher by profession. He was as wily and tough and crooked as a modern racketeer. During his campaigns before he became emperor, he was constantly in difficulties and lived by his wits. Once his enemy was surrounded by him, and threatened to boil the Emperor's old father in captivity with the enemy unless the siege was lifted. "Please do," was his reply, "and don't forget to send me some of the soup." When I was asked to write an inscription at the temple, I could not resist putting down my sentiments about that wily village bully who became emperor.

From here the motor road followed a narrow gorge along a river for about thirty miles. On the opposite side of the river we saw remains of the famous *tsan-tao* or military footway used in the ancient campaigns. The precipices closed in to the very edge of the river, and a suspended gangway was built out from the face of the cliffs for the marching armies of the Three Kingdoms. The difficulty of army transport could be imagined. For decades in the third century, battles seesawed in this region, and to the east and west, the army in Szechuen trying to conquer the North, and the army in Shensi trying to come down and challenge the South. Then, as now, the military problem was maintaining the supply line and sending reinforcements. I could understand why Chuko Liang failed, in spite of his brilliant strategy. He even invented some mysterious means of transport in the shape of animals, called the "wooden ox" and the "flouncing horse," but even these did not help him solve the problem. Measurements of different parts of these things are still recorded in history. Dimensions were given for the front and hind legs, but there was no mention of wheels, although wheels were well known centuries before. Several times he started campaigns across the Tsinling, but stopped short south of the Wei River, when his supplies ran out and he had to return. The last time, he opened settlements for his soldiers to plant grain south of the river, but before he could see the results, he died of illness.

Most traces of the ancient military footway had disappeared except chiseled marks and holes in the rocks. At the Stone Gate, a section was repaired with patches of concrete. There was a short tunnel driven through a jutting cliff. Two characters written by Tsao Tsao himself were inscribed on a rock close to the edge of the water. Here the two generals matched their wits and contended for supremacy.

Looking up at the Chicken Head Rock from the Stone Gate,
I realized how, it was said, the roads of Shu were difficult to pass.
Whither have gone Mengtch and Wuhou and the schemes of men?
Let's sit facing the cliff (in Buddhist fashion) and contemplate the past.

Chuko Liang is probably the most celebrated general in Chinese history. There is a kind of universal reverence and admiration for this man, who has occupied a place in the popular imagination through the centuries like that of King Arthur in English folklore. Like King Arthur, he failed; his ambition to restore the Han house lay unfinished at his death, and after he died, the dynasty fell. Yet like King Arthur, he was held up as a model of all manly virtues, brave and wise and kind, and as a man of great sagacity and integrity of character. For although his years were occupied with battles and campaigns, he ruled as the premier of Shu (modern Szechuen) for over twenty years, loving justice and kindness and consideration for his people. When he died, the people of Szechuen expressed their sorrow by spontaneously setting up private altars in his honor. Posterity judged him as a great statesman who had the wisdom to wait, to consolidate his rear, and to make progress in slow stages according to a fixed plan. "A great hero

173

is not judged by his success or failure," the Chinese proverb says. He was also a great scholar, steeped in the wisdom of history, and some of his writings still exist today, two being popular selections for school-children to memorize, like the Gettysburg Address. Around him grew the legend of the three famous tragic warriors, now most beloved of the people, like the knights of King Arthur.

The peasants of Szechuen today still wear white turbans. This is queer in China, because white is the color of mourning, and the white turban is ugly and difficult to keep clean, besides. Nobody knows the origin of this custom, but legend has it that at Chuko Liang's death the people of Szechuen mourned for him as for their own parents, and the custom has persisted to this day. There is a practical reason for the turban, for the Szechuen people claim that it keeps the head warm on cold, damp mornings; but the white is certainly uncalled for. Besides, Szechuen people in the country commonly wear long gowns and walk on bare feet, even in winter, which is certainly odd. Anyway, one cannot go anywhere in Szechuen without hearing tales of Chuko Liang and his warriors, and his memory still lives in parts as far south as Kweichow and even Indo-China.

The next day we passed the temple to Chuko Liang (the Wuhoutse), where there is a rather curious "relic," the stone base of a string instru-ment that he was reported to have played. There were notches on the stone for fastening the strings, and an inscription gave the date as the first year of Changwu, A.D. 231, which was during his last campaigns. It is hard to vouch for its authenticity, and the use of stone for the body of a musical instrument must be regarded as unusual. Farther on, we came to old Miencheng, connected with an episode that every theatergoer loves. The motor road cut through the city wall and a corner was pointed out as the gate where the dumb beggar, placed there by Chuko Liang, helped to mislead and confuse and frighten away the enemy, when the city was caught without enough soldiers to defend it.

A mountain marks the frontier between Shensi and Szechuen, and on the other side lies Kwangyuan. The road wound up and down over the hills. We passed passenger buses and military trucks, and the drivers would stop a minute and exchange greetings and news. Now and then we saw a line of pony carts slowly pulling up the mountain roads, loaded with empty oil drums, destined for the Yumen oil fields in northwest Kansuh.

The story of these oil drums is little known abroad. In Northwest

China, in Chungking and down to Kunming, the cars and trucks entitled to gasoline are run by gas from the Yumen oil fields, which were discovered and opened during this war. The oil gushed up in great quantities (one rough estimate is that these oil fields could produce half a million gallons a day), but because of lack of storage facilities and containers, some of the oil wells had to be plugged up. China has no steel rolling mills and cannot make steel plates for oil drums. Hence the gasoline supply is strictly limited by the number of drums available. Part of these were saved during the retreat from Burma. At Kunming, in the camps of American soldiers, I occasionally saw one of these precious drums transformed into a boiler for bath water. After the drums have served their purpose in the south, the empty containers have to be transported slowly by horse and mule carts a thousand miles back to Yumen to be refilled again. It is no wonder that a gallon of Yumen oil is sold for four hundred dollars at Kunming. Such are the problems of transportation in China.

There is severe rationing of motor fuel, of course, with the armed services having priority. The Yumen oil is of a pale yellow color, being imperfectly refined, but is the best gasoline that Chinese can get. The government trucks on the Southwest Highway, I understand, prefer to burn pure alcohol, which was also sold at about four hundred dollars a gallon but has much less power than gasoline on an upgrade. The alcohol, too, is restricted to government trucks.

The passenger buses for civilians and private commercial trucks burned charcoal gas. A Chinese engineer has invented a simplified charcoal gas tank, placed outside the front of the car, on the left, the driver's wheel being on the right in China. There is a device for pumping in air to feed the fire and for clearing the ashes, worked by turning a crank outside. Coal was not used because the fire would be too hot for people sitting near it. The charcoal gas was good enough for level country, but when more power was required, a little steam was mixed with it. On a really steep stretch, the sight was tragic. When the bus would not go up, the driver's assistant would get down and grind the crank to heat up more gas, and the bus would inch up a little. The brakes were not dependable, and three or four people would be running after the truck, each holding a wooden wedge to put beneath the tires, to prevent it from rolling backwards, in case it should stop again.

On these mountain roads, when the road was slippery, and the brakes did not work properly, a truck might roll off and overturn. In the South I saw a bus overturned down a slope, and met passengers with bandaged chins and noses and foreheads in the inn where I stopped. But even without accidents, there were all sorts of delays in inconvenient places. Coming down a mountain side toward Kweiyang, I saw a bus with a full load of passengers stuck on the road when night was falling, and I am sure that party passed the night there.

There were no filling stations in China with built-in underground tanks. The truck usually carried its own fuel in a container. At the time of refueling, the driver would get down and, after putting a hose in the container, would suck the gasoline or alcohol out of the hose with his mouth to get the flow started before connecting it with the tank. All the drivers did this expertly, and then spat on the ground, and none of them seemed to mind swallowing a drop or two. Whether it is possible to get drunk on pure alcohol this way, I have no idea, but this may explain the unusual vitality of those tireless, daredevil drivers. They were among the most adventurous souls I saw in China. Sometimes they were able to buy alcohol on the road and fill the tank by means of a washbasin. On cold mornings it was necessary to pour some precious gasoline over the spark plugs and light it with a match to heat up the engine before they could persuade the alcohol to get into action. Once in a Post Office truck, a screw got lost, and the gear shift would not work. Every time the driver wanted to shift a gear, I had to lean sideways for him to reach down to the floor, lift a plank and pull a string he had put in there. Whether these things were possible or not, I do not care to argue, but I saw them done.

The Northwest Transportation drivers were exceptional. They took excellent care of their cars; and also the highway was kept in good shape, until it deteriorated at the Szechuen border. The section on the border was the worst and most dangerous. There were hairpin bends overlooking deep canyons at the point called "Number One Pass of West Tsin." The turns were sharp and the road was narrow, in places impossible for two cars to pass. But with a careful driver, and the brakes and horn in good condition, it was safe enough.

Coming out of the giddy turns of the First Pass, the road began to descend. This is Szechuen territory. There was a complete change of landscape, and one gasped at a scene of idyllic grandeur. For here the Chialing flowed south to meet the Yangtse at Chungking.

Flying through the mountain passes of West Tsin, famed of old,
One left a cloud of "phantom horses" whirling the dust-wind.
For a glad surprise the Chialing turned up to bear me company,
With hills and ponds and fishing rafts to invite the traveler's pause.

The sunset across the river at Kwangyuan, with mists enveloping the graceful hills, was like a perfect painting of Mi Fei. I got out of the truck and stood gazing for a long time.

Across the bank the evening sun was setting behind the distant hills.
A picture untouched by a dot or stroke of the master's hand.
Whence came such a scroll of the Mi family?
I stood in the open, transfixed, until my sleeves were filled with cold.

At Kwangyuan I was to leave the truck and go on a mail bus, because the convoy was going to Chungking, while I was destined for Chengtu. As soon as we arrived, the driver, tired as he was, started to wash his truck, and the next morning he gave the engine a careful checkup. He would not accept a tip from me for the two-day service. I was greatly impressed by the way the Transportation Company was run, on a business basis, with good, efficient management. The company paid its staff well, looked after their welfare, and insisted on honesty and efficiency. I was told that in the retreat from Burma the company was able to save its entire rolling stock without loss.

A dust storm held me up at Kwangyuan for two nights. The dust storms coming from over the mountains here are notorious, and in spite of the beauty of the countryside, Kwangyuan was the dirtiest town I ever saw. I never saw so many people suffering from catarrh, and coughing and spitting about the streets, as in this town. It was, however, an important communications center, where all trucks to and from the Northwest had to pass. I saw hundreds of trucks standing in various compounds, and among them five or six American army trucks with American soldiers on them.

The provincial levies in this part were not well-disciplined, as I had occasion to see that night when I went to the theater. There was an interesting comedy about a wife punishing an unfaithful husband, played by amateur actors and actresses. Some American soldiers came in to see the show. The local commander asked them to sit in the front seats with their interpreter, and I helped to explain the play to them at intervals. We were enjoying the performance, when suddenly the orchestra on the stage came to a stop. There were shouts and the clicks of rifles from the entrance at the back. The audience stood up to look. The commander rose from his seat and shouted, "Quiet! Maintain order!" I could not explain to the American soldiers what it was about. Sensing a fire or a riot, one tall, husky American soldier was making for the stage, when everything became quiet again. Some

Chinese soldiers had got into a quarrel, demanding to come in without tickets. The play was resumed, but the American soldiers decided they had better leave the place and went out with their interpreter. They were wise, for after another ten minutes, there were again shouts and clicks of rifles, and it looked like another brawl. The audience became uneasy and some began to leave, and I left with them.

On the third day the storm abated a little. Early in the morning I went to the Post Office to see what chance there was of a mail bus leaving. The Post Office keeps a bus service running on schedule and would sell one or two tickets for the journey as an accommodation to the public. In the waiting room the bare table and few chairs were covered with a thick coating of dust, so that they were of the same color as the floor, and the wind churned the dust from one corner to another. I was told that a man had been sent out to inquire about the ferry.

At first I could not understand what the storm had to do with the departure of a bus. But I was informed that there were two rivers to cross by ferries and the boatmen refused to cross when the wind was high. Sometimes a whole line of military trucks had to wait for hours or even days on the bank. This was an important motor route, but there was no steel for building a bridge across the broad rivers.

Resigned to further waiting, I asked for a copy of the novel *Three Kingdoms* and spent the morning writing scrolls which some friends asked me to write. These are the social obligations of a traveling scholar. One of the poems I wrote was:

> *A dust storm blinds the eyes from the Kwangyuan sky,*
> *And the boatman at the ancient ferry was afraid to cross.*
> *May I ask where I may borrow a good romance*
> *Wherewith to lighten the traveler's heavy-hanging hours?*

After lunch, the news came suddenly that we were to start. It was already two o'clock and there were two rivers to cross, and each one might take half an hour to three-quarters, depending on how long we had to wait for the ferry. We would probably not be able to reach Tsutung until midnight.

There were three of us in the front seat, including the assistant who looked after the truckload of mail. The driver was a fat, jovial, and much-traveled fellow. He came from Shanghai and had been on the Lashio-Kunming run. The assistant sang opera airs all the way, while the driver followed him occasionally in snatches. The route led through enchanting scenery, the historic *chienko,* or "Sword Towers." A stretch of ten miles, between Big Sword Mountain and Little Sword Mountain, was a strategic military pass called the Sword Gate Pass. The mountains were capped by strange rocks forty to a hundred feet high, perfectly even at the top and smooth on the sides, sometimes half a mile long and looking exactly like a fortress wall. It was at this pass that Chiang Wei successfully resisted Chung Huei's army from the North. Ancient historical records speak of "flying towers" (that is, suspended gangways, I presume,) spanning the sky between the rocks, built by Chuko Liang for his army to pass through. Some take it that this is the origin of the name Sword Towers, and it may well be correct. But the rocks themselves seemed to resemble perfectly a fortress, and in places where the giant cliffs came together straight as a wall, leaving a passage looking as if cleft by the sword of some celestial giant, the term Sword Gate Pass would seem to require no further explanation.

For a long time, these strange-looking cliffs remained in sight. In the distance there were whole ranges of these cliffs facing in one general direction like sea surfs moving toward the shore, gradually rising on one side, and abruptly ending in perfectly straight precipices on the other.

When we reached Wulienyi, the earth was completely wrapped in darkness. Our truck stopped a short way outside the city, and the driver tried to refuel the car by lighting matches to look at the gasoline in that inky dark. Solicitous for his safety as well as the truck's and my own, I took out a feeble flashlight which threatened to pass out at any time, and hoped he could see clearly enough not to drink in the gasoline through his nose. Flashlights, by the way, were in little use. When I was in China back in 1940 almost everybody had a flashlight when going into an air-raid shelter, but with inflation the native-made batteries had become too expensive. I asked the driver if he was going on, and he said yes. "When shall we reach Tsutung?" I asked. "Who knows?" was his reply. "But we will get there tonight."

He told me to go to the city and find something to eat. Leaving the feeble flashlight with him, I groped in the pitch dark on an unknown road. My search for food was fruitless, and thinking that it was my duty to give him a good dinner for his obliging spirit, I groped back in the dark again and said I would rather wait for him to finish refueling and then we would find food together. By that time the flashlight had gone out, but he seemed to know his way about and had succeeded in obtaining a small oil lamp from a boy, whom he sent about as a king sends about a page.

When this was done, we went into the city together and entered a restaurant. He marched, almost like a conquering hero, into the restaurant, where everybody seemed to know him and treated him with great respect. Assuming the position of a host, I ordered a big fish among other dishes. Then the driver went to the kitchen, picking out what was good and available. When we had started eating, I began to wonder why the fish hadn't come. "I have canceled it," he said briefly, and continued eating with great gusto. After the meal, when I called for the check, I was told that it had been paid for already by the driver. The dinner cost about one hundred fifty dollars for the three of us. I insisted on paying, but he would not hear of it. The restaurant owner was on his side and refused to take my money even when I proposed to leave two hundred dollars as credit, since the driver would be passing here often. So it turned out that I was the guest and he the host. I could only present him with some packages of cigarettes, which cost fifty dollars a package, and these he finally accepted.

We started, after the supper, refreshed in body and spirit. He was feeling fine and was red in the face after a little wine. We had to cross another high mountain in the dark. For an hour I could hear the sound of our truck grinding up the hill, rumbling for miles across the valley, ripping the silence of the night. Then I dozed off careless of what might happen. When we came to Tsutung it was already past midnight. The city gate was closed and the guards had gone off to bed. After we had tooted the horn for about ten minutes, the gate was opened by a sleepy guard. A Post Office truck had the best right to demand entrance. Someone went to find a place for me to sleep at one of the hotels, and I took my small suitcase and blanket and said good-by to the jolly driver.

I think it was called the Huapei Hotel. This was my first experience at a cheap inland inn. Since everybody had gone to sleep, including the innkeeper, it took considerable knocking to get the door opened. The house was pitch dark, and it took the man another five minutes to find a match. I was not in a mood to choose, and would be thankful for a place to lie down at all. Luckily there was a room free, with two beds, one occupied by a waiter who was snoring in his sleep. The innkeeper roused him and asked him to vacate the room, which he did grouchily and somnambulantly. I wanted to wash and have a cup of hot tea, but there was nothing to be had.

The bed was of the poorest kind, a rough unpainted wooden frame with a few boards, and I did not like the look of the bedding. I peeped under the mattress and saw it was made of straw. Changing into night-clothes was clearly out of the question. I decided to put my blanket over everything and sleep on top in my fur gown just as I was, with shoes and socks on. The room was barely seven feet wide, separated from the other rooms by wooden walls only ten feet high, leaving the top part unpartitioned. I soon found that I could hear the snoring of the other guests all over the house. However, I could stretch out com-fortably and fell into sleep.

The next morning I discovered that a company of recruits had been stopping in the hotel that night. The hall bustled with men in gray, dusty uniforms with a sergeant in charge. I went out to get something to eat, and found a woman selling sweetened bean whey and eggs and ordered some boiled eggs and bean whey. While I was eating my breakfast on the street outside the hotel, the recruits gathered in the hall for breakfast. While the sergeant stood at the entrance, groups squatted on the ground holding bowls of rice congee and took vegeta-bles from a big common dish in the center.

How different from the soldiers of the North! These were recruits on their way to some distant camp to be trained before being incor-porated in the regular units. They looked more like a labor battalion. They were thin and small as the average Szechuen people are, and some were mere boys of fifteen or sixteen. I talked with some of them and learned that they had come from districts near by. They had no idea where they were going. Judged by local conditions, the hardships were not too great. They were given two meals a day, and many farmers here had two meals a day and seldom ate meat. And they were inured to marching in straw sandals. This really accounts for the Chinese soldier's endurance under physical hardships which might be considered impossible for the better-cared-for and better-fed soldiers of the West. But judged by the standards of a better-living economic society, where the general level is much higher, their conditions were deplorable. There is nothing to compare with the way in which the American Army *and the American nation* look after their soldiers.

The saddest part of the Chinese war, as I saw it during this journey, is the conscription system. It is still on a strictly primitive level, and medical supplies and facilities are woefully inadequate. Once I passed on a highway a troop of soldiers marching uphill. Marching up a hill would be nothing for a soldier in good health, and all soldiers have to march hundreds of miles. But I saw a man who was ill and unfit to walk. He lagged behind and, resting his arm on a fellow soldier's shoulder, staggered along. That was how it was. That soldier should never have been permitted to walk at all. Where, oh where, were the hospitals and nurses? You say that transportation is lacking in China, and all travel is synonymous with hardship in Chinese terms. Still these men were soldiers, fighting for our country. It was just not right. They had no leaves of absence, and once taken from their homes, their parents and wives might not see them again for years, and most probably would never hear from them, until perhaps a year after the war a son or husband might walk back home and suddenly and without notice turn up alive.

Has the status of the Chinese soldier changed? I think not. I saw everywhere slogans written on village walls, "Good sons ought to become soldiers." This was an effort to reverse the Chinese traditional proverb, "Good iron is not made into nails, and good sons are not made soldiers." When I talked with President Chiang Kai-shek about the condition of our soldiers, I made bold to remark that it was more important to "treat soldiers like good sons." I have little complaint of the Army, knowing its financial difficulties. In fact I think that the Army owes nothing to the nation, but rather that the nation owes something to the Army. The Army has done a stupendous job, under impossible conditions. It accepts lower pay than civilian government employees. It lives on rations if the merchants don't. The Army is conscious of the hardships of its soldiers and tries to do its best. In the summer of 1943, many soldiers died of dysentery and other illnesses on the roadside in Kweichow. When I was traveling there in the beginning of 1944, I was glad to find that this condition had been stopped, and that every ten miles on the road from Kweichow to Yünnan there were stations for the care of the soldiers. These were called "Stations for Co-operation between the People and the Soldiers," but Minister Ho Yingchin told me actually the money for the provisions at these stations came from the Army and not from the people. Chinese civilians do not look after the soldiers passing through but think it is the government's and the Army's business.

I hated this attitude. I suggested to President Chiang on my return that at least the schools and the Sanmin Chuyi Youth Corps in every town might make it their job to look after our soldiers' needs while in town. The Sanmin Chuyi Youth Corps always has comparatively good and sometimes spacious buildings and has a Social Service Department. It seems that social service should begin with service to the soldiers in time of war.

The Chinese Army is doing its best. Every time questions arose about raising the salaries of the civilian government employees, Minister Ho Yingchin demanded, What of the Army? The Army has about five million soldiers, and supposing a soldier costs only five hundred dollars a month to feed, which is a starvation ration, the payroll would amount to two and a half billion Chinese dollars a month. Increases were made for the wounded soldiers in hospitals, but such increases spread out among millions could mean little relief against the skyrocketing prices. An increase of thirty dollars per month for each wounded soldier's food would buy perhaps three heads of cabbage. No matter what the Army can do for the soldiers, it is never enough, and our soldiers cannot be "treated like good sons" until the social attitude toward the soldiers changes and the people, the civilians, treat them that way. No chamber of commerce can say it cannot provide a hundred thousand dollars a month for sick soldiers in its city or neighborhood. This was the greatest single difference I found between China and America at war. It is something social, rather than legal or administrative.

Yes, I wanted to see a fine-looking Chinese Army, smartly dressed and smartly equipped, parading down some avenue, with tanks and artillery, led by an exciting, heart-cheering shining brass band, with piping clarinets and deep trombones. I wanted to see Chinese soldiers passing in the streets, each walking arm in arm with two girls, and worshiped and adored and fussed over. I wanted to see the soldiers returning on leave, and an A.P.O. running the fastest and best mail system for the soldiers, bringing love and messages of good cheer from their relatives. I wanted to see the soldiers carried on the shoulders of the civilians in their home towns. All this evidently could not be. Yet these soldiers fight. Of their valor and endurance and the will to fight and give the devil his due, there is unanimous testimony. They have proved it repeatedly in the seven years of war, in their victories and in their defeats, exacting a price from the enemy for every inch of territory conquered. They proved it during the battle of Changteh, in the winter of 1943, when the most fantastic rumors were being whispered in Japanese and American "well-informed" circles that the Chinese Army had neither the will nor the physical fitness to fight. They proved it at the Salween front, with the help of some American equipment, and they proved it in the fight around Hengyang, without American training and without American equipment. Somebody is awfully wrong about these soldiers. Some American officers who visited Changteh after the battle satisfied themselves about the fighting spirit of these soldiers, but too few of them went far enough.

There must be an explanation. What one sees of the conditions of the recruits at the rear, dusty and bedraggled and often sickly and half-starved in appearance, is not true of the soldiers at the front. Once a man is incorporated in a regimental unit and sent to the front, it is the commander's job to keep him in good shape. In the front area, which extends from a hundred to a hundred fifty miles in depth, life is organized primarily for the Army. There are better sanitation facilities and medical care; the whole roadless area is under the control of the Army; there is close co-operation between the farmers and soldiers in transportation and provisions, and soldiers even grow their own vegetables. They are better fed and better cared for; they have the best of everything, although that best may not be so much. Actually, on my visit to Changsha, I learned that the nearer the front, the better the conditions and the greater the sense of security.

I left Tsutung with the mail truck for Chengtu. Now we were traveling on level, rich, and populous plains. The Szechuen landscape offered an unmistakable contrast to the plains of Shensi. Here were rice paddies and bamboo groves and sparse cypresses, never thick enough to form copses, but standing like sentinels in detail formation over the low slopes of ancient hills. The reflections of the sky and clouds in the rice paddies lent it a softness strangely reminiscent of Kiangnan (southern Kiangsu). Here, too, were fields of peas, remarkably green in winter. It was a rich and well-watered country, thanks to the genius of Li Ping, who built the irrigation system two thousands years ago. The Szechuen people boast that the farmers could have three crops a year, and without rain for a year, would still suffer no drought.

This was a country all its own, secluded in the West and fortified against the rest of China by formidable mountain ranges and the awe-inspiring Yangtse Gorges. It is a country as big as France and has a population of forty-five millions. No wonder the warlords of Szechuen were incredibly rich. I remembered that there were four hundred and seventy-three minor civil wars in Szechuen in the first twenty years of the Republic after 1912. Those warlords were reputed to have built beautiful mansions, with enameled bathtubs and white-tiled latrines imported from Shanghai, but I never saw any of them. It had been a land rich in opium, through the warlords' exacting a tax which no farmer could pay except by planting the high-priced drug. Ten or fifteen years ago, I understand, even the children of well-to-do families smoked opium. Parents thought it a good way to tie their sons to the home and prevent them from committing escapades abroad. Only in the year before the war did the influence of the Central government begin to penetrate to this province, and only since the removal of the national capital to Chungking has the authority of the government had real control here. General Yang Sen, a former Szechuen "warlord," has made his army completely a part of the national army, and he has been fighting and serving on the Hunan front all these war years.

Here is China's ancient inland, transformed now into the base of resistance. The extension of the authority of the Central government in Western China began with Szechuen. In Yünnan, the process did not start till the Japanese occupied Nanning in 1939. Even in the years when the Burma Road was open, Central control there was still incomplete, and the most progress has been made in the past two years. Right up to the time I left China, adjustments and compromises in favor of the Central government were still being made at Kunming. The last of the semi-independent regimes to come under the direct control of the Central government is Sinkiang, which made a dramatic turn in 1942. This happened through the murder of the Governor's brother by the latter's Communist wife in an effort to isolate the Governor and strengthen Soviet control of the province. But it had the opposite effect. Governor Sheng being a Chinese with the stubborn Chinese family loyalty, this produced in him such a violent reaction and hatred of the Communists that he turned completely over to Chungking, and the Chinese Communists had to decamp precipitously. There used to be a time when a Chinese traveling in Sinkiang provided with credentials of the Central government but without Communist permission did so at great risk.

The massacre of the Szechuen people by Chang Hsienchung at the end of the Ming dynasty left a permanent effect on the people of the province. Chang was a maniac for manslaughter, whose story I referred to in *A Leaf in the Storm*. These massacres practically wiped out the population of Szechuen. As late as the latter part of the seventeenth century, during the reign of Emperor Kanghsi, it was recorded that most of the old people who still survived were maimed, with an ear or an arm cut off. The story of the horrors of these days still is told with a good deal of savor in the tea shops of Chengtu. There still stands in the museum in the Shaocheng Park in that city a monument erected by the king of homicide maniacs. "Heaven has shown every virtue toward men. Man has not one simple virtue toward Heaven. Kill, kill, kill, kill, kill, kill, kill!" This was a triplet in seven-word lines. What a religious slogan for the slaughter of men! No wonder the country was ripe for conquest and the Ming house had to fall. Of all the Chinese dynasties, I have the greatest contempt for the Mings. In spite of a certain flowering of literary and artistic blossoms, it was a sad story for the people of Szechuen.

I have been puzzled by the small stature of Szechuen men and women, and have wondered where they came from. They did not mix with the *lolo* of western Szechuen. After the country-wide ravage and massacres, I suppose people filtered in from mountainous Kwei-chow and from other neighboring provinces. Once in a while, one is able to meet a man of Szechuen who claims he is a real "Szechuenese," that is, his ancestors were here before the Chang Hsienchung days.

But the land is still rich and the country populous. It has salt, sugar, rice, wheat, oil, fat, meat, fowl, and flowers, fruits, and vegetables of every kind—and a little milk. South of the Sword Gate Pass I could smell oranges, and the nearer I came to Chengtu, the more luscious and beautiful the oranges became. On the pre-industrial level, it is economically self-sufficient. As the traveler enters the province, he notices an immediate change in the abundance of things at the shops and restaurants, and sees people lounging or lolling in crowded tea shops.

At Mienyang, when our car stopped on the bank of the Fou River waiting for the ferry, I heard a brass band, a real brass band. I could not believe my own ears. Nothing could be more surprising and pleasing than that sound and the sight I saw across the river. There was a wooden bridge, fully a hundred yards long, on our right. Seven or eight companies of soldiers were coming over the bridge. They were clean and healthy-looking; their uniforms and their bamboo-matted hats were new; the rectangular bamboo baskets they carried on their backs as knapsacks were new; the rolled blankets inside were new. There was no doubt that these soldiers had just completed their training and were starting on their march to the front as replacements. What a good idea to send them off with a brass band, and what a cheerful sound it was! It was what I wanted to see being done for our soldiers. It offered a striking contrast to the recruits I had seen only that same morning at Tsutung, and I hoped they were destined for training.

Then something amusing happened. The company that had come

over halted on the bank. So did the companies on the other side. Hundreds of people who had gathered on the bank were looking at a floating black object on our left, four hundred yards down the river. It was the head of a man, bobbing above the water and slowly moving along. It was a deserter, some thought. While crossing the bridge, the man had happened to slip down and fall into the river. The river here was fairly deep, and the man would certainly have been drowned if he were not a good swimmer. Anyway, he had got that far and was still afloat. Then he came to a shallow place and stopped moving. A boat was pushed out from the bank opposite toward him, and the soldiers in the boat waded into the water and stood over him, but for half a minute he remained still. They hauled him up, and then I saw that he could walk by himself, the water there coming up only a little way above his ankles. Was he really a deserter, or had he merely fallen down by accident? By that time our car was halfway across the river, on the ferry boat punted by poles. I wanted to know what became of that man. But the mail truck had to go on its way.

The Post Office runs its mail on the Northwest Highway by the relay system, in four sections of a day's journey each. I was therefore on another truck that day. The horn of this truck did not work. The driver got down to tinker with it; he set up an elaborate system of tin cans and cardboard to keep something in contact, and then set up another elaborate system of wires and strings to keep the tin cans and cardboard in place. These drivers insisted on being called "conductor" (*szechi*, or *szechiyuan*), and woe to the man who called them "chauffeur" (*chehfu*) by mistake, for he would never reach his destination. But since they had a genius for improvisation, they deserved a special title "improvisator" to be pronounced like "imperator," rather than just "improviser." After this tinkering process, the horn sighed feebly like a good child in pain, afraid to cause his parents trouble. It worked for some time, and then refused to moan any more. A more drastic measure was required. The driver took the whole elaborate structure down and threw it on the ground as if it were no longer of any consequence. He took the cap off, cleaned the top, wiped it, blew at it, shook it, and almost kissed it. Marvel of marvels, the baby began to moan gently, but then it stopped completely.

"What are you going to do next?" I asked.

"That is nothing. A horn is not necessary," he said.

So that afternoon every time we came to a town, and there were many as we approached Chengtu, the assistant would drum on the side door with the palm of his hand as our truck rolled through the crowded streets, and the crowd always separated neatly before us. The noise was particularly loud before we turned a corner. First, it was *bang-bang,* then as the assistant's palm got hot and he used his fist, it became *dum-dum.* Finally even his fist got hot, and he changed to an iron poker, and it was *whack, bang, whack, bang,* pitched definitely on a higher key. I concluded that the crowd separated because they heard the thunderous rumble of the truck anyway and not because of the *clack-clack* or the *bang-bang,* and that all this drumming and pounding and whacking and rapping was unnecessary. So few things are necessary in life, when one comes to think of it. I found that the breaking down of the horn was among the commonest experiences with highway trucks, and that all chauffeurs resorted to this practice of pounding the side door as they came to a crowd in the street.

We therefore arrived at Chengtu literally with a bang and not with a whimper. I do not know whether the poker got hot too, but it might well have. There was certainly something triumphant about the clamor and clangor with which we entered the capital of Szechuen province.

13

OLD CHENGTU

CHENGTU is an old, old city, with a history of two thousand years. On the rich plains of Szechuen life here long ago developed an ease and comfort that Szechuen people talk about with pride, although much of that peculiar milieu and atmosphere is now gone.

The old city wall still stands, but the city gates have been torn down since an air raid early in the war, when a number of women and children were trampled to death trying to jam through them. When I was there, the site of the Southern Gate was being paved and transformed into a broad macadamized road. Two such modernized streets, fully forty or fifty feet wide, ran at right angles through the center of the town, and were lined with many shops stocked with an abundance of goods. In this section there was the atmosphere of a prosperous big city.

I put up at the *Lichihsheh,* a fine, big three-storied building, built before the war for a club which was a kind of Chinese Army Y.M.C.A. It had over sixty rooms, with a spacious lobby and dining room where foreign food was served. The building was now designated for the accommodation of the American Air Force, and some special guests, but not many American aviators had come to Chengtu at this time. Only a few people were there, including three Russian officers who had been there for several years.

Since Chengtu is flat, many rickshaws were available. After the scarcity of rickshaws and the godlike indifference of the pullers at Chungking, this was a great comfort. Riding through the streets of Chengtu early that mild December evening, I realized how the leisurely life of the city had developed. Even as the open café life of Paris was made possible by the fairly uniform climate in summer and winter, so the outdoor teahouses and night fairs grew out of the mild climate of Chengtu. The fur gown which I had worn during my whole journey proved too warm. A man can go through the winter there with only cotton padded gowns.

One of the best ways of testing a Chinese city's cultural standards is just to look at the calligraphy on the shop signs and parlor scrolls. Where the standard of excellence is high, bad calligraphers dare not show their hands, for connoisseurs pooh-pooh the second-rate. In Chengtu old scholars, poets, painters, and calligraphers still live within their stormed and much-battered fortress. Certain established artists and their followers form their cliques and coteries, and these rather resent the intrusion of an outsider from down the river. I knew a first class painter, one of the best living in China, who in criticizing the Szechuen artists raised a storm of resentment in the city conscious of its own culture.

In the shop signs I noticed a quality of sophistication associated with old cultures. I am sure this sophistication originated from the teahouses, and perhaps from the opium couch. There are two kinds of shop names, the commercial and the artistic (and in the case of English firms there are also the neutral names, like "Montgomery," "Harper's," "Abercombie," etc., which suggest absolutely nothing). Commercial shopkeepers are fond of words like *hsing, lung, sheng* (all meaning "prosperity") and *ch'uan* ("gushing spring"), *yung* ("gushing forth" of gold as water from a spring), etc. The artistic names are chiefly used by wine restaurants and places of amusement. Here in Chengtu man's fancy runs wild and becomes irrepressible. One wine restaurant is called *Pu Tsui Wu Kwei,* or "Ye Shall Not Return Home Without Getting Drunk." A famous restaurant goes by the playful and intimate name of "Sister-in-law's Show" (*Kukuyen*) and in competition with it there is one by the name of "Elder Brother's Fry" (*Kokots'ao*). I saw on one restaurant a signboard having three words, written "Mouth, Mouth-Mouth, Mouth-Mouth-Mouth." The first and last words are commonly understood, three "mouths" meaning to "sample" food, tea, or wine. But the middle word with two "mouths" is simply unpronounceable. I asked a few learned friends, and none of them knew how it should be pronounced or what it meant. They were sure the word existed in the *Kanghsi Dictionary,* which I do not doubt. But one should not be expected to consult a dictionary when reading shop signs.

A big shop selling sweetmeats had two parallel signboards, both new, having three words each, one set written with the "radicals" and the other set without. It is as though a Doubleday, Doran or Houghton, Mifflin shop were to bear two signs, the second one dropping the first letters and reading "Oubleday, Oran" or "Oughton, Ifflin." No one could tell which was the correct name of the shop. A sweetmeat shop is usually opened by a middle-aged merchant, supposed to be engaged in serious business to make money; little benefit can accrue to a shop from having two names, to be pronounced differently! This is a foggy state of mind, born on the opium couch, I fear, and appreciated by a community with the hedonistic faith that all life is just a little joke.

At the night fair, called *yehshih,* long rows of goods were spread on the sidewalks, beneath oil lamps, and a big crowd was idling along and looking at the things, more for loafing's sake than to buy anything in particular. The fair had almost everything, from fruit and candies to antiques and secondhand books. Perhaps it was not as exciting for "finds" as the Thieves' Market at night in the French Concession at Shanghai, but it was quite charming and one had the pleasure of satisfying the law-abiding instinct. As in all great old cities, there were interesting things to pick up if one had the leisure to look for them. I bought a fascinating wire contrivance that was the product of a most ingenious mind. It was not really a puzzle, but it could change at the slightest touch into twenty-eight different shapes, from a drum to a flower-vase or a perfect sphere. It was formed of interconnected rings which acted upon one another and opened or closed at different angles uniformly, and it was so well made that it would stay in any shape. The top and bottom would open out or flatten at will, and the side of the drum could be pressed out or in. Finally, the whole thing could be flattened like a collapsible top hat. Some extraordinarily clever wire puzzles have been developed in China, of which those seen in this country are only simple varieties. I also bought a complicated finger ring of four interlocked pieces fitted into a perfect pattern, which, once jumbled, would take the uninitiated more time to fit together than a five-hundred-piece jigsaw puzzle. I have seen a simple variety of this ring puzzle made in Persia, but do not know whether the Persians copied the idea from the Chinese, or the Chinese from the Persians.

Many people compare the life here to that of Peking, calling it "Little Peiping." As an ardent admirer of Peking, I object. Perhaps much of what was once the established way of living in old Chengtu is gone, perhaps the glory of its great days at the end of the Manchu dynasty has vanished. But there is only one Peking in the world; even the Japanese and the war cannot destroy the Peking way of life. What people mean when they compare Chengtu to Peking is that it has many of the charms of an old city. It has two or three streets where antiques and curios are sold. It has secondhand bookshops; there are good experts at pasting and mending old scrolls of painting, and there is still a shop that produces the most artistic handmade, hand-printed, colored letter paper. I suppose the name of this shop is resented nowadays, harking back to the olden days of *Dream of the Red Chamber*. It is called *Shihpei,* or "Maidservant of Poetry," assuming that there are a number of other pretty maidservants, one attending especially to wine, another to chess, another to painting utensils, still another to musical instruments, and a special one, in red sleeves, attending to incense. The letter paper is designed by famous artists, printed in pale tints of grey or soft green and red. I bought some of this paper, one design I chose being a copy of a Tunhwang portrait of a Tang beauty. The mouth was so well shaped and rouged that I had not the heart to write across it, but had to break the lines when I wrote letters home.

In a fascinating street of the ancient handicrafts, copper wires were drawn, animal bone was made into buttons, buffalo horn was ground and shaped into trinket boxes, and mahjong sets were carved and polished out of ivory, all as they were done centuries ago. And everywhere there were old "small restaurants," each famous for some particular dish. It would take more than a fortnight to sample all of them.

Every visitor to Chengtu must see the Black Lamb Temple (to Laotse), the temple to Chuko Liang, and the temple in honor of Tu Fu, erected on the site of his studio built in his old age—all a few miles from the Small West Gate, southwest of the city. The Tu Fu studio was situated in a cypress grove. There is irony in the fact that the grounds of this anti-war poet are used now for a military academy. His statue looks out on barracks for the cadets, and from his seat of honor he can see rows of iron helmets placed on the neatly folded bedding on the bunks. Along the long corridors were a series of drawings for teaching artillery and machine-gun tactics, so that the walls of the compound looked like an illustrated army manual. Two or three hundred cadets were sitting at desks on the open grounds taking an examination. Tu Fu was against civil war, but I am sure he would solidly support this war to preserve China's national integrity. How he would be able to write about the toils and hardships and sentiments of our people in this age, transforming the very sorrows into lines of immortal beauty!

Practically every day in Chengtu I went to Huahsipa, the site of the West China University, outside the South City. It is there that many exiled universities are located, Chilu University (from Shantung), Nanking University and Ginling College for Women (from Nanking), and the Central School of Medicine, besides the original West China University, all sharing its spacious grounds and its fine brick buildings. Dr. Kuo Yushou, American-educated commissioner of education for the province, has his home there. I saw a good deal of Lo Chungshu, dean of arts, and Nyi Chingyuan, professor of philosophy.

Professor Nyi, dressed in a foreign tweed suit and carrying a cane, and Mr. Chiang Yunkang, a well-known Szechuen poet, went with me on one particularly interesting trip. I depended very much on Mr. Chiang for local history and customs, as he knew the city well. We began with breakfast at a famous restaurant, the Tsingningkuan, in the Shaocheng Park. The park was a large, rambling place in the South City. Even at that early hour groups of young men and women and a few older people were sitting in the open tea house.

The breakfast was a revelation. The so-called Szechuen restaurants down the river and in the coastal cities are largely corrupted, and this was my first taste of genuine Szechuen cuisine at its best. I had expected various stuffed buns and dumplings, as at Soochow or Yangchow. Actually, it was more than a substantial lunch. We had a dish of *wantou* pea soup, and with the first spoonful, I was completely won over. The *wantou* is a kind of beans, and I have hated beans all my life. No one would have thought that anything that goes by the name of beans could have the creamy tenderness of whey and the taste and delicacy of "velvet chicken." But after tasting *wantou* cooked in the

Szechuen manner, fragrant and soft and mellow, caressing the palate with its inimitable tenderness, one must concede that it is one of the most delectable and fragrant foods produced by nature, and one can excuse the boasts of the citizens of Chengtu. There was also a sentimental dish, called "nine-times-twisted intestines," which was a gourmet's dream and, like unique creations of the senses, defies description by cold words. It is difficult to imagine anything richer and more satisfying all around to the palate. The reason people came here so early was to eat this dish, for by noon many of the special parts from the pigs freshly killed that day would all be sold.

Looking at the groups about us, Mr. Chiang said, "That is the teahouse culture." I asked what he meant and he explained. It is a life, not confined like "literary teas" to a coterie, but shared in public, in the open, or in rooms only partly closed, where one passes hours in conversation and loquacious peregrinations on topics that are strictly not one's own business, and in smoking the water pipe, reading newspapers, exchanging gossip, chewing melon seeds, and buying odd curios, and at certain restaurants at definite hours in the evenings, listening to musical monologues and storytelling by favorite professionals or blind minstrels. Conversations at the teahouses are supposed to be for the public, and strangers at neighboring tables are free to break in with a remark or express a difference of opinion on an overheard topic. Out of such idle chatting grew the special art of killing time called *p'ai lungmenchen,* a peculiar Szechuen expression, the nearest English equivalent for which is "playing armchair strategist." Often it is just a haphazard, rambling "bull session." By the practice of this art of conversation one learns to diagnose human motives and current politics with the cutting precision of a surgeon's scalpel. Szechuen people in general have learned to decorate their conversation with wise saws and learned instances, to a much greater extent than people from other provinces. The latter maintain that Szechuen people can always hold their own just because they can by their gift of gab wear other people down. The habit of frequenting teahouses is especially widespread, not only in Chengtu, but throughout Szechuen. As soon as I entered the province, I had noticed in every town many tea shops with low, shining, and well-used bamboo easy chairs and people lolling in them. Some "hotels" have only a few dark rooms at the back or on the upper floor, but a spacious tearoom in the lobby, which is the main thing.

By the time we got through breakfast, it was about ten. We agreed it would be wise to call it an early lunch, and set out to visit the

Wenshu Temple far out in the North City. This is a large ancient temple with an illustrious history in the past and therefore has a collection of Buddhist Thibetan classics, and various odds and ends. With Mr. Chiang as our guide, we went directly to the "relics" in a locked room on the upper floor. The most imposing exhibit was a set of sixty-one volumes of the Huayen Sutra, written in human blood. I imagine it was done by the writer pricking his finger with a needle as a form of ascetic devotion and a way to please Buddha; the blood must have had to be pricked afresh with almost every stroke, in small drops, or it would clot, and the work might well have occupied ten or fifteen years of the writer's life. The color now was a pale purple. Another curious object was a portrait of Buddha embroidered by a pious lady devotee out of her own hair.

The most interesting relic that I saw on this trip to China was a mummy, known as the "flesh body" of the Sixth Patriarch (Hui-neng, A.D. 638-713), at the Nanhua Temple, a few hours' drive from Kukong, Kwangtung, which I visited later. The mummy of this famous monk (Ch'an or Zen sect) was placed sitting erect in a shrine in the middle of the temple, and on the two sides, at a distance apart, were two other mummies of other monks, also encased in shrines. The red-lacquered face was extraordinarily lifelike, totally unlike sculptures of wood, and the body was clothed in a satin robe. The head was bent and the body drooping, but the deep brick-red shining lacquer surface gave it a frightening expression. I made some inquiries and cannot be sure how the preservation was done, but two things appear certain. It was the original skeleton preserved in the position in which the monk died; how they treated the flesh I do not know. Furthermore, many coatings of lacquer were applied, with moldings of hemp cloth as understructure, and the body was hermetically sealed as the lacquer hardened. The robe and alms bowl were among the most precious relics of the temple, which I regretted not being able to see, for they were buried safely inside a pagoda when I was there, as a precaution against air raids.

Mr. Chiang next took us to visit the Well of Hsieh Tao, a kind of Chinese Hypatia, friend of famous poets like Yuan Chen, Po Chuyi, Tu Mu, and Wei Kao, with whom she exchanged poems on many occasions. Because she was a woman, and because the Wangchianglou on the bank of the river in the outskirts of the city commanded a beautiful view, perhaps this place was even more popular with the tourists and holiday makers than the studio of the male poet, Tu Fu.

The well is the one from which she drew water to make the deep-red artistic letter paper, named after her and celebrated in her own time. A large stone tablet with the three words "Hsueh Tao's Well" stands by its side. She is supposed to have left over five hundred verses. In her old age, she put on a Taoist nun's robe and established herself in a special villa called "The Tower of Singing Verse." Here there were several covered terraces erected on the riverbank. Sailing boats passed up and down the Brocade River (Chinkiang), whose deep and broad current skirts the city wall and flows on to enrich the southeastern plains.

While we were enjoying the beautiful scene on one of the terraces, Mr. Chiang remarked that there was a *yaochin* player, an old man who had wandered here from Central China years ago and made a living by playing this ancient stringed instrument to visitors at this spot. We called him to play a few pieces for us, like *The Setting Swan on the Sand Beach*. That quiet pleasure was soon turned into a comedy. A middle-aged woman, gaudily dressed, with gold bracelets and a colored shawl, came up to the terrace and ordered the musician to play something else. The musician evidently knew her by sight and quietly took up his instrument and went away. The woman grumbled a little and said, "I have plenty of money, I have plenty of money to pay." She then sat down in the musician's chair, and opened her mouth wide and began to sing in a shocking voice for our benefit. The sublime had descended to the ridiculous. A few boys standing by laughed out loud. Amused rather than annoyed, we decided it was time to go and left her singing heartily to herself.

Going down the steps, we again met the musician, who said that she was plain mad. She was the wife of a local division commander. Her husband had taken a young and pretty concubine, which must have been the cause of her insanity; the mind in self-defense had chosen to block out all further worries about faithless Man. She was now provided with plenty of money and as I saw her that day, she was certainly happy, well fed, completely free to go about as she pleased and spend her money wherever she liked, with not a single worry for the morrow. . . . Thus passed a day, like all days, full of strange excitements.

Chengtu has become an important educational center of Free China in wartime. It has a beehive of colleges and schools. Besides those already mentioned, there is also Yenching University, removed from Peiping. But it was the middle schools, with so many keen and happy faces, that were more interesting to me.

The national program of extending education aims at establishing an elementary school in every *pao,* or village unit of sixty to a hundred families, and at least one secondary school in every county. In some provinces that I traveled through, Shensi, Szechuen, Hunan, and Kwangtung, I was told that the program had been already carried out, from 90 to 95 per cent. This is important news, very important. The aim is that 90 per cent of all children of six to twelve years old will have received an elementary education at the time when universal compulsory education will be enforced. At the same time, the schools are also to give instruction to people of both sexes between fifteen and forty-five who have not had previous schooling.

The village schools have therefore a double function in extending both juvenile and adult education, and the purpose of such education is teaching civic organization and duties and rights of citizens, as well as reading and writing. The problems of establishing elective local governments are vast and complicated in view of the backwardness of the people in the towns and country, and the enforced increase of literacy seems the most essential foundation for its success. The county schools are officially known as "Center Schools," which means that they are to serve at the same time as county centers for civic reforms, working closely with the *paochia* system in matters of improved sanitation, adult education, militia training, news facilities, etc. It is estimated that in Szechuen alone, some ten to twelve million adults have been put through these adult classes.

This is one of the most distinctive and significant achievements of China during the progress of the war. Its effects are naturally slow, but they are penetrating, and give the best assurance of changing the face of China in one or two decades. I studied the working of the *paochia* system of village government, and learned how futile it is to introduce any kind of change in democratic administrative machinery without a change of the mind. The conscription system, even with the best of rules promulgated by the government, breaks down completely under the weight of abuses in the hands of some heads of the village *paochia* system. The opening of the mind will make a difference. Once conscious of its new freedom, it will demand the stopping of abuses which directly hurt the villagers' own interests, and feel a new sense of responsibility.

Dr. Kuo, the Commissioner of Education, gave me data showing the achievements already made. The number of elementary schools in

Szechuen increased from 25,044 in 1938 to 36,317 in 1942, and the number of pupils from 1,921,735 to 3,019,489. The number of secondary schools increased from 174 in 1938 to 302 in 1943; the number of students increased from 74,671 to 141,505, and the number of teachers and officers from 3,891 to 9,651. The number of normal schools increased from 35 to 47, and the number of students from 6,425 to 12,531 in the same years. In vocational education, the number of schools showed no increase, but the number of students increased from 6,574 to 8,616, and that of teachers and officers from 576 to 1,497, between 1938 and 1943. Appropriations for education showed an increase not at all commensurate with the inflation of prices. The height of such appropriations was reached during the initial years of the new program, being 13.04 and 11.64 per cent of the total provincial revenue spent for provincial schools and colleges in 1940 and 1941 respectively, and 38.60 and 31.78 per cent of the total county revenue spent for county education in the same years respectively. In 1943, the percentage came down to 5.08 per cent of the total provincial revenue spent for provincial education and to 17.17 per cent of the total county revenue spent for county education. These are some bare facts which translated into human terms will affect the shape of things only a decade from now.

While in Chengtu I heard an interesting story about the discovery of the important Stone Library at Tunhwang by Sir Aurel Stein. This is the library of ancient manuscripts of books, made before the invention of printing in China, dating back to the eighth century and earlier, and well preserved in a stone cave at Tunhwang in the dry climate of Kansuh on the border of Chinese Turkistan. The entrance to the library was blocked up, probably by the monks in times of invasion, and forgotten about in the succeeding centuries. Sir Aurel Stein was supposed to have discovered it about 1906, and he and later Paul Pelliot, the French Sinologist, took away some of these priceless manuscripts, which are now to be found in the British Museum and the Bibliothèque Nationale of Paris.

Stein's discovery was, however, disputed by Mr. Chang Ta-chien. He is the younger brother of the tiger painter Mr. Chang Shan-tse, and is considered the more talented painter. He looks very much like his brother, with a bushy, black beard, and a pot belly enclosed in a wide cloak. I found him a fascinating talker. He had just come back after spending a year studying the Tunhwang cave paintings. He raved about the voluptuousness of Tang women and was emphatic in his assertion that women with slender waists in paintings hitherto ascribed to the Tang period could not be genuine. This was probably true, at least in the case of Tunhwang and other Buddhist paintings influenced by Indian art. I have remarked elsewhere that in the images of Buddha the face is both voluptuous and feminine, and the lips are certainly sensuous. In Buddhist paintings, too, the feminine body is exposed to a degree unimaginable in orthodox Chinese painting. I have seen many pictures of "dancing bodhisattvas," copied from these and other caves in northwest Kansuh, so sparingly clothed that they might win devotees among New York café society.

Mr. Chang's story of the discovery of the Stone Library was told him first-hand by an old priest still living at Tunhwang. There was a Taoist priest by the name of Chang (no relation of the painter). He was usually addressed as Chang "Taosze"; he understood Sanskrit, and so was invited by the Buddhist priests to teach them the classics. He used to work in one of the grottos. Smoking a pipe, he used a kind of weed, called *tsitsi* grass, for lighting it. After lighting his pipe, he would stick the long weed in a crevice of the back wall. One day he stuck it deep and found that it could go through the crevice completely. He knocked at the wall and found that it was hollow. It was not difficult for him to discover that here was a door which had been blocked up. He therefore broke down the wall and discovered the pile of manuscripts. This was in the year 1900. Apart from archeological interest, the manuscripts seemed to be of no great value, many being copies of well-known Buddhist texts and folk literature. He filled two trunks with them and presented one to the county magistrate. The magistrate looked at them and thought the handwriting most common, and said that he could do better himself. One of the boxes fell into the hands of a Belgian consular official. When Sir Aurel Stein was traveling in Sinkiang, he heard of these manuscripts and went in search of the Stone Library, and found it. Certainly Stein was the first man to realize its archeological value. Without him, the library would have been dispersed in a worse manner or sealed up and forgotten again, waiting another five hundred years for a new discoverer.

Mr. Chang told us also about the vandalism that had been going on in the Caves of the Thousand Buddhas. There were more than two hundred grottos, each filled with Buddhist sculptures, and every part of the wall was covered with paintings. Caravan travelers used to stop at the grottos and cook their meals, ruining the wall paintings with smoke. During a Mohammedan revolt the Muslims destroyed many of the Buddhas with a religious fanaticism.

Mr. Chang said he had been accused of vandalism himself. On some of the walls there were successive layers of plaster. On patches of the already ruined and smoked wall surface, he discovered, underneath, another fresco of an earlier Tang period, and underneath that, still another of Sui or Tsin. He had made about fifty copies of such paintings and was preparing them for an exhibit.

I had tea with Governor Chang Chün. As minister of foreign affairs in 1936 he had conducted very interesting talks with the Japanese ambassador at Nanking, in which I heard for the first time the voice of equality in China's foreign relations. Mr. Chang is generally considered one of the ablest minds in the government. In my long talk with him this impression was confirmed. Besides an ease in his manner of expression, I found a subtle, penetrating comprehension of world politics, tempered by tact and blended with humor, which always comes from easy mastery of a topic and clarity of point of view. He is over fifty, but he looked very young and in the best of health. His talk about future relations with the Soviets in China and Russia and about Russo-Japanese relations gave me a feeling of confidence. As a native of Szechuen and governor of the province, he had a subtle job to do in dealing with the old forces still in power. But I have a feeling that he will have a more important role to play in China's future than governor of a province.

14

OUT OF THE BAMBOO AGE

IN ONE DAY'S TRIP from Chengtu it is possible to visit the irrigation and dike system at Kwanhsien, established in 250 B.C. and still in operation today. This water control has been responsible for the elimination of floods and for irrigation of the rich regions of western Szechuen for the past two thousand years.

Kwanhsien is about forty miles northwest of the city. The name itself means "Irrigation County." Here I saw the first two of the three bamboo wonders of China: the bamboo dike, the bamboo-rope bridge, and the bamboo-operated salt wells. At least the first two were constructed without a nail or a piece of metal. I suppose it is allowable to speak of the bamboo age of China, as we speak of the steel age, and the difference between Chinese and Western industry may be measured by this difference. I am afraid that while we may point to the architectural wonders of the bamboo age with some national pride, China, if given a choice between bamboo and steel today, would without a question choose steel.

The two-thousand-year-old water control system is now in charge of a modern civil engineer who speaks in terms of "duty of water" and cubic meters of flow. In the office at the headwater there is a mud model, fifteen feet wide, illustrating the topography of the entire system. The waters from the tremendous range of snow-capped mountains of Turkistan on the northwest gather into a narrow, but powerful, stream at Kwanhsien and fan out toward the plains on the south and southeast like a horse's tail. They are divided into an Inner System on the east and an Outer System on the west, consisting of various dikes, called *yen,* for the regulation of water supply. As this system is of direct benefit to the farmers, an established custom has grown up for the annual repair and maintenance of the dikes, observed like a religious ceremony under the leadership of officials.

The architects, Li Ping (first half of the third century B.C.) and his son, now have become gods, with various titles conferred by emperors in successive dynasties. The highest title, however, is that conferred by the people themselves, *"Chuenchu,"* or "Father of the Szechuen Province." Their work has struck so deeply into the popular imagination that their characters have been surrounded with many supernatural legends. The son, called "Erhlangshen," occupies a prominent place in Chinese mythology, found even in ancient works, like *Soushenchi* and *Fengshutung,* and in popular supernatural novels like *Siyuchi.* References to the irrigation system exist in many ancient geographical works, like *Huayangkuo Chih* and the *Classic On Water* (*Shuiching*), a thesis on rivers and lakes, with a famous and beautifully written commentary (third century).

In ancient times the summer torrents of the Minkiang from the Turkistan mountains, flowing directly south toward the foot of Omei Mountain, used to cause severe floods in that region, while the regions on the southeast would suffer from drought. The first engineering problem for Li Ping was to divide and regulate the flow at the headwater. The basis of the whole system lay in cutting a deep canal through a rocky hill and diverting the water into the Inner System through this bottleneck, called "Litui." Standing on the bank of the Litui, in the Conservancy Office between the Inner and Outer Systems, one saw the broad river coming down from the mountains, passing under the 552-foot-long bamboo-rope bridge about half a mile ahead. Below the bamboo-rope bridge stood the "Fish Snout" on an islet which divided the water into the two systems. Below the Fish Snout and nearer the Litui stood the bamboo-constructed dike, known as the Feishayen, or Spillway of Flying Sands. The height of this spillway regulated the volume of water that was to go into the bottleneck for the Inner System. The canal at Litui was barely twenty feet across, but a powerful current of clear mountain water flowed through it. When the water level rose to the mark "11" which meant sufficient water for the Inner System, the flow would be 300 cubic meters per second.

The underlying principle of this water control system was expressed by its founder in six Chinese words, which mean, "Dredge where the river is deep, and build dams where the water is low." This principle, engraved at the Temple to Li Ping, has been religiously followed in all the succeeding centuries. The maintenance requires constant dredging of river beds and building of dams.

The ancient technique of building dikes was to place small boulders in cages with large meshes made of split bamboo. Each cage of boulders thus held together formed in effect a solid giant boulder of several tons that could not be washed away, while the meshes and crevices acted to soften the force of the current. As these boulders settle into position, they make a perfectly even and beautiful embankment. The use of split bamboo made periodic repairs necessary, but also made them easy. A few cuts at the bamboo strips would loosen the old cage, and new ones were placed in their stead.

Out near the Fish Snout there was also a series of wooden tripods placed across the stream for making cofferdams. The dike systems below were repaired annually, the months being apportioned separately for work on the Inner and the Outer System. When one system was under repair, the water would be turned off into the other system by means of these cofferdams. Again layers of woven bamboo plastered with mud were placed between the rows of tripods, and the empty space between was filled with pebbles, sand, and gravel. Such cofferdams could therefore be shifted easily. Successive attempts were made in different dynasties to make a permanent Fish Snout for dividing the water, including one in the form of a bronze ox, but all sooner or later were washed away by the summer floods. The engineer proudly told me that reinforced concrete has now finally solved the problem.

There is a provincial levy for the maintenance of the irrigation systems, which are known under the general name of the Tukiangyen.

Taxes are seldom of such direct tangible benefit to the taxpayer, and this is gladly paid. The area irrigated covers 3,000,000 *mu* (or 500,000 acres) and the charge of a dollar per *mu* per year besides the levy of labor is almost negligible. There are altogether 526 laterals and 2,200 sublaterals branching out from the main feeder canals, and the total length of both systems is 1,171 kilometers. Thus a sound water control for preventing floods and irrigating the fields was laid down two thousand years ago in western Szechuen, through the genius of one man and his son. But this overplentiful and never-failing water supply may account also for the heavy fog and intense humidity of Chungking and its neighboring region.

After lunch we set out to visit the temple in honor of Li Ping, and the bamboo-rope bridge, a little way up the river. The mountainside was thickly covered with a delightful mixture of green and red foliage of tall trees. We followed a street along the riverbank and soon reached the temple. I was surprised to find that the temple was more in honor of the son than of the father, by the strength of the Chinese mythology which had turned the son into a popular god, nameless except that he was called Erhlangshen, or the "Second Young Master Divinity." The temple was well kept, being evidently well endowed with funds, and there were clean, new rooms, with green-painted railings, which would make delightful summer quarters, looking out on the river and the mountains beyond.

Standing there, I was told that in the deep waters below there was an iron chain still visible when the water was low. According to legend, this was the chain by means of which "Second Young Master Divinity" had subjugated the Dragon King and enchained him in his lair after a terrific combat. The motive of the legend is the popular gratitude toward Li Ping and his second son for ridding the people of the flood pest, symbolized by the Dragon King.

The Dragon King was the chief of a savage tribe that inhabited these regions of turbulent streams, their tribal name being Tselung, or Fecund Dragon. He used to exact the offering of two beautiful girls yearly from the people of the region, and "parents were afraid to weep" when their daughters were offered up. Before Li Ping could begin his work on the rivers, he had therefore first to subjugate the monster. Having failed in overtures for a peaceful settlement, he decided with his son on a strategy to capture the Dragon King.

Li Ping sent a messenger with ceremonial gifts to propose a marriage between the Dragon King's son and his daughter, a "princess," for he was of an ancient royal family. The proposal was accepted, and he disguised the Second Young Master, or Erhlang, as the bride, accompanied by an expert archer as the bride's maid. The son was a great fighter, and used to go hunting with seven of his friends, all brave warriors, riding on a white horse and leading a white hound. The princess' procession stopped at the bank of the Peach Pass, where the Fecund Dragon had his headquarters, and had drawn up his army in battle array to receive the bride. According to custom, the bridegroom had to come over to take the bride to the wedding. The ceremony was duly performed, and a wine feast was served.

During the dinner, old man Li pretended to be greatly offended at the quality of the wine, and roared out in anger. Sensing trouble from trickery, the Fecund Dragon fled outside, and Li chased him with a spear. They were soon lost in the clouds of mists over the mountains, and both disappeared from sight.

Meanwhile the "princess" threw off his bridal dress, jumped on his white horse, and led his army in fierce combat with the Dragon tribe. They set fire to the Dragon's Temple where beautiful girls were annually offered, and defeated the tribe in a bloody fight. The river water was colored red with the dead.

After the mist lifted, two black bulls were seen fighting on the bank of the river. Soon the old man Li returned, with sweat running all over his body, and said to his officers, "It is a hard fight. You must come and help. The bull facing south, with a white band around his belly is myself, and the bull facing north without a band is Fecund Dragon." Saying this, he disappeared again, and his officers dashed into the field with spears and arrows and succeeded in wounding the bull facing north. The Fecund Dragon returned to his original shape, and tried to escape into the river. However, the second Young Master whipped out a large iron chain and caught him. Having tied him up, he securely enchained him in the deep waters below, where the Temple of the Subjugated Dragon (*Fulungkwan*) now stands.

They then proceeded to exterminate the savage tribe and set fire to their lairs in the mountain forests. The people were happy to be delivered of this cruel monster, for thereafter no parents needed to give up their daughters. And when Li Ping called for work on the control of the turbulent river, the people were glad to contribute their labor, and so his great work was accomplished.

A short distance from the temple stood the bamboo-rope bridge, which

I have called the second architectural wonder of China's bamboo age. The bridge is about a hundred and fifty yards along, consisting of spans, the longest of which I believe is about a hundred feet. Legend ascribes it to a filial son who lost his mother because when he was bringing medicine back to her as she lay dying he was held up at the ferry, and therefore vowed he would build a bridge here which should make it impossible that in the future a son would ever be held up when his mother needed help. But I believe that the bamboo-rope bridge was invented of pure necessity, because the broad and swift currents here made long spans necessary. Since they could not construct such long spans by timber, nor support shorter spans by stone arches in these currents, someone thought of the suspension principle. The high bank on one side and the islet at the Fish Snout made a suspension bridge at this point possible.

There is a gate at the head of the bridge. Here on each side are a dozen solid wooden beams one foot in diameter, with horizontal spokes used for turning the beams to tighten the bamboo hawsers which hold up the bridge. These bamboo hawsers are about five inches in diameter, made of probably a hundred strands of the best split bamboo, and could be any length desired. The bamboo, which in the mountains of China sometimes grows to a height of forty feet, has developed an extreme tensile strength; as it sways in the wind, it bends gracefully but never breaks. The ropes run along the bridge like cables in a steel bridge, providing the railing and the support for the bridge floor, which is about twelve feet wide and covered with roughhewn wooden planks.

I went out halfway to the middle of the bridge, and found that walking on it was like walking on a rocking cradle placed over three feet of marshmallows. I could imagine American boys and girls jitterbugging on it and getting the unforgettable "kick" of their lives. Trapeze actors would get the same sensation that they have when they roll on the catching nets. But men and women passed over the bridge daily, and some carried burdens on their shoulders. Anyone's tendency to caper or prance was strongly discountenanced by any who happened to be passing over the bridge at the time.

The most interesting ancient industry developed in this bamboo age is, however, the salt and gas wells of Szechuen. A visit to this ancient system of wells is both a revelation of Chinese mechanical ingenuity and a vivid object lesson on the necessity for increasing efficiency of production through the use of modern machinery.

The salt industry at Tseliuching would make a fascinating "travelog" moving picture, along with the Kwanhsien dikes and the Shen Hsin underground textile mill. But such pictures would be luxuries for a blockaded and fighting China, when even the most essential machine parts for keeping the industries going cannot be flown in. I saw a modernized salt well closed up for the simple reason that steel cables for the derricks, which require constant replacements on account of erosion by the brine, could not be secured. I learned also that China's tin mines had practically stopped operations because there was no longer Diesel oil available. We cannot afford "travelogs" in wartime, even though they might be good publicity for China. Even if some American company should send someone out to make these pictures, they would only help to burn up China's precious gasoline. So we must be contented with a word picture.

The salt wells' origin is also ascribed to Li Ping, who, according to records, was reported to have discovered the first salt well at Hwayang, near Chengtu. Since the salt industry was one of the earliest to come under government monopoly and trading control, it has a long recorded history and well-established principles of administration in production and distribution. The industry was at its height in the Tang dynasty, with wells covering sixty-four *hsien,* or counties, while in the Sung dynasty there were wells in fifty-four *hsien.* As old wells dried up they were abandoned, and new sites were located. At present, the salt district centers in Fushun and Yunghsien counties, with Tseliuching ("Self-Flow Well") the busiest district. This is a short distance from Neikiang, which is a sugar center, approximately midway between Chengtu and Chungking.

On my way from Chengtu to Chungking, therefore, I was able to see both the old-method wells and the steam-operated wells at Tawenpao in Tseliuching. I had no chance to visit the electrically operated wells at Tsekung, which was far away. The geology of the place was peculiar. I saw on the way a whole city built on a mountaintop, utilizing a long ridge of rock cliffs around the top as its city wall, reminding one of medieval times when such a fortified city, protected by natural topography, would be safe from rebellious armies or roving bandits. On the approach to Tseliuching one saw derricks dotting the horizon and realized that the whole region lived, traded, and prospered on salt.

Szechuen friends said that the prospecting and drilling of these wells had all the romance and fascination of prospecting oil in the American West. Families staked their whole fortune on a well, requiring years

205

of drilling, and sometimes went broke before they struck salt. There is a well called the Golden Hair Brooch. A family worked it for about three years, drilling to about 3,000 feet underground, and still discovered no salt. Yet salt might lie only a few feet deeper, and it was a pity to give up after the years of work and expenditure of money. The wife therefore took out her last golden hair brooch and sold it to pay the workmen for another day's work. Still they had no luck. The family, however, had treated the workmen well and fairly, and the workmen felt so sorry for them that they offered to dig another five days without pay. On the third day, they struck salt, and their years of labor were rewarded. The family was able to live on that well for a couple of generations. It really should have been called the Well of Compassionate Labor.

The old-method salt wells smelled not of brine but of cow dung, for the machine for drawing up the brine was worked by buffaloes. There are three kinds of wells: the low-grade and shallower, but most numerous, yellow brine wells; the better-grade and deeper black brine wells; and the rock salt wells, which are the best, operated by pouring water down to dilute the rock salts and drawing up the brine. The first kind is 2,000 feet deep on the average, while the other two average 3,000 feet. Consequently drawing up the brine requires a great deal of power. A team of four buffaloes is driven around a horizontal wheel about fifteen feet in diameter, which winds the bamboo hawsers dropped into a well under a derrick fifty feet away. The hawsers are made of strands of split bamboo, and the "bucket" containing the brine is made of a section of bamboo four inches in diameter and eight or nine feet long. Driving these wheels by human power would be inhuman, and it is even unbovine, if I may coin the word. The buffaloes do not live long at this strenuous work. A team can work at most three or four times a day, no more than one haul at a time, which takes two to three quarters of an hour. As the "bucket" comes up the well, it gradually becomes lighter and lighter, and as it goes down and the rope lengthens, it gets heavier and heavier. Someone has thought of the counterweight principle, and there are pairs of "yin-yang wells" where in one operation a connecting rope lets down the pipe in one well while pulling up in the other. When the "bucket" reaches the top someone pulls a valve at its bottom and flushes the brine into a big container, to be conducted to the salt furnaces by bamboo pipe lines and sold to the refineries. The derricks themselves, seventy to a hundred and twenty feet high, are made of the strongest and best timber, fastened together and strongly buttressed by subsidiary beams, in order to stand the strain of the pulleys.

I was very much interested in the method of digging and repairing these wells and of dredging them free of matter which sometimes cluttered the bottom. The hole was no more than six inches across, protected by a stone slab at the top. I saw the operation of digging a well by means of a "walking beam." On a scaffolding eight or ten feet high erected on one side of the well, a team of twelve men, divided into two opposite groups, stepped in rhythm from one side to the other. As the teams crossed over to the opposite sides simultaneously, they stepped on a beam in the middle, depressing it by their weight, and as they passed over to the other sides, the beam tilted up at an angle again. The up-and-down motion caused the rope at one end to pull up a heavy metallic drill three or four feet long and drop it down again. The metallic drill was suspended from a split bamboo rope, connected by a strong rope of hemp to a ring at one end of the walking beam. In soft formations several feet or yards could be drilled in a day, while in drilling through rocks, the progress might be as little as three or four inches a day.

Yet there was more method in the drilling than this seems to suggest. The work was begun by digging a big pit with pickaxes and hoes until a rock layer was struck. Then sections of a cut-out stone pipe were built up and joined together by native cement, a mixture of mortar, earth, and sand, and the pit was covered up again. This first stage is known as "laying the slab." Then drilling began and a wooden casing was laid down as the work progressed, known as "laying the wooden tubing." The tubing was made of a special hardwood, carved into two hollow halves of a rounded funnel, each section eight or nine feet long, and joined together section by section. As the drilling went on day by day, a record was kept of the earth formations at the successive levels for future reference in making repairs. The dredging and repairing of the wells required a set of ingenious tools, designed to pick up different kinds of matter and cut and repair or replace certain sections. The technique of working these tools is developed by workmen with years of experience. They can repair any section of a well at a given level.

The dug-up matter was taken out of the well by bamboo pipes. The layers were named according to the sounds produced when the drill hit the bottom. The "mushroom sound" indicated to the workmen soft earth, the "green peas sound" indicated gritty sand, and the "iron plate sound" indicated hard rocks. Usually they would strike rock layers at two or three hundred feet, and the work of drilling through a rock formation might take months or years, depending on luck.

A few miles away were the gas wells. These were a discovery of the middle nineteenth century, when the shortage of salt during the chaos of the Taiping Rebellion forced a revival of the salt industry. Discovered by accident, they were quickly developed as the cheapest and most natural means of supplying fuel to the salt refineries. Some wells produced only natural gas, and others both brine and gas. The gas pipes led directly to a refinery, where one could see large jets of bluish flame beneath the boiling caldrons.

Going about in this region, I saw long bamboo mains, strengthened by fine split bamboo twine wound around them, running up and down over the ground for miles. The owners of gas wells and salt wells deliver their material by these, but the mains have grown up into a separate industry, the owners collecting rent from the consumers. Where the place of origin was low, brine was pumped up into a high tower and then made to flow into the main and feed the different furnaces by natural pressure. I was told that there were also specially built pipe lines running underground and on river beds.

Of the 201 salt wells in this area, 58 are steam-operated while 143 are operated by buffalo power. But the steam-operated wells account for 82 per cent of the total production. This is partly due to the fact that the "rock salt wells" are all operated by steam. Rock salt wells produce five times more than black brine wells, owing to the higher salt content and greater speed, and black brine wells produce twice as much as yellow brine wells. The efficiency of the steam engine is apparent; it makes a haul in seven to ten minutes, whereas the buffaloes pull one "bucket" up in half an hour or more. But even steam is not as economical as electric power, and the sound suggestion has been made that the natural gas should be harnessed to run dynamos to produce the power to operate the engines. A 10,000-kilowatt generator was brought for the wells at Weiyuan, but owing to the difficulty of transportation in war time, it was left at Kunming and sold to the Kunming Power Plant under the National Resources Commission. Modern machinery to produce salt by distillation, exhaust, and vacuum methods has been installed at different places.

Considering the natural wealth of this area, the present low capacity (the average consumption of salt is only ten catty per person a year) and the basic importance of salt in the chemical industries, a thorough overhauling of salt production and better organization and improved methods are inevitable in the coming period. There should be also a better-integrated and more scientific plan for co-ordinated tapping of these resources, both in salt and in gas formations, to improve their capacity, instead of the present small-scale and haphazard drilling.

I have seen farmers on mountain roads carrying on their shoulders lumps of rock salt weighing over a hundred pounds. And I was told that, before a modern system of dikes was made, a ridiculous situation in river transportation from the salt area existed. The river below Tseliuching was full of shallow rapids and difficult for navigation. The water volume varied from one cubic meter per second in the dry season to 4,000 cubic meters per second in summer. It used to take seven weeks for a boat to make a round voyage, three weeks from Tseliuching to Tengkwan, a distance of 73 kilometers, and four weeks for the empty boat to be pulled up the rapids by workmen trudging on the banks. At places where the water was very low the boatmen had to wade in the river and literally lift the boat and help it along while its bottom grated over the pebble bottom. At places where ancient dikes were built, the boatmen might have to wait as long as seven days for enough water to accumulate before the boat could be flushed over the dikes. With the interruption of the unnavigable months, a boat could make only six round trips in a whole year.

I was therefore glad to hear of three modern locks, on the Panama Canal principle, which regulate the water levels at different stretches, and to learn that the boats could now make a round trip in one week and a minimum of forty round trips in a year. I saw one of these in operation at Kintsetang, and was all the more gratified because this work was accomplished during the war, begun in January, 1941, and completed in May, 1942. It cost $1,380,000, but the return from improved speed of transportation and saving of labor fully covered the capital outlay in one year.

After I was back in the United States, I read a news item from Chungking saying that more than two million laborers would be conscripted for road construction and more than two million for water conservancy in Szechuen. In a true sense, resistance and reconstruction have gone hand in hand in this war. Such modern improvements, once started in earnest, will gather momentum and be pushed on with greater speed in the years immediately after the war.

15

REFLECTIONS ON DEMOCRACY
AND THE FUTURE

HERE the description of my trip must end, and I must sum up my impressions and comments. My impressions of fighting China in the Northwest may be regarded as typical of what I saw in the Southwest, and I have incorporated some of my observations on the Southwest journey in the preceding accounts. I am afraid that if I were to continue to give an account of my journeys in the South, the present book would be double its present size. I shall only mention that I went south thereafter and stayed three weeks at Kunming and Kweilin, spending most of my time there visiting the American "Y" Force and the U.S. Fourteenth Air Force. There I had a chance to see the spirit of Sino-American co-operation so splendidly, ideally exemplified by Major General Claire L. Chennault himself and his staff. That man will become a legend one day in China, for he is the most popular American in China. If the Chinese people idolize him, it can be excused. I traveled through Hunan, stopping at Changsha, Yuehlu, Hsiangtan, Hengshan, Hengyang, Leiyang, and followed the Canton-Hankow railway to Kukong, the provincial capital of Kwangtung. I talked with Governor Li Hanhuen of Kwangtung and Governor Hsueh Yueh of Hunan, and with the heroes of the Changteh battle and defenders of Changsha, Vice-Commanders Li Yutang, Ou Chen, and Major General Chang Tehneng. I traveled through Kweichow and spent a week at Kweiyang, where I had a good discussion with able and modern-minded administrators like Governor Wu Tingchang and Dr. Y. T. Tsur, former president of Tsinghua University. There I spent considerable time studying the Emergency Medical Service Training School of the Army Medical Administration under Dr. Robert Lim. At Kweichow I had an exciting visit with the "Queen of the Yi" tribe, a pretty young mother, and my schedule was happily timed to watch a fascinating courtship dance of the Miao aborigines during their New Year festival. I saw the backwardness and corruption of Yünnan, the poverty and progress of Kweichow, the wealth of Hunan, and had time in Kwangtung to see an excellent group of modern-educated women, under Mrs. Li Hanhuen, who ran one of the best orphanages in China, where the orphans were taught to govern themselves, and a big relief project where seven hundred women refugees were provided machinery for spinning and weaving by which to support themselves. I talked with countless students, workers, soldiers, teachers, writers, housewives, hawkers, taxi drivers, restaurant waiters, party workers, liaison officers and interpreters for the U.S. Army, etc. After a trip of nearly two months in the Southwest, I went back to Chungking, where I stayed another month with Dr. Sun Fo before I left China. These things I must reluctantly leave out of this book, to give room for more important discussions of the problems and issues facing China today and in the future. I mention these only as providing my background for a more intimate and extended knowledge of the Chinese Army and the general problems of social and political reconstruction of China.

After this journey, I feel that on the whole, the picture of China's social and political structure which I drew ten years ago in *My Country and My People* still holds good, both as to the strength and the weaknesses of the people, and the prospect of revitalizing the nation. Many of the symptoms were chronic, and there was a balance between symptoms aggravated on account of the war and the blockade, and the bodily vitality in recovery and rebuilding of new tissues. Once more I am ready to assert that my faith in China is unshaken.

A realistic appraisal of this fighting China is needed. Just as exaggeration of military successes and concealment of casualties through a stupid censorship policy is bad for the people's morale, breeding lack of confidence at home, so also are the glamorizing or half true reports abroad.

The problems facing China today may be summed up as (1) the problem of democracy, (2) the problem of unity, (3) the problem of the Army and (4) the problem of industrialization.

(1) Democracy

The problem of democracy comes first because, looking beyond the war, the assurance of a truly democratic China is of great importance to postwar international co-operation, and is therefore of greater world interest than even the winning of the war, now that victory is certain. However, I do not think the establishment of constitutional government is the prerequisite for national unity; or rather, I do not think that its delay is the true cause of the Communist revolt, as I have shown in the chapter on "Civil War."

What does being democratic mean? Since everybody is democratic nowadays, we are terribly confused. Why is democracy extolled, applauded, contended for, and paid tribute to by every haranguing orator and every editorial writer? Democracy is a system of government based

on the association of men who believe that peace,
for all can somehow be worked out by a delegatio
freely elected bodies, provided the people can at
throw out any government that doesn't give them
justice. Fun-pokers like G.B.S. extol Mussolini an
and deny the existence of democracy in England a
It is well to have a few fun-pokers, for democracy
the people of England and the United States can
their governments that do not satisfy them, and
ernments with some slight improvements, and t
for me. Because of that, democracy guarantees pea
of opinion and interests inside a nation, and insur
of progress, however slow. I believe that is why d
mature form of government. In order to make this
be certain established habits in the government
abiding by the majority, respect for the law of t
by the people themselves, the fundamental assump
ment must be made responsive to the majority wi
certain machineries for making the will of the pe
follow electioneering and campaigning by men
love to rule others, and who praise themselves
deceive the people in campaign pledges, which a
I am amazed that such people exist. But people
and I was by nature born into the class to be r
send me questionnaires to be answered. Sometin
co-operate with these busybodies because I know
bowls depend on it and they cannot write books
and feel the democratic urge to shove the high
whether in my own or some foreign government
I am fundamentally one of that class of democr
which no democracy can survive.

Democracy means the inherent desire of private
their rulers about, and the free exercise of their
their rulers what to do and what not to do. Sin
going on the road to democracy, I must limber
I shall enjoy it, too. God bless the Chinese Repub
sen its Founder, that my intellectual muscles may

In the decade before the war, I tried my best
under a strict censorship of the press without
jail. The Kuomintang thought I had an undiscip
leftist writers thought I was only a joker, trying t

spinning and weaving by which to support themselves. I talked with countless students, workers, soldiers, teachers, writers, housewives, hawkers, taxi drivers, restaurant waiters, party workers, liaison officers and interpreters for the U.S. Army, etc. After a trip of nearly two months in the Southwest, I went back to Chungking, where I stayed another month with Dr. Sun Fo before I left China. These things I must reluctantly leave out of this book, to give room for more important discussions of the problems and issues facing China today and in the future. I mention these only as providing my background for a more intimate and extended knowledge of the Chinese Army and the general problems of social and political reconstruction of China.

After this journey, I feel that on the whole, the picture of China's social and political structure which I drew ten years ago in *My Country and My People* still holds good, both as to the strength and the weaknesses of the people, and the prospect of revitalizing the nation. Many of the symptoms were chronic, and there was a balance between symptoms aggravated on account of the war and the blockade, and the bodily vitality in recovery and rebuilding of new tissues. Once more I am ready to assert that my faith in China is unshaken.

A realistic appraisal of this fighting China is needed. Just as exaggeration of military successes and concealment of casualties through a stupid censorship policy is bad for the people's morale, breeding lack of confidence at home, so also are the glamorizing or half-true reports abroad.

The problems facing China today may be summed up as (1) the problem of democracy, (2) the problem of unity, (3) the problem of the Army and (4) the problem of industrialization.

(1) Democracy

The problem of democracy comes first because, looking beyond the war, the assurance of a truly democratic China is of great importance to postwar international co-operation, and is therefore of greater world interest than even the winning of the war, now that victory is certain. However, I do not think the establishment of constitutional government is the prerequisite for national unity; or rather, I do not think that its delay is the true cause of the Communist revolt, as I have shown in the chapter on "Civil War."

What does being democratic mean? Since everybody is democratic nowadays, we are terribly confused. Why is democracy extolled, applauded, contended for, and paid tribute to by every haranguing orator and every editorial writer? Democracy is a system of government based on the association of men who believe that peace, security, and justice for all can somehow be worked out by a delegation of their powers to freely elected bodies, provided the people can at any time peacefully throw out any government that doesn't give them peace, security, and justice. Fun-pokers like G.B.S. extol Mussolini and Hitler and Stalin and deny the existence of democracy in England and the United States. It is well to have a few fun-pokers, for democracy likes its clowns. But the people of England and the United States can peacefully throw out their governments that do not satisfy them, and organize other governments with some slight improvements, and that is good enough for me. Because of that, democracy guarantees peace in spite of clashes of opinion and interests inside a nation, and insures a steady evolution of progress, however slow. I believe that is why democracy is the most mature form of government. In order to make this possible, there must be certain established habits in the government and the people, like abiding by the majority, respect for the law of the nation established by the people themselves, the fundamental assumption that the government must be made responsive to the majority will of the people, and certain machineries for making the will of the people effective. There follow electioneering and campaigning by men who love power and love to rule others, and who praise themselves and as often as not deceive the people in campaign pledges, which are not to my liking. I am amazed that such people exist. But people are born differently, and I was by nature born into the class to be ruled by others, who send me questionnaires to be answered. Sometimes I good-naturedly co-operate with these busybodies because I know their families' rice bowls depend on it and they cannot write books. Sometimes I rebel and feel the democratic urge to shove the high and mighty about, whether in my own or some foreign government. Therefore I believe I am fundamentally one of that class of democratic citizens without which no democracy can survive.

Democracy means the inherent desire of private individuals to shove their rulers about, and the free exercise of their intelligence to tell their rulers what to do and what not to do. Since China says she is going on the road to democracy, I must limber up my muscles, and I shall enjoy it, too. God bless the Chinese Republic and Dr. Sun Yat-sen its Founder, that my intellectual muscles may be so exercised.

In the decade before the war, I tried my best to limber up myself, under a strict censorship of the press without landing myself in jail. The Kuomintang thought I had an undisciplined mind, and the leftist writers thought I was only a joker, trying to laugh off the cruel oppression of the masses. What the leftist writers could not stand was humor. One chauvinistic official, hearing that *My Country and My People* was a best-seller abroad, wittily said that I was "selling my country." I am happy to say that that man has met his due: he has become the foreign minister of the puppet government at Nanking.

It may be objected that criticism of one's own government abroad is not opportune in time of war; on the other hand, greater harm can be done, and has been done, to the cause of China by painting a half-true picture. The sooner a state of confidence is established by presenting an accurate picture of the true situation, the better it will be for my country. God knows my country is full of imperfections, but only those willing to have their imperfections known and corrected are worthy of help. The present administration has a record of as many failures as successes, exactly the kind of failures that provide ammunition for some pretty bad slugging in a presidential campaign in a Western country. The Chinese government has got to learn to take such slugging as if it were in a presidential campaign with an active and virile opposition party. It has to prepare itself, not the people, for democracy.

Yet I think the Chinese government and the nation have no reason to be ashamed of their record in this war. When the heat of political campaigning for the Chinese Communists is over, people five years from now, striking a balance sheet and taking into account all the internal factors, will find that they have done the stupendous and the impossible. They will find that both China and the Chinese government were the sinned against rather than the sinners. How difficult is a sense of balance and proportion! I know I am writing under great handicap when I wish to earn my right as an intelligent critic to refuse to fall in with the current conception that Chungking is all black and Yenan all white. I do not see how I can help myself. In the future, the fact that at present the size of American help to China is inversely proportional to the export tonnage of paternalistic advice supplied to her will be regarded as an anomaly, based neither on comprehension nor on policy, but on an offhand and lightminded thoughtlessness.

Freedom of the press is more important than the enactments of laws and constitutions. People who do not know how to talk against their government do not deserve a democracy. And the best government in the world, when it is deprived of the goading of democratic "gadflies," soon gets bored with its own virtues and dies of inanity. I sometimes think God Himself created Satan because He was so sick of the singing and flattering angels and wanted to save Himself from boredom. If the kingdom of heaven cannot do without opposition, how much less can a human secular government?

However, I must begin by defending the censors. Of all classes of beings on earth deserving pity from all of us, the first are the censors in all periods and all countries. If censors could write, they would not be censors. Like eunuchs, they can only tell other people how to do it. Their official job is not to create, but to destroy. Their weapon is the blue pencil, and unless they "kill" so much stuff per day, they cannot justify their existence to their superiors and their wives. "Dearie, what did you kill today?" the wife asks. Is he to say to his wife that his day has been wastefully spent, that he brought down no game, that in fact he did not even strike out one adjective? What does the government pay him for? Is not his job to maul, distort, wrench, and generally mess up the script that an enthusiastic reporter has sat up all night to write and polish to perfection? He has the perfectly legitimate desire to land big game if he can. What if he were able to tell his wife at lunch that he had this morning mauled Bernard Shaw or Robert Frost, or gagged Sumner Welles or Charles A. Beard?

I defend the censors. They are not all "stupid," as all newspapers say; some of them, I am prepared to believe, are quite intelligent people. They simply have an impossible job for human beings of finite intelligence. Determining what is to be passed is an extremely delicate matter. Sometimes the censors have to protect the people's morals, a subject on which many intelligent persons do differ. Sometimes they have to prevent G.I.'s from thinking about the great issues of a presidential election and provide them with the necessary vacuum of information in which they may in the most sterilized manner make their choice of the government that is going to rule their nation in the next four years. If I read correctly the American Army censorship regulations, they are desirous of maintaining freedom of thinking provided there is nothing to think with and of maintaining freedom of speech provided there is nothing to talk about.

But there is a difference between free press in the United States and free press in China. In the case of the American Army ban on works like the Beards' *Basic History,* E. B. White's *One Man's Meat,* Sumner Welles's *The Time for Decision,* Catherine Drinker Bowen's *Yankee from Olympus,* and the *Atlantic Monthly,* a few newspaper editorials started a howl and Congress took it up and the situation was at once remedied. The government responded to public opinion; that is what is good about a true democracy. American public consciousness recognized the act as wrong and contrary to a long democratic tradition. In China, the modern press being a new institution, there is no such tradition, and the Kuomintang has not given a serious start to it. All governments tend to act like children at times, and they benefit from having a free press to call their folly. The Chinese government shuts itself out from this benefit.

There is, too, a difference between censorship over foreign cables and over the domestic press. I think the censorship over the foreign press dispatches in Chungking is no worse than the censorship over the Chinese press dispatches from the United States. Foreign correspondents from Chungking, in a fighting mood, declare that Chinese censors have openly admitted that they want only good stories to come out of China, and have suppressed criticisms of the country. The American censors, too, have withheld New York or Washington dispatches of Chinese press agencies carrying unfavorable criticisms of the country, for the valid and sound reason that such dispatches will be intercepted by the enemy and used for propaganda. Chinese living in Chungking do not get a true and complete picture of America. This is war, and allowances must be made.

Yet, though bearing in mind the necessity of war censorship, I still say that in China the freedom of the press has deteriorated during the war to an undue extent. I talked with many writers and editors in China and found them irked by unnecessary restraint. When I said to a very well-educated reporter in Kweilin that the basis of all democracy is civil liberties and that American editors criticize official acts and nobody can do anything to them on account of protection of civil liberties, his eyes were wide open. In China, I must say, I did not hear of editors banned, fined, or imprisoned for criticizing officials; but since all newspaper copy is passed beforehand by the censors, this could not happen anyway. What good does it do to create a feeling of restraint and general dissatisfaction in the writing profession by an overall censorship?

The connection between censorship and stupidity is proverbial. All newspapers, magazines, and books have to be submitted to censors before publication. In the case of newspapers, this has placed the government in the odious position of being responsible for approval of all press utterances. In the case of criticisms of acts of foreign allies, Chinese diplomacy is deprived of the power of reference to Chinese public opinion as expressed in a free press. Furthermore, censors are government employees, answerable to the several authorities of the government, the party and the army, and, like all bureaucrats, they prefer to act on the cautious side, which is the murderous side in the employment of the blue-pencil weapon. The censors also tend to make literature subservient to propaganda, and authors have to alter their plays in favor of patriotic platitudes. I have heard such complaints from a playwright; he was as mad about the censorship as any American playwright in a similar situation would be. This was the more unbearable because the playwright knew that the censor himself was probably a child of eighteen who has not yet finished high school. In numerous cases, the suppression of entirely harmless and irrelevant phrases became irritating and downright asinine, suggesting that the whole nation was being put through a Sunday school class. Once censorship is established, it is difficult to escape the paternalistic spirit of allowing and forbidding the people what to read and what to think.

In practice, the Chinese people have got used to it, as the people of Soviet Russia have, except that they get bored with too oft-repeated phraseology and smile when they read it. The astounding thing is that people freely criticize the government acts in public places and private homes, everywhere except when they make a formal speech. They know "mandarin talk" when they hear it. The required submission of *all* newspaper copy and book manuscripts creates an unhealthy atmosphere, but this does not mean that the censors suppress *all* criticism of government measures. In 1940 I saw a *Ta Kung Pao* editorial which in criticism of the failure of the Price Stabilization Board quoted Tsao Tsao of the Three Kingdoms and suggested that "the skull" of the head of the Board "be borrowed to pacify the hearts of the people." There have been occasional outspoken criticisms on internal policies like that. When in Chungking this time, I read a scathing exposure of a badly run public institution and a great many articles criticizing price control, the closing down of factories, and the transportation situation.

The Communist daily, *Hsin Hwa Jih Pao,* was given more freedom than in Yenan. In February, in Chungking, I read a significantly passed attack in this paper on the Minister of Information Liang Han-chao himself, Liang's reply, *Hsin Hwa Jih Pao's* reply to the reply, and Liang's final answer. It started with a perfectly senseless quibble, unworthy of publication, which in a Kuomintang paper would certainly have been suppressed. In his comment on Anthony Eden's statement in the House of Commons on Japanese atrocities toward Allied war prisoners in Burma and elsewhere, Liang had said that such atrocities were not unknown to Chinese and the Chinese were not "shocked" by them, and went on with condemnations of the Japanese in unmistakable terms. The *Hsin Hwa Jih Pao* suggested sarcastically that he was unconcerned about the tortured masses who personally suffered these atrocities, and that he was not only not "shocked" but in fact might be quite pleased to hear about them. This is the kind of foolery that went on in the papers. Ability to talk against the government is an indication of adult democratic citizenship. Some Chinese have not yet learned it.

I think the picture of the press as I saw it and give it here is not as bad as many Americans would like to imagine from hearsay; but because of it, I also think the censorship accomplishes more harm than good. I do not think newspaper contents would be greatly altered if the editors were left to censor themselves and perhaps consult the censorship bureau only when they do not wish to decide for themselves, as in America. That is why the censorship regulations should be revised. I am glad to learn that since the summer of 1944, the Government has at last waked up to the folly of it and censorship has been greatly relaxed in practice.

The whole character of the Kuomintang government is paternalistic, but I do not think it is "fascist." It has all the evils of paternalism, over-anxious to guide and channel people's thoughts and action, and not anxious enough to let the people guide themselves; but I do not think it has the evils of regimentation of thoughts and ideas and the rule of terror and force. The reaction of the people under a paternalistic regime is one of annoyance or placid amusement; the reactions of people under a totalitarian rule are whispers, secret terrors, frightened submission, and goose-stepping unanimous praise of the government. The evils of paternalism are corrigible; the evils of totalitarianism are not. For definite evidences of the latter, one must go to Yenan.

Perhaps paternalism is to a certain extent inevitable in the "period of political tutelage," as the very name implies. Yet the declared aim of such political tutelage is teaching the people to govern themselves, and the sooner they are allowed to govern themselves in every direction and have their voice heard, the earlier will they see the results. I must allow certain positive results of this paternalistic tutelage under the Kuomintang leadership: the people have developed a national consciousness that is new and desirable; the average man has a better understanding of the Sanmin Chuyi principles and knows about the program of national reconstruction. Certainly the government has led the nation through an unprecedented war and has given them a new spirit of self-confidence and national pride. My suspicion is that if China had not had this strong Kuomintang government during this war, but a more democratic, less unified government like that of

France, the war front might have collapsed through disunity long ago. But the Kuomintang still has not made great progress in the forms or spirit of democracy. The people have been tutored too long. The Chinese people are more than anxious to take a hand in the government, but they are feeling as miserable as King Edward VII in his fifties when Queen Victoria refused to go up to heaven.

What China needs is an immediate enforcement of the Bill of Rights. I would rather see a little less paternalistic coddling of the nation and a little more attention paid to seeing the people's freedom of speech, assembly, and belief, and the *habeas corpus* enforced. It is my conviction that democracy begins, grows, and prospers with the protection of the people's civil rights, and is inseparable from it. The definition of democracy as a term meaning merely the existence of mature, self-respecting individuals living with individual dignity can oftentimes be inadequate. Certainly the Chinese people are mature, self-respecting individuals with a great deal of individual dignity. How does it happen, then, that Chinese régimes have often been corrupt and the mature, self-respecting individuals could do nothing about it until the corruption got bad enough and the regime had to be overthrown by the wasteful process of revolt and bloodshed? Individual moral dignity without the legal protection of that dignity is not enough. When individuals were arrested without trial and could not appeal to law, evidently there was not much individual dignity left.

Chinese editors are not inherently less self-respecting as individuals than American editors. Yet there is something which affects their spirit and mellows their tone; habitually they stand less for their rights than a New England farmer does. Democracy means just that difference, that when a man obeys the law no one on earth can touch him. He holds his head higher, talks louder, and sticks his chest out further. He doesn't give a damn for anybody. This quality of not giving a damn for anybody is, as I have said, inherent in the Chinese people. But when he pursues his peaceful living and yet the officer of the law grabs him by the shoulder and he knows he does not enjoy the protection of the law, then he does care a great deal. Thereafter he learns to hold his head lower, talk softer, and become wiser. He goes about doing nobody any harm, and by patient industry and thrift and drudgery makes a living, enjoys his family and lives at peace with his neighbors. In one sense, he is a democratic individual; but in the sense of organized political democracy, where every man stands for his rights and is willing to fight for them, he is not free.

The Bill of Rights is therefore more important than all the paraphernalia of elective government. When the protection of civil rights is enforced, the people do not have to learn to be democratic. There is no ground for saying that the people of China are unprepared for democracy. They are unprepared only so long as the Bill of Rights is not enforced. Any time the people can impeach officials with impunity and with some effect, they are democratic enough to do so. Any time government officials are ready to stand by the law and be impeached, the people are ready to impeach them. Any time editors can expose corrupt and lawbreaking officials with the sure knowledge that nobody can touch them except within the law, they are ready to expose them. Only when they can do that, only when this spirit is present, can true democracy arrive and the body politic be purged of its poison. Freedom of the press, of speech, belief, and assembly is the foundation of democracy.

There is no reason why freedom of the press cannot be immediately enforced now. Censorship can and should be limited only to suppressing leakage of military secrets or information desirable to the enemy. More depends on the interpretation of the censorship laws than on the letter of the law. Protection of civil liberties has been repeatedly declared in the past and is incorporated in the National Constitution drafted years ago. Only July 15, 1944, a new law of *habeas corpus* was promulgated, to become effective on August 1. Yet even this law can become a dead letter through the unwillingness of the authorities to see to its enforcement when actual instances arise. When I say authorities, I mean the local and provincial authorities wherever cases of illegal arrest or infringement of human rights may occur. Civil and military jurisdictions too often overlap. It boils down again to the general standard of the local authorities, which must necessarily undergo a gradual educational process until the idea of human rights is firmly established and recognized by all.

To show that the enforcement of civil rights is fundamental in any progress toward democracy, we may imagine that China has promulgated a constitution, formally adopted the most enlightened laws, and set up local, provincial, and national elective governments. I do not see how such governments can even come near having a truly democratic character if there is no guarantee, in practice, of freedom of the person or freedom of the press. The guarantee of the civil liberties themselves, for instance, is part of the constitution. Suppose there is in a certain province a government which begins to punish and possibly arrest editors illegally. The only remedy for such unconstitutional acts is freedom of the governed to insist that the editors' freedom be upheld. So even the maintenance of the freedom of speech depends upon the freedom of speech. Again, suppose some officials have by clever manipulation got themselves elected, and have then proceeded to violate the laws or even just break their campaign pledges: I do not see how the honesty of the government can be maintained if the people are not protected in their freedom to criticize officials and so rid the government of its abuses. Finally, we may assume that China has become a real, successfully working democracy. Even then, such a democracy must be jealously and constantly guarded. I do not see how the people are going to guard that democracy unless they have and can enforce first of all their civil rights.

The establishment of the constitutional electoral process in China, however, is a more complicated problem. Critics who ask why China does not immediately declare a constitutional government sound naïve. People who lay undue emphasis upon the declaration of a paper constitution and the establishment of an elective machinery without first building the foundations of popular local government will find themselves sadly disillusioned. Too much emphasis has been placed upon China having a constitutional government, and too little upon enforcing a Bill of Rights.

In the preparations for building the foundations of popular government, the Chinese government is unquestionably sincere. When one thinks of putting the elective machinery of self-government in the hands of a people with a high percentage of illiteracy, one realizes the size of the problem. The Kuomintang government is tackling it slowly, but methodically. First, the best earnest is the educational program being pushed through during the war and in spite of the war. It is estimated that some fifty million people have been taught to read and write in these war years. Every *pao* unit of about a hundred families is supposed to have a "citizens' school," every borough to have a "center school," and every *hsien* to have at least one secondary school. I have seen these schools; the quality is not what one would wish, but the schools are there. Secondly, emphasis has been placed on building local self-government from the bottom up. This has been done in connection with the little publicized New County System, whereby household heads are to elect the *chia* council, the *chia* heads are to elect the *pao* council, the *pao* heads are to elect the *ch'ü* (approximately borough) council, the *ch'ü* heads are to elect the county council, and the county council is to elect its "mayor," and may dismiss him. The first need is therefore the training of local government personnel, but what a task! For five years now, a stream of people have been sent up to training centers in all provinces to receive training in the methods and duties of local self-government, and one and a half million trainees have received this instruction, seventy per cent persons active in local government. The lower units are trained in provincial centers, and the personnel of the provincial governments are sent up to the Central Training Institute at Chungking. Again I doubt the efficacy of such training in the mechanics of administration, but the government is at least earnestly doing it, with a vast expenditure of money. Since self-government is to start from the bottom, theoretically, the political tutelage period will not come to an end until a majority of such elected provincial governments are in being. Actually, none of the provincial governments are yet so constituted and elected from below; but the constitutional period cannot long be delayed after the war because the party and the government have solemnly made a pledge.

Thirdly, the National Constituent Assembly was actually scheduled to meet on November 12, 1937, when the war broke out. Chinese delegates from New York and elsewhere had already been elected to attend the assembly, but canceled the trip when it was postponed on account of the war. The assembly had been postponed once before when it had been scheduled to meet in November, 1936. Conducting a national election, where there was not even a census and where local elective bodies were nonexistent, was naturally hampered with difficulties, and the postponement could be understood. I am sure that when the National Assembly is called within one year of the cessation of the war, the local electoral process will not be fully functioning, and therefore such an assembly will still be a hurried job. Even after the constitutional period is formally begun, there will be worse headaches yet, and Chinese democracy, full-fledged in form, will not be full-fledged in reality.

Perhaps electioneering apparatus is the necessary evil of an organized democracy, though I despise it. Every time I watch an election campaign in America, I lose faith in democracy. It has got to be done. But the spirit of democracy resides elsewhere. It resides in the spirit of free men who in their daily lives practice the unwritten law of democratic citizens who cannot be taken advantage of by others. It resides in the spirit of men who breathe the air of freedom in thinking and belief, and tolerate others' thinking and beliefs, and somehow by faith in the essential decency of human nature can get a government going for the common good. For this atmosphere of freedom, the Bill of Rights is the first foundation.

Democracy is a hard thing to learn both for the rulers and for the ruled. In its essence, it implies the ability of the majority to rule and the ability of the minority to criticize and abide by the majority. Even in a small group of boys playing in the streets or three office girls sharing one apartment, democracy means no more than these simple habits of thinking. When the ruling party forgets that it is only elected to rule by the rest of the group and tends to suppress criticism of its actions, it is to that extent undemocratic. When the minority group fails to abide by the majority and prefers to break away and form a separate gang, it, too, becomes undemocratic. In so far as the Kuomintang has failed to encourage liberty of criticism through freedom of the press, it is moving in the wrong direction. And in so far as the Chinese Communist party was unwilling to subjugate its partisan interests and unite with the rest of the nation even in time of war, it, too, had failed to learn the most essential of democratic habits. Since it looks as if victory will come sooner than we expected and therefore China will soon inaugurate the constitutional period, both the Kuomintang and the opposition had better learn quickly these simple democratic habits of mind. The outer form of a democratic government means nothing. The history of democracy in the German Republic before Hitler, in Italy prior to the advent of Mussolini, and in France before the final collapse, should teach us that the finest form of human government also requires some of the hardest human virtues in co-operative action, struggle tempered by restraint, selfishness held in check by a sense of fair play, and contention subordinated to unity. The Kuomintang will have the best chance to show that it is democratic by rigidly enforcing the rights of freedom and respecting the rights of the opposition, and the Chinese Communists will have the best chance to show that they are democratic by being able to abide by the majority will of the nation. If unethical tactics are employed, the government will have no recourse but to fight underground with underground, as it has been doing in the past. Twice the Chinese Communists have bolted and set up secessionist regimes, because they have not yet learned to place the nation above the party. I hope their declared intention to abolish one-party dictatorship and become a democratic party is sincere —and is lived up to.

I had the chance to discuss some aspects of China's developing democracy with Dr. Sun Fo. His position as a strong liberal leader of the Kuomintang is well known. We had many occasions to discuss foreign criticisms of the Chinese government, and I found he had the courage of honesty to admit Chinese faults when the criticism was justified, and the ability to laugh over it when it was far-fetched and grotesque, as many foreign criticisms often are. As he was heading the Council for the Enforcement of Constitutional Rule, established by the government after the decision to inaugurate the constitutional period one year after the war, there was one topic which particularly interested him. At these conferences where all political parties were represented, the question had come up as to how there could be several political parties, since all were supposed to pledge allegiance to the Sanmin Chuyi principles. The question evidently had been the subject of many lively discussions. To Dr. Sun, who was thoroughly familiar with the working of Western democracies, the question was simple. He showed them the necessity of opposition in all democracies, even though different parties might hold the same fundamental democratic beliefs, but with different party platforms. And he was very happy to have convinced them.

This brings us to what seems to me the most important question of all. Few would question the adequacy of the Sanmin Chuyi principles as the basis for a democratic government in China. Yet there is a right and a left wing to every party. Dr. Sun has conceived it as the most important thing for the Kuomintang to "return to the left," and I am sure when the Chinese constitutional government is established there can be nothing more healthy, more hopeful for the Kuomintang, than to have a left-wing party come forward and stand for the welfare of the farmer and worker. The Chinese Communists, with all their faults, have served to direct public consciousness to the claims of the primary producer, and a very large element of Chinese youth, who now fashionably style themselves as "leftists" and yet are unwilling to join the C.P., would be attracted to such a platform. Consequently, such a movement would be the revitalizing of the Kuomintang. As reported in the *New York Times,* August 27, 1944, Dr. Sun said to a training class at the Kuomintang Headquarters: "The most important task for the party is to bring about real democracy within China. We must get off the wrong track and turn back to the left. . . . We must return to our original way and proclaim ourselves with pride as true revolutionaries." Again, "Responsibility for this task must be shouldered by ourselves. Today the Communist party is in opposition. If we do not go forward, they will."

What platform such a left party will adopt I am not in a position to foretell. But I feel sure that there is urgent need for a party with emphasis on the last of the three principles of the Sanmin Chuyi, Minsheng, or the principle of a better and more abundant life for the common people. When people speak of the "reactionary" tendency of the Kuomintang, they mean that in the economic and political sense, the party's record as a whole shows it has failed to emphasize the rights of peasant and labor and the common people. Nowhere in Kuomintang China have I yet seen or heard the common people of China played up as the all-important individuals, whose happiness it is the state's final aim to look after and whose vote it is the politician's strategy to bid for. Nowhere yet have I seen the common people made to feel that they are important. Yet until the people of China are made so to feel that the "little people" are the important people, China will fail in the final analysis to qualify for the title of democracy.

I am therefore of the opinion that three things should be done. First, a Bill of Rights should be immediately and rigidly enforced. Second, the government should at once grant constitutional status to all political parties in China which are not backed by a separate army, as a preparatory step toward the coming constitutional period. This will be similar to the interim period before the final peace settlements for Europe. There are a few unimportant political parties in existence, and many important lessons may be learned in the working of party politics. The government will thus be in an unassailable position, and any time the Chinese Communist party is willing to hand over its private army to the unified national command, it will be entitled to the same status and privileges as the other parties. Third, the Kuomintang should develop within its own ranks a vigorous movement, which may be called the "left," bidding for the support of peasant and labor and the common people in competition with the Communist ultra-radical platform. This may be called the Minsheng party within the Kuomintang. The formation of such a party will be the most courageous and statesmanlike act that Kuomintang leaders can take at present.

(2) Unity

The problem of China's unity is, as I have pointed out elsewhere, exclusively the problem of the Chinese Communists. I have, in the chapter on the "Civil War," already given an account of the facts of the conflict, its cause and origin and its many twisted angles, arising from a one-sided presentation of the case before the American public.

Here I shall deal with the character of the Chinese Communist party and the possible solutions for the conflict.

But, first, it will be useful to give a brief summary of the conflict by Dr. Sun Fo. Dr. Sun is sympathetic and tolerant toward the Chinese Communists and is hopeful of a peaceful solution. For the Communists, it would be impossible to find a fairer critic within the Kuomintang than Dr. Sun Fo.

Of the present state of things and the history of the conflicts, he writes:

> As it is, the Communist power, organized separately as a government functioning in a certain area of the national territory and maintained in power as the ruling party in their occupied region by military forces answerable to the Communist Party alone, is nothing less than an *imperium in imperio*. It pays lip service to the National Government of the Republic, but the so-called 'Shen-Kan-Ning Border Region,' which incloses some 24 *hsien* located in an irregular area in north Shensi, east Kansu, and southeast Ninghsia provinces, has a government of its own organized and administered in contravention of the national laws governing provincial and local administration. National Government decrees and Executive Yuan and ministerial orders have no effect and validity within the Communist districts. The Border Government collects its own taxes and prints its own paper money. Banking and trade with other parts of the country are carried on as government monopolies. . . .
>
> The Communist armies as incorporated in the National Army in the early days of the war numbered only three divisions with a number of auxiliary units, totaling some 40,000 to 50,000 men. These were reorganized as the 8th Route Army and later renamed the 18th Army Group. This army has now grown to enormous proportions. Its members are generally accepted to be about 500,000. Such expansion is effected without reference to the orders of the Supreme Command. In fact, for some years now, the operations of this army in Shansi, Suiyuan, Hopei, Honan, Shantung, and North Kiangsu provinces have been entirely independent of the High Command. The Communist troops under their own leaders act on their own responsibility, without the least concern about the wishes and orders of G.H.Q. Nominally they are still part of the Chinese National Army, but in fact they are an independent and separate army.

The Communist 8th Army was originally assigned north Shensi, east Suiyuan, Chahar, and north Hopei provinces as its designated war zone, within which it was to operate against the enemy and puppet forces. Honan, Shantung, Anhui, and Kiangsu provinces were assigned to other Chinese armies. But instead of acting according to orders, the 8th Army went ahead with its own expansionist plans by recruiting and organizing irregular units within the zones of other commands. Friction was inevitable, and sometimes fractricidal outbreaks occurred. One by one other central government units were edged out of south Hopei, north Honan, north Shantung, and north Kiangsu provinces. Irregular units claiming to be 18th Army men were found as far south as Hupeh and Anhui provinces.

Then there was the New 4th Army, organized out of remnants of the various Communist bands south of the Yangtse River for guerrilla warfare to the south of Nanking. In the fall of 1940, orders of the High Command were issued to the 8th to move back to the north bank of the Yellow River, and to the New 4th to cross the Yangtse to north Kiangsu. The dates fixed for execution of the orders were repeatedly postponed, but to no avail. The New 4th, instead of going north to cross the Yangtse, turned south against orders and came into collision with other units. The consequences were unfortunate. The commander of the New 4th was captured and his troops dispersed and disarmed. The High Command ordered its liquidation. Yenan Communist Headquarters countermanded the High Command's order by appointing a new commander to the New 4th. This incident has caused much bad blood and brought about a situation between the government and Communists which so far has failed of an adequate solution. (*China Looks Forward,* by Sun Fo, pp. 85-86.)

A true understanding of the character of the Chinese Communist rule is necessary to an intelligent appraisal of the problem. There is no question that in a sense the Communists are "democratic." But today words have lost their meaning, which adds to the confusion. The Communists are democratic only in the sense that they have always theoretically stood for the rights of the peasants and labor, that they are ahead of Chungking in organizing the people for self-government, that they have workers' unions, peasant unions, women's unions, that they stand for the peasants against the landlords, and have reduced the interest on loans. These are democratic features. They are democratic in the sense that Soviet Russia is democratic. Yet the Soviet régime in China is no less a dictatorship, even as Soviet rule in Russia is a dictatorship, and it has all the strength and the vices of dictatorships. At best, it can be described as "totalitarian democracy" or "democratic totalitarianism"—although I would not know what such a phrase should mean. Democratic totalitarianism, or a totalitarian state working for the interests of the people, certainly has its strength, its ability for carrying through reform programs, as is amply illustrated by Soviet Russia. The question is whether that is the kind of democracy China wants.

The Chinese Communist régime has been able to mobilize manpower and resources more thoroughly than the Chungking government, because its control of the people's lives is more rigid. It has no freedom of speech, no freedom of belief; it rules by regimentation and by terror, by secret agents and local commissars in the army and in civil administrations; it goes through the farce of packed popular elections; it terrorizes the population that dares to dissent or refuses to co-operate; it enforces complete party discipline, the party dominates everything, and party members have exalted privileges; it carries out "purges," "liquidations," in a drastic and unscrupulous manner; and finally replaces the landlord and employer with the state as the master. Consequently, the people are terrorized. In Chungking, people of all classes can criticize the government freely in public places. But in Communist areas, the peasants all "praise" the régime and have nothing to say against it. The degeneration of the peasantry under Communist rule in occupied areas is, from all reports, a clear and certain fact. The final test of a régime is whether the people dare to talk against the régime, and that is a pretty good test of what we mean by "democracy." I should like to hear the foreign correspondents returning from Yenan report that they have been able to find one farmer who did not "praise" the régime as a régime of perfection.

I wish the Communists would stick to their label, of which they should not be ashamed. Certainly by "democracy" we mean something different from this. China is now standing at the crossroads, fully determined to imitate the West, but hesitating as a nation to choose between the Russian and the Anglo-Saxon model. It would make for clarity if people would speak of these models, or speak of "communism" and "democracy" as contra-distinguishing terms.

The true character of the Chinese Communist party must therefore be recognized. On this point Edgar Snow has something pertinent to say. Writing in *The Battle for Asia,* he says:

Chinese publicists, missionaries and other pro-China people did their best to convince the world that the Chinese Communists were not "real Communists" and Chiang Kai-shek himself recently told a German correspondent that there were "no Communists in China." The British Ambassador, Sir Archibald Clark-Kerr, once said to me that the Chinese Communists were really Keir Hardeians—nineteenth-century agrarian democrats—and it was regrettable their name unnecessarily frightened conservatives. Some think that because the Chinese Reds are now fighting for democracy and national independence they cannot be bolsheviks but are "only a peasant reform party." How all these people reconcile such interpretations with the Chinese C.P.'s loyal adherence to the Comintern I do not know.

But if I understand Mao Tse-tung correctly he would not be bothered about these aspersions cast upon his Marxism. He would chuckle and say that if it would solve the contradiction in the sentiments of liberals who want to be known as pro-China but anti-Stalin they might call him anything they liked—so long as they did something to stop America from arming Japan and helped China and the Eighth Route Army to win victories.

My personal feeling in the matter is that liberals who would build up hopes that the Communists of China are "different" and "only reformers" and have abandoned revolutionary methods to achieve their program, are doomed to ultimate disillusionment. These men are nationalists because they are in a nationalist united-front phase of revolution, and they are perhaps strong enough in their own right not to fear becoming submerged as puppets of anybody. But their religion remains international socialism and if conditions change they may adopt whatever methods they believe necessary in order "to stay on the locomotive of history." (Edgar Snow, *The Battle for Asia*, pp. 290-291.)

"From beginning to end the Chinese Communists are believers in Socialism," wrote Wang Chia-hsiang, Politburo member and vice-chairman of the former Soviet Government, in a recent official publication of his party (1939). "They will never abandon their ideals and the theories of Marxism and Leninism. The whole program of the Chinese Communists consists of two parts: (1) the maximum program, for the overthrow of capitalism and the establishment of socialism, and for radical emancipation through the elimination of classes; (2) the minimum immediate program of the national democratic revolution. . . . In order to realize socialism, the Chinese proletariat must first of all secure the emancipation of the Chinese nation. . . ." (Quoted by Edgar Snow, *The Battle for Asia*, pp. 294-295.)

This was written in 1940 and published in 1941. Perhaps the most interesting part is Edgar Snow's remarks about the widely different methods and tactics. The Chinese Communists have made about as many sudden chameleon-like changes in the past seven years as the American Communists, just as embarrassing to themselves as to American Communists, including the Chinese Communist defense of Stalin's recognition of Japan's "Manchukuo" frontiers. They have again changed their strategy now, breaking the United Front and actively attacking Chungking, and they will change their tactics again after they have decided to join the fold. But however they may change in strategy, they will find it hard to reverse their Marxist ideology or take down the sickle from their flag and the portraits of Stalin and Lenin from their halls of worship. Ideas indoctrinated into the minds of their members for two decades cannot be condemned all of a sudden by their leaders without some sense of ridicule. Perhaps they may be able even to make and enforce such reversals, as totalitarian leaders are able to do, and take down the Russian portraits and the Soviet flag, while keeping their Marxian philosophy underground, as a gesture of condescension toward the backward Anglo-Saxon democrats who do not know that "scientific Marxism-Leninism" is the last word of Western social philosophy and Lunacharsky the last word in literary criticism. But as late as 1943, Chen Pai-ta, in his *Critique of Chiang Kai-shek's Book: "China's Destiny,"* still proudly flaunted his banner: "We Marxists usually despise those who try to conceal their political opinions." (P. 4, reprinted by *The Communist,* January, 1944, New York.)

My own estimate of the character of the Chinese Communist party is as follows: It is a party with about the same aims as those of a labor party in a western democracy, plus the ideology, the methods, the organization, and the paraphernalia of a totalitarian dictatorship. It has the following chracteristics: *First, it is not communist* in the Leninist sense of the word. That is, it is no more genuinely communist than present-day Soviet Russia is communist. *Second, it is Marxist* in ideology. That is to say, its whole intellectual outlook is based on materialistic dialectic; it believes in the necessity of class struggle and social revolution; it is inimical to religion and family and all bourgeois

229

institutions. It talks and thinks in communist symbols and Marxist clichés; communist writers indulge in foreign-looking terms like *ao-fu-ho-pien* (German *Aufheben* for "upheaval"), *pu-lo-ta-li-ya* ("proletariat"), "petit-bourgeois habits," "Sinoized scientific Marxism-Leninism," etc. In China this opposition to bourgeois institutions takes the form of a sharp anti-Confucianism. Therefore, *third, it is anti-nationalist in ideas.* The Chinese Communist party and Communist literature are for a complete uprooting of the social structure of China's past, and of all tradition. Mme. Sun Yat-sen sums up the Communist position well when she says, "Confucian teachings are feudalistic and autocratic from beginning to end. We must realize how deeply Confucian influences have been imbedded in our art, literature, social sciences and morals. *We must make great efforts to uproot Confucian ideas out of every nook and corner of our life and thoughts.*" (Quoted by Edgar Snow, *Battle for Asia,* p. 224, italics mine.) *Fourth, it is a totalitarian dictatorship,* and its methods and techniques are definitely copied from the Russian model. The party rules over everything, and party agents penetrate and control every military and civil organization. It calls any critics "Trotskyites" and sends them to colonize uninhabited, primitive regions, the Chinese equivalent of Russian Siberia. It has the same check and countercheck spy system, it has the same "purges" and "liquidations" carried out by the same refined and to us tortuous technique. It holds the same "small group" conferences at night, even obtains "confessions" and self-condemnations (as in the case of Wang Shih-wei) which are alarmingly similar to confessions at the Soviet trials.* *Fifth, it owed allegiance to the Comintern* to its

* This seems to me an amusing and insignificant literary incident magnified out of all proportions. Mr. Wang is a Communist party member of sixteen years' standing. He translated Eugene O'Neill's *Strange Interlude* and was once a contributor to my magazine of humor, *The Lunyü,* and writes a quietly sarcastic style. In March, 1942, he published a series of four articles, in the paper *Chieh Fang (Emancipation)* at Yenan, expressing dissatisfaction with affairs in Yenan. The four articles were called *Wild Artichoke,* whose meaning, according to his own explanation, was that it was a kind of flower found on the mountainsides of Yenan and that although it was slightly bitter in taste, it had certain medicinal properties. The articles in themselves were not important, about 2,000 words in all, chiefly complaining about the bad food, and were written in a casual, chatty style. They quoted an overheard conversation of two girl comrades walking in the open at night, criticizing the Communist party members, mentioned "the feeble, low voice of dissatisfaction made in the dark," expressed the hope that "this voice of dissatisfaction of the youth of the lower ranks" might be heard through more open criticism, and finally criticized the discriminations in food and living between the higher and the lower ranks and between party members and non-members, proposed the situation should be "slightly" improved so as to obtain greater co-operation, said that there were "three classes of uniform and five classes of food," that he was not "sour grapes" because he himself was entitled to the "small kitchen,"

last day. Whatever the Comintern thought of the Chinese Communist party, the latter thought very well of its mother. Now, however, it is orphaned through the mother's decease, and a frantic effort is made to father it through some other Western nation.

Actually, the situation is not so frightening as this seems to forebode. The Chinese Communist party is caught in the process of a transformation, not by Kuomintang argument, but by the shape of events of this war. Russia began to talk differently when she began to ask and receive American war supplies; so will the Chinese Communist party when American help and supplies are desired by them. The tone of their attacks on capitalist thieves and imperialist butchers will be softened considerably. Marxian ideas are not being modified by the words of Tom Paine and Thomas Jefferson, but by the force of events and by certain Communist leaders realistic enough to see it. One of the most interesting lessons of this war is that the national instinct is deeper than the class instinct. According to Marxian dialectic, the German Communists should have proved useful to Stalin. They weren't. England should have fought with Germany against Russia because of capitalist affinities. She didn't. American labor should have approved of the American Communists' loyalty to Moscow in its attitude toward the European war, both during Stalin's pact with Hitler and after. It discredited them. Russia herself should have gone on with the Comintern. She dissolved it. Even as Russia moves toward democ-

---

but that "the young students had two meals of thin congee, and when asked whether they had eaten enough were required to reply, 'We have eaten enough.'" The articles produced a great commotion in Yenan, and for a month and half many people expressed sympathy with the writer's point of view. The articles became the talk of the town, and a serious view was taken by the authorities. After a three-day and three-night deliberation, May 15-17, Wang was expelled from membership in the Anti-Japanese Writers Association, with the chairman, Miss Ting Ling, announcing that it "was a general session of the literary circles, making a good reckoning of Wang Shih-wei's Trotskyist thoughts, and a session of the greatest educational value in reviewing the surviving petit-bourgeois ideology among the writers." From May 27 to June 1, the Yenan Central Research Institute held a continuous six-day session, trying to rectify Mr. Wang's thoughts, and, according to the published minutes found that Wang was unquestionably "a Trotskyist, . . . practicing the same tactics as was once used by the Trotskyists in Soviet Russia." Wang begged to cancel his membership in the Communist party on June 2. However, the affair had attracted too much public attention, and agents were sent to dissuade Wang from the decision. On June 3, Wang announced that "he was touched by the love of his most highly respected friends," and that "he formally and seriously took back the demand he had made when his mind was abnormal." The chairman of the Central Research Institute took the trouble to answer his criticisms point by point, and there were four or five articles from the official Communist agents on the subject, published in a "special edition" of the paper *Emancipation*. The material is reprinted in the magazine *Ch'ünchung (The Masses)*, published in Chungking, vol. 7, nos. 15, 16, 17. Mr. Wang has now escaped to Chungking, I am informed.

racy, nationalism, private property, the family, and the church—that is, away from Marxism—so will the realistic Chinese Communists. Even as Russia begins now to sing songs of its ancient national heroes instead of the *Internationale,* so the Chinese Communists in time will go back to the family and Confucianism. They will say, All we were trying to do was to imitate Jeffersonian democracy and we never meant proletariat dictatorship when we said it. If they *had* advocated Jeffersonism, it would not be recognized as "foreign," because it would be so close to Chinese humanism and the traditional character of Chinese thought. Unfortunately for them, Marxism sounds "foreign" to Chinese ears, and the Chinese family and Confucianism and pride in one's own historical heritage will be too strong for them. They will then, as I have said, become as pro-Confucian and pro-nationalist as the Kuomintang Minister of Education, Chen Lifu. This truculent, affected anti-nationalism cannot last long. So history will play pranks with men's ideas.

Lastly, it must be noted that, in the eyes of the Chinese people as a whole, the character of the Red régime in China is far different from what it appears to Americans. Indifferent and unsympathetic to the Kuomintang as many Chinese are, they care even less for a Red régime over China. It is true that many Chinese youths are so-called leftists, and they are strong even in Chungking. This is due to almost two decades of influence of Russian thought. The trend of the majority of writers has certainly been toward the left in the last twenty years. But many of the so-called leftists are so partly because it is the fashion and partly because if they are to avoid concerted attacks by the leftists they have to join them. More important than that, they are for the left, not because they are really secret Communist party members, but because of their dissatisfaction with the failures of the Kuomintang rule. These people are progressive and "revolutionary" as all youths are, and incidentally they all accept Marxian materialism and economic determinism as a philosophy even if they do not go all out for a communist rule over China. The writers over thirty today in China read nothing but Communist literature in their school days in the nineteen-twenties.* If they lack perspective in social philosophy and maturity in general outlook, they cannot be blamed for it, for in China, the introduction of anything new is apt to be thought of as the last word in Western science, which is what they believe of Marxian materialistic dialectic today. In science, they still believe in nineteenth-century mechanistic physics; in psychology, they believe that Sigmund

---

* On the influence of Russian literature in China, see *My Country and My People,* pp. 284-5.

Freud represents the most advanced interpretation; in history, the fashion is to talk of economic causes of all human events; in literature, they think Upton Sinclair the most important contemporary American author. Their knowledge of the West is necessarily limited by the translations available to them. While they thus fall generally twenty years behind Western thought, they are about ten years behind Soviet Russia in their reorientation toward nationalism and capitalist-democratic institutions. Confucian humanism is mentioned only to be pooh-poohed as feudalism in ideas. It is singular to note that not one English- or American-educated Chinese writer can be counted among the Communists, or even among the leftists in China. People educated in the United States or England, especially England, easily fall in with the conservative-evolutionary point of view because they have greater respect for tradition and cultural values. They have heard of not one, but several, social philosophies; their academic background is better rounded out, and their critical sense is better developed. I doubt that if Mao Tse-tung were a Harvard Ph.D. or General Chu Teh were a West Point graduate, either of them could have fallen so hard for Marxism as the newest gospel of Western "science."

But for the average Chinese people, their conception of the Red régime is not based on books by American travelers who depend upon Communist youth as interpreters but on personal stories from their friends and relatives who have lived under it in the last eighteen years. They have heard of the Red régime and reign of terror in Kiangsi, Anhwei, Fukien, Hunan, and the hair-raising massacres of Liuyang, Liling, and Changsha before the war and of the present régime in the occupied territories. Their impression is, on the whole, that of something incomprehensively foreign to them, a régime characterized by bloody massacres, wholesale executions, commissars ruling over magistrates and spies penetrating into the households of the countryside, breaking up of the family, wives turning against their husbands, sons against fathers, brothers against brothers, and a fifteen-year-old boy reporting on the hiding place of his seventy-year-old grandmother who was led out and butchered in the streets. Finally, it is characterized by the greatest regimentation of the people's lives and ideas and suppression of individual liberty that they have known in the four thousand years of China's history. They have learned about the Chinese Communist régime, not by reading *Red Star over China,* but through a hundred lives and a thousand deaths. The truly totalitarian régime and really thorough one-party dictatorship in China is in Yenan, and not in Chungking.

The government has wisely and definitely decided that the Communist issue is a political one and will be settled by political means. During 1943, after several severe conflicts, including the capture of Governor Han Tehchin, for which the Communist commander Chu Teh officially said, "So sorry," the Communist issue was officially discussed at the People's Political Council and the Eleventh Plenary Session of the Central Executive Committee of the Kuomintang. Similar decisions were embodied in (1) President Chiang Kai-shek's message before the Eleventh Plenary Session, September 13, 1943; (2) "Resolution of the Eleventh Plenary Session of the Central Executive Committee of the Kuomintang Concerning a Report on the Case of Sabotaging the War and Endangering the Nation by the Chinese Communist Party," of the same date, and (3) "Resolution of the People's Political Council Concerning That Part of the Military Report Regarding the Eighteenth Army Corps," September 26, 1943. The first two declared that there were "no other demands on the Chinese Communists, except the hope that they will forsake their military separatist occupation and cease their past activities in attacking the National Army and sabotaging the war"; the People's Political Council expressed it as a hope that "the Chinese Communist party and the Eighteenth Army Corps, realizing the enormous sacrifices of our army and people in the past six years and the difficult tasks facing us in national reconstruction hereafter, will live up to their pledge, observe strict discipline, and not indulge again in actions hindering national unity and affecting the war." All three hoped that they would "live up to their declaration of 1937 and carry out the four points mentioned in the declaration, viz., (1) They will fight for the realization of the Sanmin Chuyi principles; (2) They will stop the policy of violence and the Communist movement for the overthrow of the political power of the Kuomintang and will stop the policy of confiscating the land of landlords by force of violence; (3) They will abolish the present Soviet government and carry out democratic political principles, with the aim of establishing a national political unity; and (4) They will abolish the Red Army and foreign names and be reorganized as the National Revolutionary Army, taking orders from the Military Affairs Commission of the National government, and hold themselves ready to mobilize to their assigned duties on the war front against Japan." The Kuomintang Resolution says that "as to the other problems, the present session has already decided that one year after the close of the war, a National Assembly will be convened and a constitution promulgated, when they can be brought up for discussion and solution at the

National Assembly." The brief official report by the Military Affairs Commission to the People's Political Council on some of the outstanding cases of war sabotage, with official telegrams from the front, has been published in a special pamphlet for private circulation only.

I believe this is a sound and clearsighted policy, and no other policy is possible for settling the dispute short of a civil war. The Chinese Communists, in establishing their own separate régime, did so out of a sincere conviction, and their aim is to improve the lot of the primary producer. On this fundamental aim there is no ground for difference; the difference between the Kuomintang and the Chinese Communist party lies in the method of carrying out the social revolution, whether by gradual reforms or by methods of violence and a proletariat dictatorship. In any modern democracy, such political differences should be settled by democratic means. The Chinese instinct for compromise is strong. No matter what the Chinese Communists have done, all will be forgiven when they are willing to unite with the rest of the nation.

On the solution of this problem, Dr. Sun Fo says:

> There can be only two solutions to the Communist problem in China. . . . Outside of a few hotheads in the Kuomintang or the Army, opposition to a military solution of the problem is well-nigh universal. The Kuomintang C.E.C. in plenary session has repeatedly resolved, in 1942 and again in 1943, to bring about a satisfactory termination of the deadlock by political and peaceful means. . . .
>
> The Kuomintang, as the ruling party, has formally and solemnly made public its pledge to the nation that convocation of the National Assembly will mean the termination of party tutelage, and the restoration of sovereignty to the nation. Generalissimo Chiang Kai-shek, as Leader of the Kuomintang and President of the Republic, has unequivocally declared to the world that China will be a democracy in the full sense of the term. He unmistakably stated in his opening speech before the Eleventh C.E.C. Plenum that, when constitutional rule is inaugurated in this country with the meeting of the Constituent Assembly, the Kuomintang will retire to a position of equality with any other party in China. Let me conclude by quoting his own words on this point. "After the enforcement of Constitutional Government, our Party should hand over the government to the people. . . . After the enforcement of Constitutional Government, our Party should be on equal legal footing with other ordinary parties and the common citizens, and

should enjoy equal privileges and rights, fulfill equal obligations, and receive equal treatment from the state under the principles of freedom of assembly, organization, speech and publication in accordance with law." (*Ibid.,* pp. 87-89.)

Yet there is a graver question. Political democracy is a matter of slow growth, and Americans should not expect too much from the declaration of a paper constitution, as if democracy could be conferred upon a people overnight. There will be struggles ahead as in the history of all republics. In the United States, where democracy is well rooted, one can hardly appreciate the Communist menace in China, which as a nation is in the process of transformation. Frankly, if there were two major parties in the United States, and the second party were not Republican or Democrat, with more or less the same faiths and ideals, but a powerful American Communist party, and if the state of the Union were still in flux and uncertainty, Americans would be howling less impatiently for China to grant constitutional liberties to the Communist party backed by a Communist army.

The government will after the war, I am quite certain, declare the promised constitution and then demand the abolition of the secessionist army. The first move has to be made by the government, and the choice offered to the Communists. It is then up to the Communists to choose between secession and unity, and on that choice depends China's progress, rapid or slow, toward national unity. If the answer is secession, the government will then have to make the choice between having a nation, one and indivisible, or tolerating in a modern state a separate administration backed up by a separate army. The American republic had to face the issue of secession and unity in 1860; the Chinese nation has to face the same problem now.

On August 5, 1944, the *Ta Kung Pao* of Chungking published an important editorial on the solution of the Communist problem, written upon the return of the press party from their visit to Yenan. I regard it as the best summary of the Chinese people's point of view regarding the whole Communist question; it is representative of the opinion of the nation and I agree entirely with it. The *Ta Kung Pao,* as is well known, is a nonpartisan paper; it is authoritative and represents the peak of present-day Chinese journalism; at times it has criticized government measures and policies fearlessly, competently, and intelligently. Its tone of courteous restraint toward the Chinese Communists is typical of what appears in the Chungking papers, and while it champions unity and support of the present Chinese leadership, it urges reform both in the administration and in the Yenan opposition. Much of course may be read between the lines of this dignified and sober editorial expression.

The press party to the northwest was arranged mainly at the request of foreign correspondents in Chungking who wanted to see Yenan. Chinese pressmen including a representative of this paper also went. During their 43-day stay in northern Shensi, it was quite impossible for them to see everything and the picture they got is at best a hurried one. Furthermore, what has been printed about the trip in the Chinese papers in no sense presents the whole picture, because there are things which the press is either unwilling or unable to print. These shortcomings in the Yenan reports must have been noticed by the reading public. We should like to give here our own conclusions drawn from the reports of the Yenan trip.

The world war in which we are involved is one waged between the democracies and Axis aggressors. China's traditional spirit is democratic and so are the principles on which the Chinese nation has been founded. Being the first to arise in arms against Axis aggression, the Kuomintang and the National Government have repeatedly declared that their policy is to carry out China's democratic ideals toward constitutionalism. The Communist party in China has similarly avowed its aim to struggle for the realization of democracy. All these signs show that China and her two main political parties are trying to keep abreast with the world's march toward democracy.

Yenan today is the nerve center of the Communist party in China. What can be seen there is typical of Communist activities, even though it is incomplete. It is most striking that behind all the activities seen at Yenan the Communist party is the motivating party. This bespeaks the omnipotence of the party and the Communists are particularly insistent on vesting their party with almost *carte blanche* powers over all political and military affairs. From the standpoint of the Communists themselves who naturally hold the interest of their party dearer than anything else, there seems to be nothing open to criticism. But from a standpoint of a democracy-loving citizen of the nation, one cannot help feeling that there is something wrong somewhere in the state of affairs existing in Yenan. The power of the party cannot be upheld as supreme unless at the expense or even the total sacrifice of the liberty of the individual. This power of placing the party above everything else runs counter to the principles of democracy which place primary emphasis on the respect for the liberty of the individual.

There are in all other democratic countries political parties, but those parties are active within the constitutional law. They contest with one another in open and legal campaigns for election to government. In spite of political rivalries, there is a spirit of mutual respect both among the parties and members within each party. From the standpoint of true democracy, we feel that the problem of political parties as it exists in China leaves much to be desired. There should be more respect given the individual rather than such unqualified emphasis placed on the authority of the party.

China today is a united nation, simply because she must be a united nation if she wants to succeed in her revolution, in her resistance, and in her national reconstruction. For the sake of these important interests of the nation, we have no other alternative than whole-heartedly to support national unity and strongly to oppose any split. The National Government and President Chiang Kai-shek constitute the pivot of this essential national unity. This pivot should be most dear to every Chinese heart because it was achieved through a bitter struggle of more than thirty years and through much bloodshed on the part of the Chinese people. Speaking in the interests of the nation, we as common citizens cannot but do our honest best to uphold and strengthen this pivot in the hope that China may soon win victory in the war and success in her national reconstruction. It is inconceivable that this pivot should collapse and leave the nation and its people with several more decades of bitterness and bloodshed ahead.

Through seven years of bitter fighting, China has now achieved the status of equality with the leading powers and is looking forward to an early victory. This to a large extent must be credited to the National Government and President Chiang Kai-shek. Until the final triumph comes, we have to fight on. In the postwar world we will have to strive for the completion of our reconstruction program and for the mobilization of our nation. In all these endeavors this pivot of national leadership will be indispensable. To replace it with a new one may again plunge China into the retrogressive status of a semi-colony. We have as a warning before us the example of Jugoslavia and Marshal Tito in whose footsteps we must not follow. If the Central Government has certain shortcomings we should urge reform rather than complete overthrow.

No government of any nation can by law or logic tolerate the existence of another government within the nation nor another organization with armed forces independent of the national army system. The right of the Central Government of China in advocating unity of military command and unity of political administration cannot be questioned. Purely as citizens we uphold this platform. At the same time we hope that the National Government will on its part more completely fulfill its moral obligations. A government, according to the explanation given by Dr. Sun Yat-sen, is the organization which handles people's affairs. To handle such affairs efficiently, the government must be able to solve people's problems. The government must feel duty bound and morally obliged to put everything in order, political, military, and legal. Therefore, we uphold the National Government, and at the same time we hope that it will overcome what shortcomings it has and seek improvement in its administration.

During the visit to Yenan, the position of the Chinese pressmen was not entirely the same as that of the foreign correspondents. Yenan is a Chinese city and the Communists there are all our fellow countrymen. Our pressmen visited Yenan as Chinese visiting a Chinese city and met the Communists as brothers meeting brothers.

Judging by what the press party heard and saw during its trip to Yenan, there apparently has existed a political problem which is harmful to the nation's unity and strength. It is natural to ask, "Is a solution to this problem possible?" Our answer is definitely in the affirmative, simply because a solution must be made possible. The resolution adopted by the Eleventh Plenary Session of the Central Executive Committee of the Kuomintang to seek a political solution is most appropriate, though little progress has been made after the lapse of more than a year. With the presence of Lin Tsu-han* (Communist delegate) in Chungking, the time is opportune now for reaching a satisfactory solution.

A political solution does not mean an empty promise. The road for its ultimate realization has been paved by the decision on the part of the Kuomintang and the National Government to estab-

---

* Lin Tsu-han was the political commissar of the Communist army under General Cheng Chien; as such he was responsible for the killing of foreigners in Nanking in 1927. This was the only antiforeign outbreak in the National Revolution.—Author.

lish a constitutional government in which all political parties may participate in government by legal means. The conflict between the two parties will then automatically disappear, and what has been known as the Red Army in China will be nationalized. National unity and cooperation among parties will be assured.

Democracy is becoming the mainspring of world politics. It is truly the most effective system for national progress and political efficiency. A most striking example is found in America in which all the racial complications and divergence of opinions among political parties are dissolved through democracy. Today America is the leading power of the United Nations. The same thing has been true with Great Britain which, thanks to democracy, has been able to pass through the most critical stage in her history and is now coming close to final victory. The world is on the way to democracy. So is China. (Reprinted by *Contemporary China,* September 4, 1944, published by Chinese News Agency, N. Y.)

Political sense means intelligent foresight into the larger shape of events as developed by the present actions, policies and tendencies of our own time. Some people have got this political sense and some haven't. It is evident that the present American attitude toward the problem of China's unity cannot be devoid of grave consequences. Such consequences ought to be carefully considered and the choice intelligently weighed. There has been enough reckless talk, and exaggerated claims are being made for the Chinese Communist régime. It is quite possible that some Americans, failing to get Washington to switch its recognition from Chungking to Yenan, as suggested by their reference to Mikhailovitch and Tito, will be campaigning for the recognition of two separate states in China, in the same manner that the British are sympathetic toward Jinnah's claims for a partition of India. According to a dispatch from Yenan to the *New York Herald-Tribune* of July 26, 1944, the Communists are steadily pressing their claims, openly and publicly, to all occupied territory, covering not only northern Shensi, but the whole of Shansi, Hopei, Shantung, and areas from Inner Mongolia in the north to the island of Hainan in the south, with "bases" in Honan, Anhwei, Hupeh, Kiangsu, Chekiang, and Kwangtung, claiming the allegiance of 86 millions, in the same sense and manner that Jinnah claims the allegiance of 90 million Muslims in India. The Communists have been fairly successful in expanding into Hopei and Shantung against Central guerilla units and government agencies operating in those provinces, but even in these provinces, the

Communist control is far from complete. Central guerrillas and regulars are in operation in all the other areas mentioned, and the guerrillas operating in the island of Hainan are government and not Communist guerrillas. But the very fact that the Communists are putting forward such claims shows their political ambitions. Now that such claims are openly put forward, it is important that before raising the bogey, one ought to be sure of one's ability to allay the ghost conjured up. For in present-day political strategy, ghosts can become political realities if properly assisted by political favoritism and official propaganda.

American opinion certainly has encouraged the Chinese Communists to make new demands upon the government as a rival contending state and make a peaceful settlement more difficult. If left unsolved, and if encouraged by foreign powers, the problem will certainly reach the magnitude of the problem of a Chinese Jinnah and a Chinese "Pakistan." I think that the Washington support for Chungking, which the Chinese Communists are trying their best to undermine, and the sending of three tank division equipments to the Chinese Army, which the Chinese Communists so fear, would not have the political tendency to precipitate an open civil war in China, but rather have the opposite effect, to avert it.

Political sense would seem to indicate that a politically split China would not be to the advantage of her Allies in peace, unless it were based on a well-thought-out policy to keep China in a disunited and therefore weak state, resembling the situation in India. According to orthodox imperialist politics, the best way to obtain a leverage to divide and rule is by encouraging a minority, so that dissension can be prolonged. Since nothing is further from the minds of China's Allies, the championing of the weaker contending party would seem to suggest no policy at all. That is the more pity; for Americans certainly desire to aid China's reintegration into a strong state, rather than her disintegration. Yet, without thinking of the consequences of their action, they have lightmindedly encouraged, not a normal political party, but one that has established a *de facto* secessionist state, backed by a separate army. In this war against Japan, American interests are principally in seeing China's fighting power increased through a resolution of this conflict. Yet American opinion seems sympathetic to the Communists' keeping their separate army, which is the stumbling block to all Kuomintang-Communist negotiations, and to military unity. All Chinese are conscious of the defects of the Kuomintang government, yet all Chinese believe with the *Ta Kung Pao* that in the coming period this "pivot" of leadership, dearly bought with years of bloodshed, should be strengthened rather than destroyed.

Summing up the situation, it would seem that President Chiang Kai-shek, as head of the Chinese state, possesses that political sense of the larger shape of things in the future of China to an extraordinary degree, and American friends might well put themselves in Chiang's position, with responsibility to decide whether China shall be a nation, one and indivisible, or whether to allow the course to drift until the problem becomes insoluble or precipitates a conflict. No one can doubt that President Chiang Kai-shek wishes to avoid a civil war after the victory, when China will desire more than ever to assume the position of a united nation and command the respect of others. So far, during this war, Chiang has shown extreme tolerance and tact and forbearance, hoping still for a peaceful solution. I have confidence that he is the one man most competent and most tactful to deal with the Chinese Communist problem. He prefers to regard it as still an internal problem. His past record of political sagacity requires that one leave him a free hand.

(3) The Army

The problem of the Chinese Army in time of war is naturally of first importance, although I have preferred to deal with the background problems first. As I see it, it is principally a question of supplies for China. I am glad that the Burma Road is being reopened by the strength and heroism of American-equipped Chinese soldiers, planned and courageously carried out by General Joseph W. Stilwell, who with Major General Claire L. Chennault has unshaken faith in the Chinese nation and her soldiery. I am glad that my contention that the Himalayas were not too high and air transport could be increased has now been proved by the heroic efforts and sacrifices of American pilots in 1943. The opposite contention that the Himalayas could not be licked, which was the reason advanced for failure to do anything about it throughout 1942, has been completely proved false. The thesis that reopening the Burma Road through the jungles is impossible has been disproved by the energy of one man. Incidentally, I am glad also that my thesis in *Between Tears and Laughter,* that imperialism and power politics and balance of power must inevitably bring about another world war, and that peace is not a material but a spiritual problem and cannot be reached by a system of mechanics, has been championed by other voices worthier than mine, including Sumner Welles and Archibald MacLeish. I still disagree with a certain statesman who said that the critics of imperialism have been completely discredited in America. And I violently disagree with that dear, pig-headed individual who said in 1943 in answer to a question about supplies for China, "China as a war front was washed out a year ago. Why throw in good money after bad?"

I am not so happy that what I wrote in the spring of 1943 in *Between Tears and Laughter* has come true:

> A hurricane will blow. President Roosevelt announces the intention to use China as a base to invade Japan—the only logical base, but between that announcement of intention and actual planning, there will be another time lag of years. Events will happen and the complex situation will become more complex still, while we say nothing in the Far East matters until Hitler is defeated. . . . For Japan was listening when President Roosevelt declared China as the only base for invasion of Japan. Besides, the Japanese know the map of the Orient pretty well, even if the others don't. (P. 111.)

It is not the purpose of this book to discuss foreign politics. But the question of supplies for China seems yet to labor under a new heavy handicap. I refer to the vicious, grotesque, and irresponsible rumor, constantly repeated, that if Chungking were given supplies, it might hoard them up and not use them to fight Japan. This makes the fantastic assumption that Chungking, after seven years of stubborn war record and unswerving purpose amid disheartening circumstances, is not interested in fighting Japan, or is more interested in fighting Chinese Communists than in fighting Japan. It assumes that the Chinese Army is practically a deserter from the cause of the Allies, and worse than that, it assumes that Chiang Kai-shek himself is such a deserter, for he certainly controls the military operations. Such low rumors against a man who kept faith with the Allies in their darkest hours should not be repeated by men going about in long pants without some basis in fact or plausible reasoning. The obvious implication of such rumors is that Chungking's armies should not be strengthened even at the risk of losing the Chinese Army for the coming big fight against Japan. In the columns of Drew Pearson, however, rumor changes as all rumors change, and the fear has become a fact stated in the past tense: American supplies "were hoarded up," not to fight the Japanese, but to fight the Chinese fighting the Japanese, that is, the Communists. I am sorry that Americans have co-operated in this baseless rumor and in the connected and equally grotesque Communist rumor that the Chinese Minister of War, Ho Yingchin, is pacifist and pro-Japan because he is anti-Communist.

This vicious rumor never had a sponsor who was willing to put his signature under it. There was not a hint as to how much was hoarded, where it was hoarded, who hoarded it, and when. The plain fact is, there wasn't anything to hoard. American commentators aware of the state of transport into China up to now should be able to provide some figures as to what has been given to the Chinese Army to hoard, let us say, in terms of so many guns or tanks or bullets. Minister Ho Yingchin informed me in February, 1944, that about 10,000 tons of material had been given to the Chinese Army, which had arrived at Kunming. Every ounce of it is now being used at the Salween front to wrench back control of the Burma Road, with Chinese blood, sweat, and tears. So far, not enough supplies have been given to the Chinese Army and not enough planes to the Chinese Air Force to give them a chance to prove what they could and would do with them. The fact is that the Chinese Army, Chinese-equipped and Chinese-trained, fought stubbornly for forty-seven days in the defense of Hengyang and did the best that could be expected of any army similarly equipped.

The first task of a nation at war is to fight. Any nation at war, being not in position to start a counteroffensive, no matter whose fault it is, is naturally and by legitimate human reactions held up to ridicule. It is the first duty of a boxer to deliver a good punch; it is the first duty of a baseball batter to hit the ball into the field; it is the first duty of a race horse to win on the track. The crowds on the grandstand are not in a mood for explanations. I am of the firm opinion that all the cynicism and all the idle twaddle about China have one sole primary origin, that the Chinese Army hasn't got big guns and hasn't been able to get things going. When the big guns begin to roar, and the Chinese cease to be outshot and outgunned at every point by the enemy, and the counteroffensive gains momentum, all such old wives' gossip will disappear. The unforgivable sin of China is that she hasn't got big guns. The next sin is that she hasn't got good gin. To certain observers the combination of lacks of good guns and good gin is fatal.

I am deeply concerned that in the great land combats for the destruction of the Japanese army, China should be given a chance to do her part as an equal ally. China threw all she had, her planes, her artillery, her modern troops, into the battle of Shanghai. Now everywhere except in mountainous regions, her troops can be outshot and outgunned by the enemy. She has done her best by adapting her weapons to the terrain and has held mountainous regions wherever the enemy came. She can, with terrific losses, recapture points like Ichang, as indeed she did once, but she cannot hold them, when enemy guns and poison gas arrive. To demand that the Chinese Army take the initiative without better equipment is unreasonable, and to blame it for "not fighting Japan" owing to the lack of power of military initiative is unfair. Foreign praise of the heroism of Chinese soldiers and foreign criticism of their fitness and organization and morale do not touch them; the sending or withholding of supplies does.

These are not idle replies to idler gossip. So far, the viewpoint expressed by Hanson W. Baldwin, the well-informed military analyst of the *New York Times,* of planning the defeat of Japan without the Chinese Army, seems to reflect correctly the thinking and the general strategy of the Allies. China does not count except for the use of air bases, which theoretically exist in a kind of inoculated and invincible vacuum. The Allies have been shown, rather vividly in the battle of Hengyang, how the whole shape of the war against Japan may be altered, and sacrifices made greater and the war made longer and more difficult than it would have been if they had not gone on the stupid theory of counting without the help of the Chinese ground forces and had started to send some guns by increasing the air transport in 1942, which I was howling and screaming for in *Between Tears and Laughter.* Events have now conclusively proved that the Allied plan to defeat Japan without the Chinese Army and with only the help of China's air bases, formulated as far back as 1942, has been a costly mistake. Now if land battles develop against the Japanese army in China, as they certainly will, and if the strategy is planned to defeat Japan without the Chinese Army, Americans will wake up to the gravity of the cost too late again. It may not be America's choice to fight Japan's army in China, but it will most probably be Japan's choice to fight her last battles in China. It looks as if China, the first to fight the fascists in this war, will be the last to come out. Since every month of prolonged war is costing the American nation some seven billion dollars, I suggest that the shortening of the war by even three months through a better-equipped Chinese Army may save the Americans twenty billion dollars. They will also save themselves the chagrin of the grandstand over the failure of a baseball shortstop to stop a ball, not because he meant to muff it, but because he was given a worn-out glove.

But there is also a political reason for sending the supplies in earnest now. The United States failed to deliver supplies at first owing to the fear of offending Japan. The Chinese understood that without any trouble. Then the Allies lost Burma through being contented to fight only a delaying action and preventing Chinese soldiers from coming into Burma as long as they could. The Chinese understood that, but not so well. Then Burma was cut off, and there were great, though not insurmountable, difficulties in flying in supplies. The Chinese understood that, too. The failure to do something about it throughout 1942 could not be understood, since the few hundred planes required had nothing to do with defeating Hitler first. Now that vast relief is in sight through victory in Europe, should the Allies find yet another reason for not equipping the Chinese Army, the Chinese will completely fail to understand.

From the Chinese point of view and the point of view of future historians, the strange concatenation of events in China's war against Japan, and the succession of excuses, both good and bad, for leaving China out on a limb during seven grim years of war, seem so incredible and yet so natural that they will have to ascribe it to the will of God. I am at present in just about the position to accept God's will. For the inevitable "disappointing and vexatious" results of a man-made disappointing and vexatious policy, however, it would be wrong to place the blame on God. I am quite sure that when the liberation of China begins after Hong Kong is liberated first, the results will not be vexatious, but encouraging.

"All the universe is an inn; seek not for a special retreat of peace. All the people are your relatives; expect therefore trouble from them." I thought of this old Chinese proverb constantly during my journey. I liked its noble ideals and its sweet hard realism. It means that we are transient birds of passage, on a journey somewhere, whose destination is unknown. It means that no country and no nation can have peace at home without peace abroad. It means that other peoples of the world are China's cousins. And nations, like cousins, have to borrow from and lend to one another, and lendings and borrowings always cause some unpleasantness. As between neighbors, we have to learn to get along with one another, and understand one another enough not to be afraid to borrow a fire extinguisher when one's own house catches fire and, in better days, to borrow lawnmowers from each other. If the neighbor is slow about lending the fire extinguisher while the house is on fire, one gets irritated; if it were not so, he would not be human. There was such a fire in China. She wanted to borrow only a small fire extinguisher. None came, in 1937, 1938, 1939, 1940, 1941, 1942. Now that there is some hope of getting fire extinguishers, a neighbor's boy says, "There's no use lending him fire extinguishers. He

246

will hoard them and not fight the fire." That is a mean boy, she thinks: what has she been doing all these years? But too constant borrowing of fire extinguishers and lawnmowers is bad for neighborly relationships. "Why don't you get a fire extinguisher or a lawnmower yourself?" the neighbor has the perfect right to ask. The only answer is that he is going to, very definitely, this time.

Granting that the Chinese Army is going to receive supplies after the Burma Road is open and assuming that there will be big land battles in China before the Japanese army is crushed, the problem seems to me less one of training than of proper food and medical care and transportation for the soldiers, and of replacement by a more efficient conscription system. I am confident that as soon as big guns and tanks arrive, there are sufficiently trained Chinese units to handle them, and an immediate change in the military situation will be apparent, with the recapturing of one city after another. The Chinese officers have kept up in their military academies the German training technique, and moreover, officers have all taken short turns learning the American technique at the Artillery Training and Infantry Training Corps at Kunming. I have seen both Chinese and American training in artillery and infantry tactics, and do not think the basic training is so different. Once I asked War Minister Ho why he allowed Chinese officers to go through the basic training for raw recruits from ABC up under the American instructors, his reply was that not all of them had had the same training and whatever additional training they could get was all to the good. Such training as was really required would be in handling the new weapons like bazooka rocket guns, which is not too big a problem. The training received by the "Y" Force operating now in Burma will serve as the basis for other similar units to be equipped later.

The Chinese Army, organized on the principle of defense in depth on a more or less stabilized front, will face new problems of transportation and food supplies when the front begins to become fluid again. There is, I am afraid, not very much that can be done for improvement of their food, considering prices. However, an army moving back on a counteroffensive liberating the land would get the enthusiastic support from the civilians which it had in 1937-38, and which it did not get when the front was stabilized. On the other hand, the improvement of transportation facilities must be one of the first and foremost objectives after the reopening of the Burma Road, and an expanded army medical service, built on the excellent basis planned and developed by Lieutenant General Dr. Robert K. S. Lim, is of the greatest importance in saving lives and China's fighting power. I hope Washington will see medical supplies for the Chinese Army as urgent help to conserve Allied manpower, and not as gratuitous charity. The sad lack of surgical supplies and lack of transportation, when soldiers are literally marched into thin skeletons over hundreds of miles, partly forced upon the Army by the blockade, should no longer be tolerated after the supply route is open.

Strange as it may seem, the problem of the replacement of soldiers is a grave one, not because of shortage of manpower, but because of abuses in the selection and care of the selectees. This is the darkest aspect of the whole China war. The draft system completely breaks down in the hands of the village heads (*paochang,* or chiefs of *pao* units); they have arrested villagers at night without notice and held it as a weapon over people who offend or defy them, although official draft rules provide for regular periods of selection and notification; they have often accepted bribes for substitutes and connived at returning deserters; they have not followed the regulations and have turned in required numbers of selectees with false names and without regard to the health and age limitations. A magistrate told me that he believed a high percentage of the draftees came under false names. The draftees are marched, ill-clad, ill-fed, and without proper medical care, across mountains to a different province, and many fall sick on the way. Such hardships encourage desertion, which in turn causes some sergeants responsible for delivery at the camp to treat recruits like prisoners while on the way. These conditions discourage enlistment, which in turn encourages the selling of substitutes by the village heads. Such are the terrible abuses of the conscription system.

I have already mentioned what the Army is doing to improve the situation. But it seems to me that a thorough reform is required, and I suggested to President Chiang Kai-shek that the first step is to take the matter out of the hands of the village gentry. Periodic drawings under the direct joint supervision of the Army Draft Stations, the local magistrate, and representatives of the provincial People's Political Council, protected by a system of fingerprint identification, would make such abuses impossible. In the absence of transportation facilities, selectees should be trained, organized, and shaped into some sort of physical fitness before they are sent out of the province, thus shortening the hardships in the period between selection and induction into a regular unit.

Brooks Atkinson reported on August 19, 1944, from Chungking:

At a protracted conference in Generalissimo Chiang Kai-shek's country place Chinese military leaders recently adopted plans for the most thorough reorganization of the Chinese armies since the war began in 1937. Although the number of men in the Army will remain unchanged the number of units will be reduced and divisions will be reformed at full strength under the command of China's best combat officers. For several years many Chinese divisions have been under strength. Area commanders will be relieved of their political responsibilities. Heretofore, many have been serving as governors of the provinces. A number of other changes in the organization of the army are designed to result in more compact fighting units with two steps eliminated in what has been a cumbersome system of transmitting orders from the top to battalions. Many officers will be reclassified and reassigned or be sent to training schools for further study.

Changes are being made to raise the living conditions of soldiers by improving and increasing the supply of food and of medical services and by reforming the conscription system which has been subject to many abuses.

One of the most radical changes will be the conscription of students for training as noncommissioned officers in combat units. Until about a year ago university students were exempt from military service on the assumption that China would have great need for all her educated persons during the reconstruction after the war. Recently China began the conscription of students for interpreters and for other services behind the lines. Now, to raise the intelligence level of the army, about 10,000 students will be conscripted yearly for combat duty.

The Army, having the lowest pay among all government employees, is hardest hit by the inflation. The feeding of five million soldiers at the starvation ration of five hundred dollars per person, giving them rice and a little vegetable, is costing the nation two and a half billion dollars a month. Steadily mounting prices mean that revised budgets can never keep up with them. Yet inflation is to a certain extent psychological, and the reopening of the Burma Road should stabilize prices, if not lower them. At Kweiyang, soldiers were being inspected for physical fitness before they were sent to the Burma Expeditionary Force. They were told that the soldiers of this force were given four ounces of meat a day. I was told by the medical officers under Dr. Robert Lim that some of those who had failed to qualify wept like children. The Chinese Army is using over a hundred trucks to transport the selectees to Yünnan instead of letting them march, and a chain of stations has been established to look after their comfort and food supplies on the way.

These soldiers of China are underfed, underclothed, and underequipped, and they go through unbelievable hardships. Still they fight with a stolid indifference to danger and physical discomforts, and they have an imperturbable good cheer when their stomachs are satisfied. Few of them smoke or drink, they are honest citizens, and certainly I have never heard of them looting or molesting women. The soldiers' job is to do or die, and have little fun, besides. What they can do, if given the guns, is being proved on the Salween front, and what they can do on the Salween front they can do elsewhere in China when the offensive begins.

(4) Industrialization

There remains the problem of industrialization, which means bringing about a better and larger life for the people, the final goal of the Sanmin Chuyi and of democracy. I have watched the American pattern of life and have constantly made mental comparisons. A drinking fountain is not just a drinking fountain to me, and a children's playground is not just a children's playground, but something I mentally place in my own country and visualize with some effort of imagination. I see girls in fine woolen sweaters and mothers in cotton prints, and ask myself, Do the Chinese women have these, the average housewives and their daughters? I have seen the American slums and pictures of "poor white trash" and I have heard of Mayor Hague, but still the total impression is that there is plenty of fun in America. The five-and-ten stores are probably the best index of a manufacturing country turning out things cheap enough for the poorest housewife to buy, and therefore the most interesting phenomenon in this country for an Oriental. The cheap things, the soaps, perfumes, inks, pencils, kitchen utensils, lampshades, are very good. All these things I have to transplant mentally to my country. Out of the better and larger common life that is already multiplying in this country, I have to weave it into the ancient agricultural and handicraft pattern of China.

In *Between Tears and Laughter* I took some pains to destroy the picture of heaven as a concrete storehouse filled to the roof with canned goods, and to warn against the fallacy that there is any materialistic, mechanistic solution to the problem of a lasting world peace. I still do not think "a quart of milk for every Hottentot" will establish world peace, but will rather destroy it by inevitably bringing about another world war, if other, spiritual conditions do not exist. I protested against the view of man as an economic biped searching by animal instinct in the direction of potato supplies. This was addressed to the Americans and it was all a question of emphasis.

When it comes to China, the emphasis has to be laid elsewhere. America is having too much material progress, and China is having too little. If my paragraphs about raising the standards of living of the common men were interpreted to refer to China, I would rather take them back and preach at the top of my voice for raising the standards of living in China. This was what I did when I traveled in China, so much so that I seemed a materialistic prophet. I said that in spite of all its evils, industrialization had to come and this handicraft age had to go. I said the sin of China was not dirt, but poverty, and that dirt was not a moral problem, but one of water supply and sewage system and enameled bathtubs. How the Chinese soldiers loved a shower bath, when they could have it! How they loved to have their dusty uniforms steamed and deloused as was done for them by Dr. Robert Lim! How grateful they were for the disinfection of well water!

These economic problems pained me as I traveled through China. Having grown up on the rich southeastern coast of China, I did not know that the people of the inland West could be so poor. Familiar as the Chinese streets were to me, I could not, after coming back freshly from America, help making mental comparisons. And I had a distinct feeling of relief when I reached the rich province of Hunan, when the countryside approached the level of the southeast. I was ashamed of the general health conditions, and the people's dresses and shelter. President Roosevelt said one-third of the American nation was under-housed and underfed; I decided he probably meant they had no enameled bathtubs, although I understand there are twenty-five million in the world altogether, of which twenty-two and a half are in America. Reckoning at four in a family, there are some eleven million American families without enameled bathtubs. My statistics may be wrong, but that is about it.

Coming back to China, I saw what I do not see in America—farmers and their wives everywhere wearing mended clothing, with patches of new deep blue on gowns of faded blue. I knew it was no shame in China, but a sign of thrift, deliberately encouraged as virtue by the national tradition; the strong native homespun cotton made of coarse twill could last for years, and it would be an outrage to throw it away when by some patching and mending it could serve another three years. I was not surprised or shocked as Americans would be, because I had seen farmers wear it from my childhood, and mended clothing could still be kept clean—the wives saw to that. Still if China produced enough cotton goods, they would become cheap enough for the farmers to buy new gowns every two or three years.

It is all a question of increased production. The nation could increase production fifteen to twenty fold with modern machinery. If there were no power and no hydraulic machines and no diesel engines, there would be nothing to be said, and China could go on carrying burdens on her shoulders and be content with carving ivory and burning pewter oil-lamps. But the power is here and the machines are here, and it would be a sin to deny them the increase of their productivity. I know Chinese would use flashlights instead of torches and Chinese ladies would use lucite combs instead of combs of buffalo horn and would even take aspirin for headaches and plasmo-quinine and atabrine for malaria. If China did not produce these things, she would buy them from abroad and use them anyway. So let the industrial age come.

The Kuomintang constantly uses a phrase, *"fu, ch'iang, k'ang, lo,"* meaning a "wealthy, powerful, peaceful, and happy" nation, to represent China's ideal. My idea is that the Sanmin Chuyi, the "three principles" of nationalism, democracy, and better livelihood, is a dream that this nation shall be put right within this generation, and that our people shall be better clothed, better fed, better housed, and have better means of transportation, and as Dr. Sun Yat-sen added, have better amusements and pleasures. These four—*i, shih, chu, hsing*—are materialistic aims. They mean new and unmended clothing for the people; brick cottages with bright green or red trim and white curtain; meat for the farmers, clean broad streets and beautiful bridges and long motor highways and railways spanning the width of the land. This is something to be enthusiastic about.

I believe that of the three principles of the Sanmin Chuyi, nationalism, democracy, and people's livelihood, the last is the true goal of the Kuomintang doctrine. The principle of nationalism is like the blood of a body. The principle of democracy is like the internal organs, without which the body cannot function properly and purge itself of waste and poison. But the principle of the people's livelihood is health itself, as shown in a firm skin, a ruddy complexion in its cheeks, luster in its eyes and a spring in its steps. This is the final goal, the goal of health, of a happy people in a happy land. And I really don't care which party of men shall bring this vision about.

Chungking papers and parlor talks buzz with discussions of postwar industrialization schemes. I still have not mastered them. But I got the definite general impression that there will be a balance between planned economy and private enterprise. Certainly the whole program must be state-planned. China cannot afford the haphazard development of free enterprises which may make many wasteful mistakes and will take decades, because she will have no time to lose in this period of national reconstruction. Certainly the basic communications, resources, and heavy industries needed for national defense will be state-planned and state-owned, while the production of consumer goods and light industries by private firms will be encouraged. The main railway systems and main water transportation lines will be undertaken by the government, while subsidiary feed lines will be left to local enterprise. Generally the development of agricultural production, steam and electric power, basic mineral resources, and communications will precede manufacture. President Chiang said that after the war he would transform the military army into an industrial army. The training of technicians and mechanics is a vast problem, and Chinese students in agriculture, medicine, and engineering are given scholarships in the government colleges and practically trained free. Philosophy and literature fall to third place, and Chinese college students seem all to go for banking and engineering.

Foreign help will be needed and desired. But if loans are made, they will have to be made chiefly to the government and bank on the government. In order to attract foreign capital, the Chinese government will have to make concessions for security. At the same time, with the passing of the era of extraterritoriality, foreign firms fall under Chinese jurisdiction and foreign business men will have to recondition themselves to a new psychology and a new state of things. Some of the foreigners in Chungking still talk like missionaries and crave their whisky. The earlier the Old China Hand attitude passes out, the better for Sino-foreign co-operation.

Negotiations should be entered into now between the Chinese and the American governments for absorbing the vast American ammunition and army equipment that will certainly be locked up and stored away to become outmoded, and also to absorb the first three months' war production after the armistice. China should also stipulate definitely now, before Armistice Day comes, for the conservation and handing over of Japanese warships, submarines, merchant marine, shipyards, steel works, airplane factories which still remain at the time of the armistice and which the Allies wish to take away from Japan, as part of the reparations for China's incalculable losses. For I do not believe Japan will have much cash left, and enemy property could not be disposed of to better constructive purposes.

As I write, I would like to shut my eyes and go into sleep, to wake up twenty-five years from now, like old Rip van Winkle, to see what China will look like then. It will be such a crazily happy picture that I dare not think too deeply about it. . . . But I also want to remain awake and see the drama of a nation rebuilding and transforming itself, and not miss the show. Perhaps it is better to keep awake.

I am fully awake now. It seems to my mind's eye that the nation has been keeping a long night of vigil before the Festival of the Fruitful Corn. The night has been long and strange and full of fateful portents, tense with expectancy and the silent wishes and prayers of men for an abundant year. On the eve before the festival dedicated to the God of Earth and the Fruitful Corn, a thunderstorm struck and the people hastily gathered in the corn from the field. The sky darkened and the clouds on the mountaintops gathered and thickened, threatening to destroy the fruit of the sweat and labor of men.

All night the farmers have sat watching, in expectation of the great day. The sacrifices have been made, the bulls and rams, all pure, have been offered on the altar, and the smell of incense rises from the tripod. Because of the storm there have been weepings and sorrow, and haunting specters of hunger and death. But steadily through the night the sentinels have kept watch, the bells and drums have sounded, and the candles have been kept burning bright. In spite of the storm, the people have not lost hope and have gone on with the ceremonies and the sacrifices in good cheer. They sing a song, handed down from their ancient ancestors in days of old:

> *They clear away the grass and the bushes; and the ground is laid open by their plows. In thousands of pairs they remove the roots, some in the low wet ground, some along the dikes.*
> *There are the master and his eldest son; his younger sons, and all their children; their strong helpers and their hired servants. How the noise of their eating of the viands brought to them resounds! The husbands think lovingly of their wives; the wives*

*keep close to their husbands. Then with their sharp plowshares
they set to work on the southern acres.*

*They sow their various kinds of grain, each seed containing
in it a germ of life. In unbroken lines rises the blade, and, well
nourished, the stalks grow long. Luxuriant is the young grain, and
the weeders go among it in multitudes.*

*Then come the reapers in crowds. And the grain is piled up in
the fields, myriads, and hundreds of thousands, and millions of
stacks; for the spirits and for sweet spirits, to offer our ancestors,
male and female, and to provide for all ceremonies.*

*Fragrant is their aroma, enhancing the glory of the state. Like
pepper is their smell, to give comfort to the aged.*

*It is not here only that there is this abundance; it is not now
only that there is such a time; from of old it has been thus.**

The night is calm now; the storm has passed. The bells and drums
have sounded; the officer of the prayers retires. As the night wears on,
the candles burn low, and some, the lazy ones and the fainthearted,
have fallen into sleep. But for those who are awake, the sky is excitingly beautiful and the air is tense with the excitement of the coming
of the new day. They prepare themselves for new and fruitful labor,
when they will not have a moment's pause, for much depends on the
abundance of the year. Some are seemingly asleep, but they are not,
and are merely waiting patiently as the hours pass.

Out in the dark, some sentinels have been standing watch under the
storm and under the now starry sky, watching the fateful portents,
wondering at the shooting-meteors and the mystery of the eternal procession of the skies and the solemn grandeur of the night, holding and
foreboding so much. They have stood all night in the open to keep
sharp lookout, or taken turns to sleep in their armor, pillowed on spears,
to wait for the dawn. They are curious about the intermittent streaks of
light shooting up from the black horizon, and if they listen well, they
might hear strange music in the air, breaking in upon the solid dark
silence of the night.

The hour approaches. It is the fifth watch. The sentinels will soon
be relieved of their posts and the night-long vigil will be over. The
light in the woods already changes its hues and a pale luminescence
is tinting the eastern sky. The candles will be snuffed out and the
night watchers will go forth into the open, in a long and solemn pro-

* Ode of the Chous, the *Tsai Shu*, probably twelve hundred years before Christ and
seven hundred years before Confucius.

cession to the top of a hill to greet the dawn. The great Festival of the Fruitful Corn will begin. There will be great rejoicings and merry-making and the singing of songs. The daughters of Chungking will put on red pajamas and dance in the streets with the soldiers, those soldiers who stood in the storm in the threatening night. For the long watch is over, the day has come, and the night shall not fall again. So shall pass the Vigil of the Nation.

INDEX